FARM JOURNAL'S
HOMEMADE
BREADS

FARM JOURNAL'S HOMEMADE BREADS

By the Food Editors of Farm Journal

Alice Joy Miller, Editor

Joanne G. Fullan, Assistant Editor

Margaret C. Quinn, Home Economist

Galahad Books · New York

Published in 1994 by

Galahad Books
A division of Budget Book Service, Inc.
386 Park Avenue South
New York, NY 10016

Galahad Books is a registered trademark of Budget Book Service, Inc.

Published by arrangement with Doubleday, a division of Bantam, Doubleday, Dell Publishing Group, Inc.

Library of Congress Catalog Card Number: 84-45565

ISBN: 0-88365-875-5

Book Design: Michael P. Durning
Consulting Art Director: Alfred A. Casciato
Illustrations by Nancy Burpee

Printed in the United States of America.

CONTENTS

Introduction

It was a custom of my mother's, whenever she visited the home of a newly married couple for the very first time, to bring certain housewarming presents. In the summertime, she included a bouquet of fresh flowers from her garden; in the winter, she cut a handful of evergreen boughs from the fir trees in our back yard. Aside from these, the other items in her gift package always remained the same.

With her gift to the newlyweds she presented a note of explanation: "These are for both of you and for your new home. This new straw broom is given so that your home will always be spotlessly clean. Accept this box of salt so that you'll have good fortune and never be in need of money. The dozen eggs bring the hope that your home will be filled with many healthy children. The loaf of homemade bread is given so that there will always be a bounty of food on your table. The flowers are from our home, and with their fragrances, it's our family's wish that your new home will be as happy as ours."

In keeping with this custom, the Food Editors of Farm Journal offer these recipes—collected from experienced farm and ranch bakers all across America. It is our wish that this book will provide you with enjoyable baking experiences as well as wholesome bread for your table.

ALICE JOY MILLER
Food Editor

1
Ingredients

Round or flat, sweet or savory, moist or dry—bread may have many different textures and flavors and may take many forms. The "personality" of a loaf of bread is determined by its ingredients and based on how they are mixed. This chapter tells all about these ingredients—the many varieties of flours, meals, liquids, fats, leaveners and sugars that you can use to make bread.

Before you begin to prepare any of these recipes, especially for the first time, it's a good idea to read the recipe from beginning to end. Then you'll be able to determine how much time you'll need to make the recipe and whether you'll need any special ingredients or utensils.

MEASURING INGREDIENTS

The key to successfully making golden flaky biscuits or any other baked goods is to measure accurately. Many of us can remember our grandmothers who had the special knack of making a whole week's worth of bread by the simple method of "look and feel"—a spoonful of this and a handful of that. Less-experienced cooks must use other methods of measurement, but the fact is that every cook measures just a little differently.

Here's a rundown on standard methods of measurement—the ones we used to measure recipe ingredients in this book.

To measure liquid ingredients, whether they be milk, honey or vegetable oil, use a liquid measure—a clear glass or plastic cup marked with colored lines, often red, indicating measurements of ¼ c., ⅓ c., ½ c., ⅔ c., ¾ c. and 1 c. Liquid measures are sold in various sizes (1 c., 2 c. and 4 c.), usually with handles and spouts for easier pouring. We find the 2-c. and 4-c. sizes extra helpful for measuring large amounts, and the 4-c. measure can be used as a small bowl.

For example, if you are making muffins and need ⅓ c. vegetable oil, place the measure on a level surface and slowly pour the oil into the measure until it reaches the line that's marked ⅓ c. *Always read the line of the measuring cup at eye level to check the volume in the measure.* At any other angle, the level may appear correct, but it actually will be either above or below the line, depending upon your angle of view.

To measure dry ingredients such as flour, granulated sugar or oats, use a set of graduated measuring cups. These are often sold as ¼-c., ⅓-c., ½-c. and 1-c. measures, and they're usually made of metal or plastic. They have small handles and will stack neatly for easy storage.

If you're making waffles, and need 1⅔ c. *sifted* flour, sift the flour first. Then, *lightly* spoon the sifted flour into a 1-c. measure, filling the measure until it overflows. Using the straight edge of a metal spatula or knife, level off the surplus. Don't pack or shake down the flour or tap the side of the cup; if you do, you may add too much flour and your waffles will be heavy and tough. Next, repeat this procedure, this time using the ⅓-c. measure. Repeat once again, using the ⅓-c. measure, for a total of 1⅔ c.

For small amounts of both dry and liquid ingredients—less than ¼ c.—use measuring spoons. A standard set consists of ¼ tsp., ½ tsp., 1 tsp. and 1 tblsp. Most cooks own two sets of measuring spoons. This eliminates the need to stop and wash one set of spoons when measuring liquid and dry ingredients.

If a recipe requires 1 tsp. salt, measure the salt just as you do flour: fill the 1-tsp. measuring spoon with salt until it overflows and then level off. For liquids such as vanilla, pour the vanilla just to the top of the measuring spoon without letting it overflow.

Some ingredients need special measurement techniques. Brown sugar, both light and dark, is moist, so you must pack it into the measuring spoon or cup with the back of a spoon, then level it. When you remove the sugar, it should hold the shape of the spoon or cup.

It's easy to measure butter or margarine if you purchase it by the pound in stick form. Each pound contains four sticks, with each ¼-lb. stick measuring ½ c. Each stick is marked off in tablespoons. Use a sharp knife to cut off the number of tablespoons needed, following the guidelines on the wrapper.

If you buy butter in 1-lb. or 2-lb. blocks, or if you need to measure shortening or peanut butter, firmly pack the butter or shortening right to the top of the measuring spoon or cup. Level with a knife or spatula.

How many teaspoons in a tablespoon? How many tablespoons to a cup? Use this guide to find the answers to these questions and more.

Equivalent Measures

dash = 2 to 3 drops or less than $\frac{1}{8}$ tsp.

1 tblsp. – 3 tsp.

1 fluid oz. = 2 tblsp.

¼ c. = 4 tblsp.

⅓ c. = 5 tblsp. plus 1 tsp.

½ c. = 8 tblsp.

⅔ c. = 10 tblsp. plus 2 tsp.

¾ c. = 12 tblsp.

1 c. = 16 tblsp.

½ pt. = 1 c. or 8 fluid oz.

1 pt. = 2 c. or 16 fluid oz.

1 qt. = 4 c. or 32 fluid oz.

½ gal. = 2 qt. or 64 fluid oz.

1 gal. = 4 qt. or 128 fluid oz.

BASIC FLOUR AND MEAL INFORMATION

The major ingredient in all breads is flour or some type of meal. It's the most important ingredient, too. Without either a flour or a meal, bread just wouldn't be as we know it.

In the following two sections of this chapter we describe more than 30 different types of flour and meal. You'll find all of the wheat flours—all-purpose, whole-wheat flour and cracked wheat— in the section called "Wheat Flours and Meals." Buckwheat flour, rye flour, corn meal and more are included in the section called "Other Whole Grains, Meals and Special Flours."

While each flour and meal has unique characteristics, there are a few things all flours and meals have in common, especially when it comes to making bread.

The flour that's made by the old-fashioned milling method of crushing grain between two round millstones is called stone-ground. Besides whole-wheat flour, you'll find buckwheat flour, rye flour and corn meal are sometimes stone-ground. These coarser-textured flours are available at some supermarkets and at specialty food stores.

The modern method of milling flour is to pass the grain through hot steel rollers—resulting in a finely textured flour. Most commercial flours, such as all-purpose, are "steel-ground" and are available in supermarkets in 2-lb., 5-lb., 10-lb. or 25-lb. bags.

All flours—all-purpose flour, whole-wheat flour and rye flour, just to name a few—can vary from season to season according to the amount of moisture in the air. In humid weather, flour absorbs moisture from the air, and the reverse is true during dry weather and in arid climates. For this reason, we give a range of flour measurements in our yeast bread recipes. It's best to start with the smaller measurement, then slowly stir or knead in just enough flour to make the dough smooth and no longer sticky. Use the larger measurement as a maximum. (For quick breads and batter breads, we list an exact flour measurement; the moisture content of the flour isn't an issue for these doughs and batters, because they have so much more liquid than yeast breads.)

Some cooks don't believe in sifting flour, but we do. Most all-purpose flour is labeled "presifted," but during transit and handling at the supermarket, the flour settles and becomes compacted. Sifting flour before measuring will give you the same good results each time you make the recipe.

Coarse flours, like whole-wheat, cracked wheat and rye, are stirred before they are measured. The same is true for fine-textured flours like soy, rice and triticale.

Store flour in an airtight container in a cool, dry place to preserve moisture and freshness. All-purpose and bread flours can safely be kept at room temperature up to six months. Temperatures above 75°, especially when coupled with high humidity, invite spoilage and infestation.

Flours and meals that contain the oil-rich germ, such as whole-wheat flour and wheat germ, will turn rancid quickly, so store these flours and meals in your refrigerator. You can freeze any type of flour for long-term storage: wrap the bag carefully in moisture-proof material and freeze. Always bring chilled flour to room temperature before using.

For years bread has been made with many different varieties of grains and meals. If your favorite supermarket doesn't carry a particular flour or meal, you probably can purchase it at a specialty food store.

WHEAT FLOURS AND MEALS

Wheat is the most important of all grains, especially when it comes to baking breads. Wheat flour provides the framework of almost all baked goods. The wheat kernel is used to make over a dozen different types of flour and meal, and in this section, you'll discover just how unique this tiny kernel is.

The most common wheat flour is a blend of hard and soft wheats and is called all-purpose. As its name implies, it's suitable for all cooking and baking. All the quick bread and yeast bread recipes in this book have been tested with all-purpose flour, unless otherwise specified.

When freshly milled, all-purpose flour, bread flour and cake flour are slightly yellow. Upon storage they will oxidize and become the milky-white color that you're accustomed to. Since this whitening process takes a long time, food technologists developed a chemical process to bleach wheat flours and improve the appearance of baked goods. The bleaching of wheat flours, either commercial or natural, doesn't reduce its nutritional value.

Wheat flours are treated with potassium bromate to strengthen the protein and improve baking performance. Untreated wheat flours or unbromated flours tend to be soft and sticky.

Flours made from a high proportion of hard wheat contain more protein and are excellent for making bread. Soft wheat flours are lower in protein and are excellent for making cakes, cookies and pastries.

One way to check the type of flour you have is to read the nutritional information on the package label. Flours with 12 to 14 grams of protein per cup are great for making yeast breads. Some food companies manufacture and sell flour especially formulated for making bread, called bread flour. But remember that while these high-protein flours are ideal for making bread, they may make cookies or pastry a little tougher than you would expect.

Flour that's made from wheat contains high-quality gluten proteins. When wheat flour is mixed with water and then kneaded, these proteins form an elastic substance called gluten. It's gluten that gives doughs their structure and elasticity.

As a yeast dough made with wheat flour is mixed or kneaded, the gluten develops, forming long, elastic strands that trap the bubbles of carbon dioxide released by yeast or other leaveners. This is what makes dough rise.

Because it takes time to develop the gluten, most yeast breads must be kneaded at least 5 to 10 minutes. Don't worry about overdeveloping the gluten in yeast breads, especially if you're kneading by hand—it's almost impossible. But in quick breads such as muffins and biscuits, mixing and kneading must be kept to a minimum and done with a light hand to avoid overdeveloping the gluten. Quick breads leavened by baking soda or baking powder can become tough if they're overmixed or overkneaded.

All wheat flours are high in thiamine, riboflavin, niacin and iron, but the protein content varies. Flours such as whole-wheat, which contains the entire wheat kernel, are good sources of fiber.

Here's a brief description of the wheat flours and meals that can be used in making bread.

All-purpose flour is milled from selected blends of wheat kernels and can be used in all types of baked goods, from breads to cakes. Enriched with iron and B vitamins, all-purpose is the most popular flour. You can purchase it either bleached or unbleached. Sift before measuring.

Bread flour, milled from a blend of hard and soft wheats, is higher in protein than all-purpose flour. Bread flour has about 2% more protein than all-purpose, so it's better for making breads. It's bleached and bromated. This flour generally absorbs more moisture from the air than all-purpose. When making yeast breads, if you substitute bread flour for all-purpose flour, you'll find that you use a little less. Sift before measuring.

Bulgur is made by boiling whole wheat berries in water until they triple in size. Then they're dried and milled. They're ground in three grades: fine, medium or coarse. Bulgur should either be soaked or cooked before using it in bread recipes.

Cake flour is milled from soft wheat. It's low in protein and best suited to recipes for cakes and pastries, in which high gluten development isn't desirable. Sift before measuring.

Cracked wheat flour is made by coarsely crushing wheat berries, and is high in fiber and phosphorus. Store in your refrigerator.

Quick-mixing flour is a granular form of all-purpose flour. It pours freely and dissolves quickly in cold liquids—ideal for making sauces and gravies.

Self-rising cake flour sometimes is confused with regular cake flour. Because it contains leavening agents, self-rising cake flour *cannot* be substituted for cake flour.

Self-rising flour is a mix of all-purpose flour, leavening agents and salt. One cup of self-rising flour contains the equivalent of 1½ tsp. baking powder and ½ tsp. salt. Detailed instructions for using self-rising flour in baking are included on the package label.

Unfortunately, there's no general rule for substituting this flour for all-purpose flour and leaveners. While it produces flaky biscuits and delicate cakes, it's not recommended for making popovers. Sift before measuring.

Semolina is a high-protein flour milled from durum wheat. Usually mixed with white or whole-wheat flour, it's great for making yeast breads, dumplings and machine-made pasta. Stir before measuring.

Unprocessed bran is the outer layer of the wheat kernel and is used in small amounts to add fiber and flavor to breads. It's very coarse, and should be stored in the refrigerator. Unprocessed bran (which can be found in specialty food stores) can be used interchangeably with high-fiber bran cereal buds; we used both for the recipes in this book.

Wheat berries are whole, entire wheat kernels. Wheat berries can be ground to make cracked wheat and whole-wheat flours. Soak and cook them as you do rice, or sprout them as you would mung or soybeans.

When whole kernels are added to bread dough and baked, they add a chewy texture and a nutty flavor. For long-term storage, be sure to refrigerate.

Wheat germ, the embryo or germ of the wheat kernel, is produced as a by-product when flour is milled. It has a nutty flavor and is sometimes toasted to enhance its flavor. It's an excellent source of protein, iron, B vitamins and Vitamin E. Serve it topped with milk as a breakfast cereal; add it to baked goods; or use it to coat meats, like chicken, before cooking. Wheat germ must be stored in the refrigerator because of its high fat content.

Whole-wheat flour is milled from the entire wheat kernel including the bran, so it has a coarse texture, is light brown in color, and is higher in fat than all-purpose. It's often called *graham flour*, after the Nineteenth Century American nutritionist Sylvester Graham, who encouraged the use of whole-wheat flour in making breads.

Bread made exclusively with whole-wheat flour tends to be heavy and compact. You'll get a better structure, volume and finer texture in your homemade bread if you mix whole-wheat flour with some all-purpose.

Don't sift whole-wheat flour before measuring; this tends to remove some of the bran. Simply stir the flour before lightly spooning it into the measuring cup. Because this flour contains bran, it needs to be stored in the refrigerator.

Whole-wheat blend flour is a mix of whole-wheat flour and unbleached, all-purpose flour. You can substitute this flour for all-purpose in most baking recipes, but it will give cakes a much coarser texture and darker color. Stir before measuring and store in the refrigerator.

OTHER WHOLE GRAINS, MEALS AND SPECIAL FLOURS

Here are some whole grains, meals and special flours that can add flavor, texture and extra nutrition to breads. Although many are good sources of protein, few of them contain gluten-producing proteins, so they are usually mixed with all-purpose flour to make well-leavened breads.

Whole grains contain the oil-rich germ, so to ensure their freshness, it's best to buy them in small quantities. In humid weather and hot climates, all whole grains, seeds and flours are less likely to become rancid if you keep them refrigerated.

It's not necessary to sift whole-grain flours, special flours and meals; simply *stir* the flour or meal to aerate it. Then spoon it into your measuring cup, leveling off the excess with the straight edge of a knife or metal spatula.

Barley was one of the first cereal grains to be cultivated. Throughout its history, barley has been used in many countries to make malt syrup, a vital ingredient in brewing beer.

The outside hull or husk of barley is inedible, so it's removed by a process called pearling. Barley is available whole-pearled and quick-pearled. Quick-pearled barley is crushed slightly to expose more surface area of the barley kernel, so it cooks faster than whole-pearled barley. Barley is a good source of protein, calcium, phosphorus, potassium, iron and B vitamins.

Barley meal is coarsely ground barley, and *barley flour* is a finer version of barley meal. You can use both the meal and the flour in combination with wheat flour in baking.

Buckwheat is actually an herb and a member of the rhubarb family. The triangular seeds of the buckwheat plants are called groats, and in Russia and Eastern Europe, groats cooked in water are called kasha.

Buckwheat groats can be ground into a dark flour that is clay-like in texture. It's low in gluten and is usually mixed with wheat flour for baking. Buckwheat flour has a strong, unique flavor and is a good source of protein, fiber, calcium, phosphorus, iron and B vitamins.

Corn meal is made by crushing dried kernels of corn into meal. In the Midwest, you'll find corn bread made with yellow corn meal, and in the South, you'll find corn bread made with white corn meal, but the only difference between yellow and white corn meal is the color. Corn meal is a good source of Vitamin A and niacin.

Stone-ground corn meal leaves the germ intact. This nondeger-minated, or "bolted," corn meal is high in fiber and is an important ingredient in salt-rising bread.

Grits are a coarser kind of corn meal. *Corn flour* is a finer grind of corn meal and is made from corn grown especially for flour. *Cornstarch*, used primarily to thicken sauces and gravies, is made by wet-milling kernels of corn to extract the starch.

Millet is a small round grain that resembles mustard seed. This nut-flavored seed can be ground into flour and is an excellent source of iron, fiber and B vitamins.

Oats are processed in various ways to produce a variety of choices for the breakfast and dinner table.

Whole oat kernels are steel-cut to form a meal that's similar to cracked wheat. These steel-cut oats are then crushed and rolled to form large flakes called *old-fashioned oats.*

When old-fashioned oats are rerolled and cut more finely, they become *quick-cooking oats.* As a rule, old-fashioned and quick-cooking oats can be substituted for one another in baking recipes. Either can be used in our bread recipes.

Finally, when quick-cooking oats are partially cooked and then dried, the product is *instant oats.* These are manufactured as a convenience item—for a bowl of oatmeal, just add boiling water and stir.

Oat flour is made by grinding old-fashioned or quick-cooking oats into flour. You can easily do this in a blender or a food processor: Place uncooked old-fashioned or quick-cooking oats (1 c. at a time) in a blender or food processor container. Blend at high speed or process until a fine flour forms, about 60 seconds. Homemade oat flour *must* be stored in the refrigerator.

Oat flour can be used to replace up to (but not more than) one third of the total amount of all-purpose flour in bread recipes. The finished bread will have a coarse texture and a nutlike flavor.

Oats are an excellent source of protein and are high in iron, potassium, phosphorus and B vitamins.

Potato flour is made from mashed potatoes that have been dried and crushed. This powdery flour is very hard to find on the retail market as it is used primarily in commercial baked goods.

Potato starch is available in supermarkets and is not to be confused with potato flour. Potato starch is used to thicken soups, stews and gravies, but is not used in making bread. It's produced by extracting starch during the processing of instant potato products.

Rice flour is milled from both white and brown rice. Because it contains no gluten, it can be used to make bread for those who are allergic to gluten. Rice flour breads are compact and dense, but acceptable. Rice flour is an excellent source of B vitamins, especially thiamine and niacin.

Rye flour is made by grinding whole rye berries. Because it's milled in various grades, the color ranges from pale to dark tan. All grades are interchangeable, but the darker the flour, the more pronounced the flavor.

This flour, though high in protein, contains very little of the protein that produces gluten, and it becomes sticky and tacky when mixed with liquid. Because of this, rye flour usually is mixed with wheat flour for making bread. You may find a coarser grind of rye flour, called *rye meal*.

Rye flour and meal both are good sources of protein, phosphorus, potassium, iron and B vitamins.

Soy flour, or *soya flour*, is milled from soybeans. The beans are sometimes lightly toasted before milling to produce a stronger soy flavor. This flour is high in protein and is often added in small amounts to bread dough to increase its nutritional value.

You can easily make homemade soy flour by grinding soybeans in your blender. Follow the same directions for making *Oat flour* (see preceding page) substituting soybeans for oats.

Soy flour also is high in iron and adds a characteristic sweet, sprout-like flavor to breads.

Triticale flour is milled from a hybrid grain that's a cross between durum wheat and rye. It has a high protein content and is excellent for making bread.

Breads made with triticale flour should be kneaded gently to develop the delicate gluten structure without breaking it. These breads will take a little longer to rise than wheat flour breads.

This flour is highly perishable, so purchase only what you need and store any leftovers in the refrigerator or freezer. This light, tan-colored flour is a good source of protein, fiber and iron.

LEAVENING AGENTS

The highest and lightest loaves of bread all have two ingredients in common, and they're free—lots of air and steam. Air is incorporated as you mix the batter or knead the dough, and the heat of the oven causes the liquid ingredients to form steam.

While they are important, very few breads are leavened by air and steam alone. Other leaveners are used—yeast, baking soda, baking powder or starters. All produce bubbles of carbon dioxide gas that help bread rise and give each loaf its unique texture.

Here's how each of these leaveners interacts with other ingredients to make bread rise.

Yeast, a microscopic plant that lives all around us in the air and soil, needs air, moisture and sugar or starch to grow, and it thrives in the moist, sticky environment of bread dough. As yeast grows, it converts sugars and starches into carbon dioxide and alcohol in a process known as fermentation.

Of the many different strains of yeast, bakers' and brewers' yeast are the most important for food preparation. Bakers' yeast is a mix of yeast strains selected for flavor and their ability to produce carbon dioxide. Brewers' yeast is used to brew beer, and never substituted for bakers' yeast in making bread.

Bakers' yeast is available in two forms: active dry, and compressed, sometimes called fresh yeast. Some bakers swear that compressed yeast produces a better baked product, especially in flavor and texture. We have used both forms to make the same recipe and were unable to discover any difference, so for convenience we have used active dry yeast in our recipes.

Active dry yeast is about 8% moisture and can be stored for months, unopened, on the pantry shelf. It's sold in ¼-oz. foil packages and in 4-oz. vacuum-packed jars for big-batch home bakers. Once opened, these jars should be stored in the refrigerator.

Compressed yeast is sold in 0.6-oz. and 2-oz. cakes. A 0.6-oz. cake equals 1 (¼-oz.) package or 2½ tsp. active dry yeast. Because it is about 70% moisture, compressed yeast is highly perishable, and must be kept in the refrigerator. It should be stored no longer than two weeks. Compressed yeast also may be frozen up to two months. If you see a slight browning on the edge of a cake of compressed yeast, this indicates drying, but the yeast is still active enough to use. One way to test it is to crumble the cake between your fingers; if it breaks easily, it's still good, but if it feels mushy or soft, it should be discarded.

Both compressed and active dry yeast are packaged with expiration dates; check the date on the package before buying.

Be sure to bring yeast to room temperature before using. Never measure active dry yeast with a wet measuring spoon.

There are two methods of adding yeast. The use of either method is determined by how the dough or batter is mixed. As a rule of thumb, use about ½ pkg. (1¼ tsp.) to 1 pkg. (2½ tsp.) active dry yeast for every 4 c. flour.

In the Conventional Method, active dry yeast is sprinkled over warm water that ranges in temperature from 105 to 115°. This mixture is stirred until the yeast is completely dissolved. It's then mixed with the remaining ingredients to make a batter or a dough.

In the Rapidmix Method, active dry yeast is mixed with some of the dry ingredients. Then very warm liquid—the temperature should range from 120 to 130°—is gradually beaten into the yeast-flour mixture, using a mixer. The very warm liquid will not kill the yeast because the yeast is surrounded by flour and is not in direct contact with the very warm liquid. This mixture must be beaten for about two minutes until all of the yeast is dissolved before adding the remaining ingredients.

Both of these methods—Conventional and Rapidmix—are explained in detail in Chapter Six, "Basics of Yeast Breads."

Because it's high in moisture, the only way compressed yeast can be incorporated into a batter or a dough is by the Conventional Method. Simply crumble the compressed yeast into the warm water and stir the mixture until the yeast is completely dissolved.

Recently, more-active strains of dry yeast have become

available, variously called "fast-rise," "quick-rise" or "rapid-rise" yeast. If used correctly, this type of yeast will cut the rising time of the dough in half. These more-active, stronger strains of yeast are finer, so they absorb liquid at a much faster rate. They also blend more readily with flour, which makes it unnecessary to dissolve them directly in water. For the greatest timesaving, it's recommended to use quick-rise yeast in recipes made by the Rapidmix Method (see Index).

In all of our Rapidmix recipes, you can substitute quick-rise yeast for active dry yeast, measure for measure. Your bread will rise in about half the time, so be sure to check the dough often, especially during the last half of the rising time. For more information on quick-rise yeast, see the package label.

No matter which yeast you use—compressed, active dry or quick-rise—the yeast feeds on the flour and sugar in the bread dough. As it feeds it will ferment, producing carbon dioxide and some alcohol. The carbon dioxide can't escape the sticky, heavy dough, so it collects in small bubbles throughout the dough, causing the dough to rise.

When the dough has doubled in size, it's time to punch it down to release some of the gas. Punching down the dough and letting it rise a second time produces bread with a fine, smooth texture.

Baking soda, or bicarbonate of soda, was the first chemical leavener used in this country. It must be combined with an acid, such as buttermilk, yogurt or molasses, to produce the carbon dioxide that makes dough rise. Baking soda reacts immediately when moistened and always should be sifted or mixed with dry ingredients before liquid is added.

Baking powder is a mix of baking soda, an acid such as cream of tartar, and an absorbent such as cornstarch. When mixed with liquid, baking powder releases some carbon dioxide immediately. Like baking soda, it must be sifted or mixed with dry ingredients before being added to liquid.

In this book, the recipes that call for baking powder were tested with double-acting baking powder. At one time, single-acting baking powder was the only type of baking powder available. To be effective, it had to be mixed into the batter quickly and immediately baked. Double-acting baking powder works twice: It releases a small amount of gas when it's first mixed with liquid, and more gas when it's exposed to heat.

Baking powder is perishable, so it's a good idea to purchase the smallest can available and check the expiration date on the can.

To test for freshness, combine 1 tsp. baking powder with ⅓ c. boiling water; if it bubbles actively, it's still usable.

Starters such as sourdough starter, beer starter and salt starter are unpredictable at best. Before yeast became commercially available, cooks would set a mixture of flour and liquid in a warm place in the hope of capturing the yeast that's present in the air. In a few days, with luck, the starter would begin to ferment and bubble, and then it could be used to make bread.

Starters were kept "going" by replenishing them each time bread was made. Sometimes starters produced big, high loaves of bread, and sometimes not. That's why once the integrity of the starter was proven, it was passed along to neighbors and friends.

In this book you'll find a recipe for a sourdough starter made by adding active dry yeast to a mix of flour and water (see Index). After it has fermented for a day you can use it to make bread, biscuits and pancakes. Because of its characteristic taste, sourdough is the most versatile and well-known starter in this country, especially in San Francisco.

A starter made from a mix of rye flour, water and yeast is used to make two loaves of Jewish Sour Rye Bread (see page 159). It ferments for three days, producing a wonderfully pleasing sour-rye starter. It's not difficult to make this starter and it's well worth the wait.

Salt-rising starter is a mixture of whole-grain corn meal, sugar and water. You must use whole-grain corn meal because it contains the corn germ, which is necessary to attract the right yeast from the air. This starter has a cheesy texture and flavor—not at all salty, as its name implies. However, years ago, crocks of starter were placed in beds of heated rock salt to keep the starter warm enough to ferment—hence the name.

Salt-rising starter is by far the most temperamental and unpredictable. To eliminate the guesswork in making our Salt-Rising Bread, we added a package of yeast to the starter after it fermented. While this bread is not technically a salt-rising bread, it won't disappoint you, because it will rise every time you make it and produce three handsome, firm-textured loaves. And this bread makes excellent toast!

LIQUIDS

To moisten dry ingredients, to dissolve yeast, and to stimulate the formation of gluten, liquid ingredients are needed to make bread. The ones you choose also will affect the bread's flavor and texture. These are the common liquids used in bread recipes.

Water brings out the flavor of grains and creates a crisp crust. Breads such as French or Italian, in which all the liquid is water, are chewy, coarse-textured and crusty.

Milk and milk products—yogurt, sour cream and heavy cream—produce yeast breads with a fine, velvety texture. In general, breads made with milk keep longer than breads made only with water. Milk produces a soft, golden brown crust and adds to the nutritional quality of the bread.

Whatever type of pasteurized milk you normally drink, feel free to use it as an ingredient in baking—whole, low-fat and skim milk can be substituted for one another. It used to be necessary to scald milk before adding it to yeast dough to denature the protein that plays havoc with the gluten formation. Pasteurization makes that unnecessary, but if you use raw milk, fresh from the dairy, it must be scalded and cooled before using it to make yeast dough.

Nonfat dry milk can be used in bread recipes and is generally added with the dry ingredients. If a recipe calls for 1 c. milk, substitute 1 c. water and add ⅓ c. nonfat dry milk.

Buttermilk is the liquid that remains after milk or cream has been churned and the butterfat removed. Today you can purchase cultured buttermilk in the dairy section of most supermarkets. It's added to many bread recipes, especially biscuits, pancakes and waffles, for its characteristic "sour" flavor. We used this type of buttermilk in testing our recipes.

You also can substitute a mix of whole milk and vinegar for buttermilk: to equal 1 c. buttermilk, add enough whole milk to 1 tblsp. cider or white vinegar to make 1 c. In some supermarkets you also can purchase buttermilk powder to use in place of fresh cultured buttermilk. You can use either substitution in our recipes that call for buttermilk.

Fruit and Vegetable juices add flavor and body to breads. For years, country cooks have been in the habit of saving the water in which they cook potatoes and using it to make breads. Potato water adds flavor and produces a fine-textured bread. If you'd like to use potato water in your bread recipes, just substitute it for the amount of liquid that's required. If you've stored it in the refrigerator, be sure to warm it slightly before using it. Because potato water is high in starch, your yeast dough will rise more quickly.

Beer and liquor make smooth-textured breads and add flavor. The alcohol will evaporate as the bread bakes.

FATS

The softest and most moist breads are made with butter, margarine, vegetable oil or shortening. Yeast bread made with one of these fats also will keep longer than yeast bread without.

Use these four kinds of fats interchangeably in dough for yeast breads—but not in quick breads!

EGGS

Eggs enrich bread; add to the liquid and fat content; and also contribute to the structure, flavor, color and leavening of bread. An egg bread will have a golden brown crust with a fine-textured, pale yellow crumb. We used large eggs in testing our recipes.

SWEETENERS

Granulated sugar, light and dark brown sugar, honey, light and dark corn syrup, molasses and maple syrup are added to doughs or batters to provide food for yeast. Often just 1 tsp. sugar will be added to a yeast mixture to activate the yeast.

When sweeteners are added in larger amounts they bring out the flavor of bread and produce a brown crust. Brown sugar, honey and molasses often are used for their characteristic colors and flavors, especially in dark bread.

SALT

Salt enhances the flavor of bread and helps stabilize the yeast fermentation. If you're on a low-sodium diet, you can eliminate salt from your bread recipes. Your bread will rise, but it will taste bland and flat. During the recipe testing of this book, we used only enough salt to stabilize the yeast fermentation and make an acceptably flavored bread.

OTHER INGREDIENTS

Raisins, dried fruits, nuts, seeds, cheeses, spices, herbs and flavoring extracts enhance the flavor of bread. All these ingredients can be added in small amounts without affecting the way your bread bakes.

STORING, FREEZING AND REHEATING

Here's how to keep your homemade coffeecakes, rolls, yeast loaves and quick breads "oven-fresh."

After baking breads or rolls, let them cool completely; they should not be wrapped while still warm. After they've cooled to room temperature, wrap them tightly in foil or plastic wrap, or place in plastic bags. When using plastic bags, press excess air from the bags before sealing tightly.

An old-fashioned, well-ventilated bread box is an ideal place to store breads at room temperature. Breads and rolls that contain no fat will become stale in just a few days. Those that are made with fat will keep longer, about three to four days.

Most breads and rolls don't benefit from storage in the refrigerator. In fact, the cool temperature causes breads and rolls to become stale even faster than at room temperature. If you can't use a loaf of bread within three to four days, consider freezing it.

Breads, rolls and coffeecakes will keep up to six months in the freezer, especially if wrapped well. Wrap them in heavy-duty foil or freezer-proof plastic wrap or plastic bags. Press out as much excess air as possible and seal tightly. Label, date and freeze.

Add icing and glazes to coffeecakes, sweet breads and rolls after thawing. If you forget and ice or glaze your sweet bread—freeze it first before wrapping. Then, wrap it and return it to the freezer. Bread with icing should be unwrapped before thawing.

Or, try what one experienced Alabama baker does: She slices her bread before freezing. Then she can remove and thaw the number of slices she needs—the slices thaw quickly at room temperature. For breakfast she takes bread slices right from the freezer and pops them into her toaster.

Waffles, French toast and thick pancakes can be frozen and reheated in the toaster, but it may take more than one toasting cycle to thaw and heat them.

Breads and coffeecakes should be thawed in their original wrappings and unwrapped just before serving. Bread will take two to three hours to thaw, depending on the warmth of the room and the size of the loaf.

Foil-wrapped breads may be thawed and warmed in a 375° oven in about 20 minutes. Rolls will take about 8 to 12 minutes. Unwrap crisp-crusted breads or rolls the last 5 minutes of heating to crisp the crusts.

2
Utensils

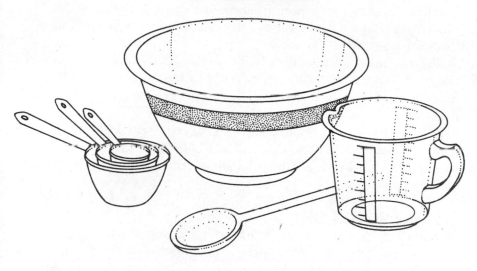

To make even the most sophisticated bread recipe, you probably already own all of the equipment that you'll need—a mixing bowl, a set of measuring cups and spoons, baking sheets or loaf pans, a reliable oven and most important, two eager hands. That's all—except, of course, the ingredients and the time it takes to make the bread.

The most essential bread-making tools are your hands. Without them, it would be next to impossible to make bread. So don't be afraid to use them! Most yeast doughs are meant to be kneaded, shaped and patted, and your hands are just the right tools.

There are a number of kitchen gadgets and appliances that will prove helpful in preparing bread. How these tools are used is as important as having them. The more you make and bake bread, the more you'll be able to determine just exactly what you'll need. Here's some information on using the right utensils for making and baking bread, plus a few baking tips for those of you who live in high-altitude areas.

USING A FLOUR MILL

Grinding grains and seeds right in your own kitchen has several advantages: You can custom-grind seeds and rice to make unusual flours such as millet flour and rice flour. By doing your own milling, you can control the texture of the ground grains or seeds from coarse to fine. Home-ground flours tend to be fresher and therefore more nutritious than store-bought flours.

But there's more to milling flour than meets the eye—first you must own a flour mill. There are two types, manual and electric.

Manual mills are relatively inexpensive and easy to clean. But like hand-cranked ice-cream freezers, it takes a lot of muscle power to use them and a lot of effort to grind enough grain into flour for one loaf of bread.

Electric mills, quite naturally, are easier on the muscles, but can tax the budget. They generally cost about four times as much as hand mills, but in just seconds you can grind enough flour to make two loaves of bread.

Flour mills are worthwhile if you bake regularly with unusual flours. If you're an occasional baker, it's probably more practical to purchase hard-to-find flours locally or through mail-order food catalogues.

USING A MIXER

Most of the recipes in this book can be made by stirring the batter or dough with a wooden spoon. To save time and effort, though, we suggest that you use your mixer to beat and possibly knead yeast doughs.

Portable hand-held mixers are great for mixing cake batters or whipping heavy cream. But these lightweight appliances usually aren't powerful enough to mix and knead thick batters and yeast doughs without damaging their motors.

Larger mixers mounted on stands can safely be used for the beginning stages of mixing yeast doughs.

You'll notice that many of our breads use the mixer to combine the liquid ingredients with about half of the flour, producing a heavy batter. This batter is thick enough to allow the gluten to start forming, but thin enough not to harm most standard mixers.

Heavy-duty mixers are equipped with larger motors and can easily knead yeast dough. These are sold with special accessories called dough hooks. The beater-like attachments can be used for the last addition of flour and for kneading yeast dough. Kneading an average yeast dough will take 3 to 4 minutes at low speed. The dough will come away from the side of the bowl and will be smooth and elastic. (Be sure to follow the directions that came with your mixer when using these attachments.)

If your mixer has difficulty beating dough or makes "laboring sounds" while kneading a yeast dough, it's a good bet that there's too much dough for the machine to handle. Turn off your mixer and finish mixing or kneading the dough by hand.

USING A FOOD PROCESSOR

The food processor is truly a timesaver in mixing bread batters and doughs. In this book you'll find several bread recipes that can be made in your food processor, including Muffins and Scones (see Chapter Five) and Processor French Bread and Pizza Dough (see Chapter Seven) to name just a few.

The method for using the food processor differs a little from standard procedure. Here are some guidelines if you wish to adapt bread recipes to take advantage of your food processor.

When you make quick breads in your processor, measure all the dry ingredients into the work bowl. Using the sharp metal blade, process the dry ingredients for about 10 seconds to mix and aerate them. If nuts are one of the ingredients, add them to the dry ingredients and process a few seconds, just until they're chopped.

Mix the liquid ingredients in a small bowl. While the processor is running, pour the mixture through the feed tube. Process only a few seconds, just until the batter or dough is moistened and blended. Don't overprocess, or your quick bread will be tough. Pour the batter into the pan and bake—it's that simple!

Before making yeast bread in your food processor, check your processor's instruction book. Processors vary in their capabilities, and not all can handle the same amount of dough; some are not even suitable for making yeast bread. Most standard-size food processors can handle doughs made with 4 c. flour. A few larger models can handle doughs made with as much as 8 c. flour.

Refer to your processor's instruction book to determine which blade to use (either the sharp metal blade or the plastic dough blade) and insert the correct blade in the work bowl of your processor.

Begin with by placing all the flour, sugar, salt and other dry ingredients into the work bowl. (If butter or margarine is an ingredient, add it with the dry ingredients. If vegetable oil is an ingredient, add it later, right after adding the yeast.) Process 5 to 10 seconds until the ingredients are well mixed.

For processor breads, yeast always must be dissolved first in ¼ c. warm water (105 to 115°). While the processor is running, pour the yeast mixture through the feed tube in a slow, steady stream before adding the remaining liquid.

The temperature of the remaining liquid when added must either be cold or ice cold; this is a considerable departure from most yeast bread recipes. It's necessary because the heat from the processor motor and the blade action warm the dough. If the dough is too warm, it will rise too quickly and its flavor won't have time to develop. Adding cold liquid keeps the dough cooler.

Add this remaining liquid only as fast as the dry ingredients can absorb it.

Even though you add cold liquid, you'll notice that a bread kneaded in the food processor will rise faster. This is because the dough is warmer at the beginning of the rising, which causes faster yeast growth.

When all the liquid ingredients are added, the dough will form a ball around the blade. At this point, continue processing for an additional 40 to 60 seconds. Your dough should be uniformly soft, pliable and slightly sticky. The dough should always leave the side of the work bowl.

Sweet yeast doughs are an exception to the rule. Because these doughs have more fat and sugar, it takes the processor only about 25 to 30 seconds to knead these doughs. A sweet yeast dough will not leave the side of the work bowl after kneading.

Processor-kneaded doughs are soft. If the dough is too moist and doesn't leave the side of the bowl, add more flour, 1 tblsp. at a time, processing 10 seconds after each addition until the dough leaves the side of the bowl. If the dough is too dry to form a ball, add water, 1 tblsp. at a time, processing 10 seconds after each addition until the dough forms a ball.

If your processor motor slows down, you may be processing too much dough. Divide the dough in half and process each half separately.

Once the dough is kneaded in your food processor, follow recipe directions for the rising, shaping and baking of the dough.

CHOOSING BAKING PANS

Baking pans are available in a dazzling assortment of sizes, shapes and materials (from popover pans to French bread pans), but you can produce an amazing variety of baked goods with just a few basic pans.

High-quality baking equipment will last a lifetime, so when you choose a new baking pan, purchase a good heavy one if possible. Thin pans tend to warp and bend after numerous uses. In testing recipes for this book, we most often used metal pans to bake bread, but exceptions are noted in the recipes.

Here are some of the most common materials used to make baking pans.

Aluminum is the best all-purpose metal for home baking pans and is moderately priced. It's easy to clean, doesn't rust and is a good conductor of heat.

You'll find that aluminum baking pans are either highly polished or dull and dark with a gray finish. Breads baked in dark, heavy aluminum pans will be browner and have thicker crusts than those baked in shiny pans.

In a pinch you can use disposable foil pans. They're convenient for gift giving or taking breads to a party or church social—no need to remember to take your pan home!

Cast iron baking pans are heavy, but very durable and not expensive. These pans heat evenly and retain heat for some time. However, they can rust if not properly cleaned. Cast iron is most often used to make Dutch ovens and skillets, but you'll also find cast iron griddles, muffin pans and corn stick pans.

Glass and ceramic baking dishes are easy to clean and versatile, especially if they're microwave-safe. They can double as casseroles, and can go from freezer to oven and from oven to table.

Ceramic and glass dishes retain more heat than metal pans. To avoid overbrowning and overbaking your breads, we suggest reducing the oven temperature by 25° when you use these dishes for baking.

Whenever we used a glass or ceramic dish to test a recipe for this book, we have said so and have made the necessary temperature adjustments in the recipe.

Nonstick baking pans have metal bases and a smooth coating. Some of these coatings scratch easily, so be sure to follow manufacturer's use-and-care directions. These pans clean easily and breads tend not to stick to their sides or corners. They still need to be greased when the recipe specifies.

Baking sheets, also called cookie sheets, are flat sheets of metal that may have at least one slightly raised edge. Usually made of aluminum, sometimes with a nonstick coating, they're used to bake free-form loaves, rolls and coffeecakes.

When baking at high temperatures, sweet buttery breads such as croissants and Danish pastry may brown on the bottoms before the centers and tops are done. Professional bakers solve this problem by "double panning." This simple technique of stacking two baking sheets creates a thin layer of air that slows down the browning process so that the delicate breads will bake evenly.

Whether or not the baking pan is greased makes a big difference. Whenever it's necessary, our recipes say so; if the recipe doesn't mention greasing the pan, you need not do it.

When a baking pan does need to be greased, you have several choices. You can use a piece of waxed paper to add a little solid shortening, butter or margarine to the pan; use a pastry brush to apply vegetable oil or melted shortening, butter or margarine; or simply spray the pan with an aerosol vegetable spray.

Many breads, such as some batter breads and muffins, are baked in muffin-pan cups. You'll notice that most of our recipes instruct you to pour or spoon the batter into greased cups. However, in some recipes we suggest using paper liners (often called cupcake liners). Those recipes were tested in liners because the breads are tender and need the help of the liners to prevent sticking.

SUBSTITUTING BAKING PANS

Each recipe in this book specifies a pan size, and this is the size that should be used for the best results. But even if you don't have the correct-size pan, you still may be able to make the recipe. You may have another size pan that will work just fine. Here are some tips and a chart to help you improvise with the equipment that you already have.

If you don't have:	Use:
1½-qt. casserole, or 6-c. ring mold, or 6-c. fluted tube pan, or 4 (4½x2½x1¼") loaf pans, or 12 to 15 (2½") muffin-pan cups	8½x4½x2½" loaf pan (5½ c.)
2-qt. casserole, or 1 gugelhupf or turk's head mold, or 8x8x2" baking pan, or 9" tube pan, or 9-c. fluted tube pan, or 2 (1-lb.) coffee cans, or 2 (7½x3¾x2¼") loaf pans, or 14 to 18 (2½") muffin-pan cups	9x5x3" loaf pan (8 c.)
3-qt. casserole, or 10" tube pan (angel food cake pan), or 10" fluted tube pan (12 c.), or 2 (9") round pans, or 2 (8x8x2") baking pans, or 3 (1-lb.) coffee cans, or 22 to 30 (2½") muffin-pan cups	13x9x2" baking pan (15 c.)

When we call for a baking *pan* in our recipes, we refer to one that's made of metal; a baking *dish* is made of glass or ceramic material.

When substituting one pan for another, try to substitute one that has similar dimensions or volume for the specified pan.

To measure a pan or dish, place a ruler straight across the top and note the length and width from the inside edges. Measure the height or depth from the bottom of the pan to the top.

To determine the capacity or volume of a pan, dish or mold, simply count the number of 1-c. measures of water it takes to fill it to the very top.

Pans and dishes should be filled about one-half to two-thirds full with batters or doughs before baking. Changing the size of the pan or dish will alter the depth of batter, so baking time can be 5 to 10 minutes more or less than the stated baking time.

Keep in mind that glass cookware absorbs and retains heat, so food cooked in glass dishes may be done a few minutes sooner. Again, if you choose to substitute a glass or ceramic dish for a metal pan in our recipes, we suggest reducing the oven temperature by 25°.

BAKING IN A CONVENTIONAL OVEN

Before you set the oven dial, first position the rack so that the tops of the pans are in the middle of the oven. Then, check how your pans fit on your oven rack. Use one rack when you have at least 2" of space between each pan and between each pan and the oven walls.

Otherwise, you'll have to bake on two racks. Stagger pans on the two racks and reverse them from top to bottom and from front to back once during baking. If you do this, your breads will bake and brown evenly.

Chances are that even if you're using a brand new oven, the cost of your recipe ingredients, plus your valuable time, will be wasted if you fail to preheat your oven and double-check the temperature.

Always remember to turn on your oven 10 to 15 minutes *before* you plan to use it. This allows plenty of time for your oven to reach the proper temperature.

All the recipes in this book were tested in conventional gas or electric ovens—ovens the same size as the ones you and your neighbors have in your own kitchens. It doesn't matter whether your oven is gas or electric, or whether it's a brand-new model with digital touch pads or a 20-year-old economy model with a manual dial. What does matter is the temperature—and it's important to remember that in any oven (even new ones, sad to say) the temperature setting on the dial and the temperature of the oven may not match.

You can easily check the accuracy of your oven's temperature setting by using an oven thermometer. If you don't already have one, it's well worth the money to purchase one. Look for this most essential baking tool in the housewares section of hardware or department stores. Here's how to use one.

Place the oven thermometer on a rack in the middle of your oven. Set the oven temperature as recipe directs. After about 15 minutes, or as soon as the preheat light on your oven has gone off, check the temperature on the oven thermometer. Then make any adjustments needed to compensate for the difference in temperature.

If you own a self-cleaning oven, be sure to remove the thermometer before cleaning; it will break if it's exposed to the extremely high heat of the cleaning cycle.

BAKING IN A CONVECTION OVEN

This oven differs from a conventional oven because it has a fan to move the hot air around the food. Because there are no "hot spots" in a convection oven, breads and coffeecakes brown evenly, without having to rotate the pans or moving them from one shelf to another during baking.

Since hot air is constantly moving in the convection oven, baking temperatures for bread should be lower or the bread will burn. The general rule for convection oven baking is to reduce the baking temperature by 75°, but the temperature should never be reduced lower than 300°. For example, croissants bake at 425° in a conventional oven, so you would bake them at 350° in a convection oven. Or, if you want to bake graham crackers which bake at 350° in a conventional oven, you would bake them at 300° (not 275°) in a convection oven.

If you correctly adjust a convection oven's temperature, baking times will be the same as for a conventional oven. As every experienced baker knows, it doesn't matter which oven you use—it's always a good idea to check your bread 5 to 10 minutes before it's due to be done.

Professional bakers have been using convection ovens for years, and countertop models are available to home bakers.

All of our recipes were tested in conventional gas and electric ovens. If you plan to use your convection oven to bake any of these recipes, be sure to follow the manufacturer's directions for baking temperatures and baking times.

USING A MICROWAVE OVEN

The microwave oven is great for thawing or reheating baked breads, but when it comes to baking, this marvelous appliance has its limitations.

Breads do not brown, nor do they form a crust, and they rise unevenly when microwaved. The microwave oven's speed is not much of an advantage in baking, since most breads bake conventionally in 30 minutes. Because we feel the appearance, texture and flavor of microwaved breads suffer in comparison to those baked conventionally, you'll find very few microwave directions for the recipes in this book.

However, the microwave can be helpful in preparing bread recipes. Use it to defrost, to soften or melt butter, and to heat the liquid you use to make yeast bread dough.

The 2-c. and 4-c. glass liquid measures are ideal for mixing the liquid ingredients for yeast bread dough. Following recipe directions, first measure the milk, using a large microwave-safe measure. Then add the recipe's other liquid ingredients to the milk. Microwave this mixture at high setting (100% power) 1 minute.

Insert a yeast thermometer into the liquid to measure the temperature. If too low, continue to microwave at 15-second intervals until it reaches the correct temperature. Unless your thermometer is microwave-safe, remember to remove it before microwaving.

As a guide, to heat 1 c. cold milk to 105 to 115°, microwave at high setting (100% power) about 1 minute 15 seconds. The same amount of milk will take about 1 minute 40 seconds to reach 120 to 130°.

You can let the yeast dough rise in the microwave oven to save time. But before you do so, use this test to see if you can use your microwave oven for this purpose. Unfortunately, not all ovens have low enough temperature settings—too high a temperature will kill the yeast, and your dough won't rise.

Here's how to test your oven: Place 2 tblsp. *cold* butter in a microwave-safe custard cup. Microwave at lowest setting (10% power) 4 minutes. If the butter *melts completely* in *less* than 4 minutes you can't let yeast dough rise in your microwave oven.

If your oven passes this test with flying colors, follow these rising directions, which are designed for yeast doughs yielding two loaves. Smaller amounts of dough will take less time.

• When letting yeast dough rise in your microwave oven, watch it carefully and check the rising progress every few minutes to make sure that your dough doesn't overrise.

• Pour 3 c. water into 4-c. microwave-safe measure. Microwave at high setting (100% power) 4 to 6 minutes, or until water is steaming. Move measure to back corner of oven.

• Place kneaded dough in greased large microwave-safe bowl, turning over dough so that top is greased. Cover with waxed paper. Place bowl next to water-filled measure in oven.

• Microwave at *very low setting* (10% power) 16 to 20 minutes, just until dough is almost doubled. (If you are using quick-rise yeast, microwave only 8 to 10 minutes.)

• Punch down dough and let rest. Shape as recipe directs and place loaves in greased 8x4x2" microwave-safe loaf dishes.

• Microwave same 3 c. water at high setting 4 to 6 minutes. Cover loaves with waxed paper. Place loaves in oven next to water-filled measure.

• Microwave loaves at very low setting (10% power) 6 to 8 minutes or until almost doubled. (If you are using quick-rise yeast, microwave only 4 to 6 minutes.)

• Bake in a conventional oven according to recipe directions, but reduce oven temperature by 25° since you are using glass dishes.

Quick defrosting of store-bought or homemade frozen yeast dough can be done in your microwave oven, too: Place one loaf of frozen bread dough in greased 8x4x2" microwave-safe loaf dish, brush top with vegetable oil and cover with waxed paper.

Microwave at very low setting (10% power) 15 to 20 minutes or until dough is defrosted, rotating dish one-quarter turn every 5 minutes.

After thawing, follow package or recipe directions for letting the dough rise conventionally in a warm place. Further rising of thawed dough in the microwave results in an uneven loaf with a tough crust. Again, when you bake the loaf, remember to reduce the oven temperature by 25° whenever you use a glass dish.

Warming rolls and thawing frozen breads and rolls can be done in a flash in your microwave oven. For the best results, use the defrost setting for warming and thawing breads. You might be tempted to microwave breads and rolls until they're piping hot, but if you heat them too long, the result may be tough breads or rolls.

Most microwave ovens have a defrost setting; if yours doesn't, use a setting of low (30% power) or medium (50% power). These lower settings are best because they allow the oven to cycle on and off, and during the ''off'' periods, the temperature of the breads has a chance to equalize for more even heating and thawing.

Another reason why we suggest warming and thawing breads at a low setting in your microwave is that many breads, especially sweet breads, have sweet glazes and fillings. Microwaves are attracted to the sugar in the glazes and fillings. These sugary fillings and glazes may be bubbly hot before the surrounding bread begins to warm or thaw. By using a low setting, the microwave cycles on and off allowing even warming and thawing of your sweet bread.

To warm, place fresh or frozen bread or rolls on a paper towel and cover with another paper towel. The towels will absorb any excess moisture. When warming or thawing rolls, arrange three rolls in a triangle on a paper towel; place four or more rolls in a circle on a paper towel.

When defrosting a whole loaf of bread, it's best to rotate the loaf one-half turn, halfway through thawing. Breads or rolls may not be completely thawed in the times given below. They'll need to stand, covered, a few minutes to thaw completely.

Use the defrost setting (30% power) to warm or thaw the breads listed below. If your microwave doesn't have a defrost setting, use medium setting (50% power) and cut the microwave time suggested in the chart in half. For example, if you defrost a large coffeecake such as a Viennese Striezel at medium setting, check the coffeecake after 2 minutes to see if it has thawed.

To freshen stale bread, fill a microwave-safe custard cup two-thirds full with hot water. Set the cup in the corner of your microwave oven when you are reheating stale bread.

Another trick, especially useful for French and Italian breads, is to place the dried-out bread in a clean, brown paper bag that has been heavily misted with water. Close the bag and microwave at high setting (100% power) no longer than 30 seconds.

Warming and Thawing in the Microwave Oven

Bread	To Warm (minutes)	To Thaw (minutes)
1 whole loaf	4 to 5	9 to 10; stand 2
1 slice	30 seconds	1
1 small coffeecake	1 to 2	3 to 4; stand 2
1 large coffeecake	3 to 4	4 to 5; stand 2
sweet dinner rolls or doughnuts		
1 to 2	1 to 2	2 to 3; stand 1
4 to 6	2 to 3	3 to 4; stand 1

USING OTHER TOOLS

Here's a list of additional kitchen equipment that'll help you in making and baking all types of bread. You'll find that these items can be used in making most other baked goods, too.

Aluminum foil—Used to wrap baked breads for storage. A tented sheet of foil also is used to cover coffeecakes and breads during baking to prevent overbrowning.

Atomizer or plant mister—Used to spray a fine mist of water over risen dough before and during baking to give bread a crisp crust.

Baking tiles—Used to line the oven so that you can bake bread directly on the hot tile surface to produce thick crusty loaves. These tiles are placed on the lowest rack of the oven before preheating. The tiles create a "brick oven," much like the ones professional bakers use. You'll need a large flat wooden paddle to transfer the risen loaves to the hot baking tiles.

You'll find baking or quarry tiles in lumber or hardware stores. Purchase enough to line one rack in your oven.

Flat baking stones, also called hearth stones, are sold in department stores and by mail-order catalogues. These stones are usually sold in a kit consisting of one large flat stone (big enough to accommodate two loaves of bread) and a wooden paddle.

Cooling racks—Made of wire, or sometimes wood, and designed to let air circulate around and underneath the freshly baked breads and rolls as they cool. You'll need at least two large cooling racks.

Dough scraper—A rectangular piece of steel with a wooden handle that looks like a paint scraper. It's used to clean the work surface and comes in handy when you first begin to knead yeast dough. A large metal spatula can be used in place of a dough scraper.

Flour sifter—Needed to sift dry ingredients before measuring and to help mix the dry ingredients. A large sieve will do just fine.

Kitchen towel—Used to cover yeast dough during risings. Use one made of any material except terry cloth. (The little loops on the terry cloth have a tendency to stick to the rising yeast dough.)

Measuring cups and spoons—Used to accurately measure all types of recipe ingredients. For dry ingredients, use a graduated set of four measures: ¼ c., ⅓ c., ½ c. and 1 c. For liquid ingredients, use a cup measure made of see-through material with a spout and cup measurements marked on the side.

For small amounts of both dry and liquid ingredients, use a set of measuring spoons. Be sure to see *Measuring Ingredients* in Chapter One for more detailed information.

Mixing bowls—Can be made of stainless steel, glass or earthenware. You'll need several sizes, ranging from 1-qt. to 4-qt.

Oven thermometer—Necessary to check the accuracy of your oven.

Pastry blender—A wire utensil used for cutting solid fat, such as shortening, margarine or butter, into dry ingredients. If you don't have one, improvise by using two knives in a scissor fashion.

Pastry brush—A necessary tool used to brush dough with egg washes and to apply glazes. Use a soft brush between 1 and 3" wide.

Plastic wrap—To cover yeast dough during rising and keep it moist. It's the only suitable cover for yeast doughs that rise in the refrigerator.

Rolling pin—Used to roll out the dough before shaping. Choose one that's heavy and fits easily in your hands. We especially like the ones made out of wood with ball bearings in the handles— they're so easy to use.

A stockinet cover for the rolling pin will make the rolling even easier by preventing the dough from sticking to the pin.

Rubber spatula—Shaped like a flat paddle with a wooden or plastic handle. Since the rubber paddle is flexible, it's a handy tool for scraping down the side of a bowl and turning out the dough onto the work surface.

Ruler—For measuring the dimensions of pans and especially the thickness of rolled dough. If you want truly professional-looking biscuits and crackers, a ruler is essential.

Timer—A must, unless you can remember to watch the clock.

Wooden spoon —Used for stirring batters; stirring the last addition of flour into dough, and for stirring down the risen yeast batter. A wooden spoon is preferred over a metal spoon because wood doesn't chemically interact with acid ingredients in dough.

Work surface—A smooth, flat surface used for kneading and rolling out dough. Wood, formica and marble are all suitable surfaces.

Some bakers prefer to knead on a pastry cloth, because once flour is rubbed into the cloth, there's little chance that the dough will stick to the work surface as it is kneaded or rolled.

Yeast thermometer—To accurately measure the temperature of the liquid in which yeast is dissolved. Some bakers do this by feel, but it's well worth spending the few dollars to own one and eliminate any guesswork.

When purchasing a thermometer, look for one that measures temperatures between 100 and 400°. This versatile, three-in-one thermometer can be used to measure liquid temperature for yeast bread, sugar mixtures for candy-making and hot oil for deep-fat frying.

Most meat thermometers also can be used to measure the temperature for yeast liquids.

BAKING AT HIGH ALTITUDES

If you're accustomed to baking at sea level, baking at high elevations can be frustrating. At high altitudes the rate of evaporation is faster; the boiling point of water is lower; and leavening gases expand more and at a faster rate.

The change in atmospheric pressure affects the preparation method of certain foods, sometimes making it necessary to adapt your favorite lowland recipes.

If you're a newcomer to the mountains, you may wish to contact your county Cooperative Extension office. You also might want to talk to a neighbor about baking in your area; you're bound to get first-hand information, and it's a good way to make new friends.

Although you may not need to make adjustments at elevations as low as 2,500 feet, you'll definitely notice a difference at elevations above 3,500 feet. Here are some guidelines.

Because of the increased rate of evaporation at high altitudes, flour tends to dry out during storage and therefore absorb more liquids, especially in making bread. At high altitude, store all flours in an airtight container. In yeast bread recipes add only the minimum amount of flour listed, gradually adding more flour only if your dough is too sticky to handle.

The lower boiling point of water affects the deep-frying of moist foods such as doughnuts and fritters. These moist batters and doughs may appear to be done on the outside, but their centers may be doughy and undercooked.

To fry these breads evenly, you'll need to lower the temperature of the hot oil 3° for every 1,000 feet above 2,500 feet. It's best to experiment with one fritter or doughnut first before frying all of them: cut the fried fritter or doughnut in half to see if the center is cooked. It may be necessary to lower the temperature of the oil a few degrees more.

High altitude has a pronounced effect on the leavening of both yeast and quick breads. Carbon dioxide gas expands faster and therefore has a greater leavening action.

But, before you make any adjustments in your recipes, try filling your pans no more than half full with batters and doughs, or use a larger pan. For example, if your recipe calls for an 8½x4½x2½" loaf pan, use the larger 9x5x3" loaf pan to allow for the increased rising action during baking.

Yeast doughs can rise in half the time at high altitude. Check your dough halfway through the suggested sea-level rising time to make sure that your dough doesn't overrise. You'll want the dough to rise just until it doubles. For better flavor and texture, some experienced high-altitude bakers suggest letting yeast dough rise a second time before it's shaped.

Quick breads are usually firm-textured enough to withstand the faster leavening action of baking soda and baking powder. But if your quick bread has a bitter or alkaline taste, it's probably due to the inadequate neutralization of the baking powder or baking soda in the recipe. When this happens, try reducing the amount of baking powder by one-quarter. Always reduce baking powder before reducing baking soda. Recipes that call for baking soda usually have enough acid in them to neutralize the baking soda's bitter taste.

3
Basics of Quick Breads

Muffins, biscuits, popovers, crackers, tea loaves, pancakes and waffles—any bread that's made without yeast is a quick bread. These simple and fast-to-make breads require no experience on the part of the baker for perfect results, time after time.

Because these breads are generally leavened by either baking soda or baking powder, or a combination of both, you don't have to wait hours for quick breads to rise. These breads do all of their rising in the oven while baking. The key to success in making quick breads is fast but gentle mixing.

Basically there are two kinds of quick breads—those made from batters and those made from doughs. In this chapter you'll discover how easy it is to make quick bread batters and doughs by following our illustrated directions. In Chapter Four and Chapter Five, you'll find more than 70 recipes for naturally good quick breads, and most can be made in less than an hour.

QUICK BREAD BATTERS

Muffins, corn bread, quick coffeecakes and tea loaves are all examples of quick breads that are made from batters. You don't need any fancy equipment to make them—just two bowls, a fork and a spoon.

The dry ingredients are stirred together in one bowl and the liquid ingredients are stirred together in the other. Then both sets of ingredients are quickly stirred together to make a batter.

It's that simple, which is why batter-type quick breads are the easiest breads of all to make. It actually takes more time to measure the ingredients than it does to mix them together.

This procedure of mixing the dry ingredients with the liquid ingredients is called the *muffin method.* Many quick breads are made using this method.

Though the muffin method is basic, there are certain techniques that need further explanation. So, we've included an illustrated recipe for *Step-by-Step Muffins,* which follows. In addition, you'll find a section called *Muffin Tips.* This section of questions and answers will help you discover the causes of many common mistakes, so you'll know how to correct them the next time you make muffins.

Tea loaves are similar to muffins because most tea loaves are made using the muffin method. However, they have a few unique characteristics. For this reason we've included a special section in this chapter that's called *Tea Loaf Tips.*

Step-by-Step Muffins

Whether plain, or flavored with good things like fruits, nuts, cheese or even vegetables, properly mixed muffins should be tender, light and slightly moist. Their crusts should be golden brown and their pebbled tops should be slightly rounded—never peaked. Elongated holes, called tunnels, should not be evident when the muffins are broken open.

This is how perfect muffins are made:

2 c. sifted flour
⅓ c. sugar
1 tblsp. baking powder
½ tsp. salt
1 c. milk
⅓ c. vegetable oil
1 egg

Step 1: Into large bowl, sift together the flour, sugar, baking powder and salt. Sifting helps to evenly distribute the sugar, salt and especially the baking powder throughout the flour.

Step 2: In a small bowl, mix the milk, oil and egg until well blended. A fork works well for this; you also may use a rotary beater or wire whisk.

Step 3: Add the milk mixture to the dry ingredients all at once. Stir just until moistened. *Do not overstir.* This is the single most important thing to remember when making muffins. Don't try to stir out the lumps—the batter *should* be lumpy.

Overstirred muffin batter will produce tough muffins. These muffins will have smooth, peaked tops. Their interiors will be fine-grained and riddled with tunnels.

Step 4: Spoon the batter into 12 greased or paper-lined 2½" muffin-pan cups, filling each about two-thirds full. To help prevent additional mixing of the batter when filling the cups, use an ice cream scoop instead of a spoon.

As a general rule of thumb, fill any size muffin-pan cups two-thirds full. Remember that the baking time may vary if you are using muffin-pan cups of a size different from those specified in the recipe. Smaller muffins may bake more quickly; larger muffins, more slowly.

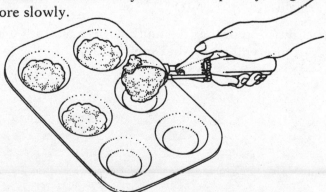

Step 5: Bake in preheated 400° oven 25 minutes, or until golden brown and a toothpick inserted in the center comes out clean. Muffins should be baked on the middle rack of the oven to allow heat to circulate evenly around them.

Step 6: Immediately remove the muffins from the pans. If the muffins are allowed to cool in the pans, the steam will make them soggy. Serve muffins at any temperature—piping hot, warm or cold. Makes 12 muffins.

Muffin Tips

As you can see from the following questions, the most common cause of poor muffins is overmixing. If you stir the batter *only until it is moistened*, then it is practically guaranteed that all your muffins will be successful.

The tops of my muffins were smooth and peaked—why?

The batter was overmixed. Remember to stir only until the batter is moistened.

The insides of my muffins were very fine-grained and full of tunnels—why?

Once again, these are caused by overmixing the batter.

My muffins were heavy and tough—why?

Too much flour in the batter can result in heavy muffins, but this also can happen if the batter is overmixed.

My muffins were dry—why?

Your oven was too hot, or the muffins were baked too long. Too much flour also will make your muffins dry.

Tea Loaf Tips

The muffin method is used for making many tea loaf batters. Some bakers feel that tea loaves are even easier to make than muffins, since the batter is baked in one or two loaf pans, eliminating the task of filling individual muffin-pan cups. However, tea loaves have certain distinct characteristics, because they are baked in larger pans.

Fill the baking pans about two-thirds full. The batter will nearly double in volume when baked, and the loaves shouldn't sink when removed from the oven.

Don't be alarmed if you see a crack running down the center of the top of the finished loaf; this crack is characteristic of many tea breads.

Because tea loaves bake for a longer time, it's wise to check the loaves 15 minutes before the baking time is over. Check by using a toothpick: Insert the toothpick in the center of each loaf and remove. If the toothpick comes out clean, the loaf is done. If there's any batter or sticky crumbs adhering to the toothpick, continue baking until it tests done.

If you find that the loaves are browning too quickly during baking, cover them with a tent of foil to prevent overbrowning during the remainder of the baking time.

The loaves should cool in their pans about 10 minutes. Then remove the loaves from their pans and cool them completely on racks before slicing.

A good tea loaf is tender and moist, but not oily. Its texture should be slightly crumbly. Tea loaves are best served at room temperature.

Unlike other baked goods, many tea loaves improve in flavor if wrapped tightly when cooled, and stored at room temperature overnight. They also will slice better on the second day.

Here are some answers to the most commonly asked questions about preparing and baking tea loaves.

My tea loaf was soggy and sunken in the middle—why?

This can be caused by either too much liquid or too much sugar. Not enough baking powder or baking soda also can be the cause.

My tea loaf was dry and bulged in the center—why?

Not enough liquid or too little shortening in the batter will cause this to happen.

My tea loaf had a coarse, very crumbly texture and a bitter aftertaste—why?

This is caused when too much baking soda or baking powder is used. A tea loaf also may have a bitter taste if the baking powder or baking soda is not sifted or thoroughly mixed with the dry ingredients.

My tea loaf was greasy and the edges of the loaf were very crisp—why?

Too much shortening in the batter will cause this.

The crust on my tea loaf was thick, porous and much too dark—why?

This happens when there is too much sugar in the batter. You also may see tiny, light specks of sugar on the surface of the crust.

QUICK BREAD DOUGHS

Biscuits, Scones, Irish Soda Bread and many crackers are all quick breads made from doughs. Just as you would make pastry for a pie crust, a solid fat—shortening, butter or margarine—is cut into the dry ingredients. The liquid is then added and the mixture is stirred until a soft dough forms.

The dough is gently kneaded on a lightly floured surface. The kneading is brief, usually about 10 times—just long enough so that the dough is neither lumpy nor sticky, and the ingredients are well mixed. This technique for making quick bread dough is often referred to as the *biscuit method.*

You'll find illustrated directions for using this method in the following section, *Step-by-Step Biscuits.* For more information on biscuits and other quick bread doughs, be sure to read *Biscuit Tips*, following the step-by-step recipe for biscuits.

Step-by-Step Biscuits

Savored piping hot from the oven and spread with butter or jam, biscuits rank high among all-time quick bread favorites. They can be served at any meal—morning, noon or night—and the memory of their flaky goodness will linger long after the rest of the meal has been forgotten.

Whether you cut the biscuit dough into rounds or hearts, squares or triangles, baked biscuits should have level, fairly smooth, golden brown tops, without yellow or brown spots. Their sides should be straight and lighter in color than their tops. When baked, the biscuits should be 2 to 3 times higher than the unbaked ones. Their crusts should be crisp but tender. Inside, biscuits should be slightly moist, tender and flaky.

Here's how they're made:

 2 c. sifted flour
 1 tblsp. baking powder
 2 tsp. sugar
 ½ tsp. salt
 ⅓ c. shortening
 ⅔ c. milk

Step 1: Into large bowl, sift together the flour, baking powder, sugar and salt. Sifting helps to evenly distribute the sugar, salt and especially the baking powder throughout the flour.

Step 2: With pastry blender, using a chopping motion, cut the shortening into the dry ingredients until coarse crumbs form.

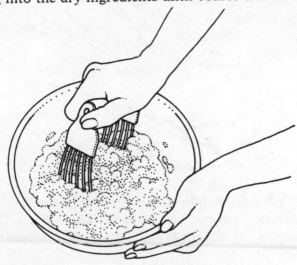

Step 3: Add the milk to the shortening mixture all at once. With a fork, stir until the mixture forms a soft dough that leaves the side of the bowl. Keep the stirring to a minimum. The dough will be soft and slightly sticky.

Step 4: Turn out the dough onto a lightly floured surface. Lightly flour your hands and knead the dough 10 times. Kneading helps to thoroughly mix the dough. (For more detailed kneading directions see Steps 7 through 9 in the recipe for *Step-by-Step Yeast Bread* in Chapter Six.)

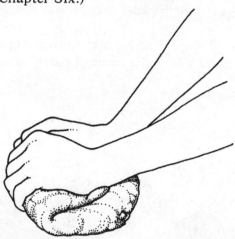

Step 5: With a floured rolling pin, roll out the biscuit dough to a ½" thickness. Use a ruler to check the thickness. If you don't have a rolling pin, just pat out the dough with lightly floured hands to a ½" thickness.

Step 6: Cut the dough with a floured 2½″ round biscuit cutter. Biscuits should be cut close together, leaving as little dough as possible for rerolling. For tall, straight-sided biscuits, cut the dough using a straight, downward pressure and avoid twisting the cutter. If cutting biscuits with a sharp knife, use a straight, downward pressure and avoid dragging the knife through the dough.

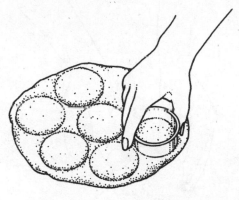

Step 7: Using a metal spatula, carefully lift the biscuits and place them on an ungreased, shiny baking sheet. For crusty-sided biscuits, place them 1″ apart. For soft-sided biscuits, place them close together with their sides just touching.

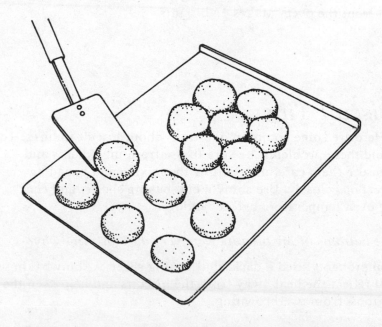

Step 8: Handling the dough lightly, gently press the scraps together; reroll and cut. Though the rerolled biscuits may not be as uniform in appearance, they will be tender if the dough is handled as little as possible.

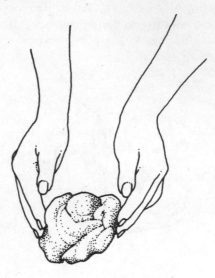

Step 9: Bake on the middle rack in a preheated 450° oven 10 to 12 minutes or until golden brown.

Step 10: Serve immediately. Biscuits are best when served piping hot from the oven. Makes 12 biscuits.

Biscuit Tips

Here are some common questions about biscuit failures. To avoid these problems, be sure to use fresh ingredients and measure them carefully. Follow the mixing and kneading directions closely. Use shiny metal baking sheets, and check the oven temperature before baking.

The bottoms of my biscuits were very dark brown—why?

You probably used a dark, dull baking sheet. A shiny baking sheet will reflect the heat away from the biscuits and help keep the bottoms from overbrowning.

My biscuits were not very high—why?

Poor volume can be caused by several things. You may not have used enough baking powder or the baking powder may be old; you may have undermixed or even overmixed the dough; or your oven temperature may have been too high.

There were yellow or brown spots on the tops of my biscuits—why?

This can happen when the ingredients aren't thoroughly mixed together. The spots are actually particles of baking soda or baking powder that weren't moistened. It also can happen when too much baking powder or baking soda is used.

My biscuits were tough—why?

Too little shortening, too much flour or liquid, or too much mixing or kneading of the dough all can cause toughness.

My biscuits were crumbly—why?

Too much shortening can cause biscuits to crumble, but this also can happen when too much baking powder is used.

My biscuits weren't flaky—why?

If you didn't use enough shortening, or if the shortening is cut into the dry ingredients too finely or too coarsely, your biscuits won't be flaky. The shortening should be cut in just until the mixture resembles coarse crumbs.

My biscuits were heavy and soggy—why?

Most likely they were underbaked, but overmixing or too much liquid or flour can cause this problem, too.

My biscuits had a bitter flavor—why?

Too much baking powder can cause a bitter flavor. The same thing can happen if the baking powder is not sifted or thoroughly mixed with the dry ingredients. You also may notice a bitter flavor if the dough is not thoroughly mixed.

My biscuits tasted rancid—why?

The culprit is probably less-than-fresh shortening.

4
Coffee Breads and Tea Loaves

In between cakes and yeast breads is the simple, yet wonderful world of quick breads. Generally moist like cakes and shaped like yeast breads, quick breads require little preparation time and bake in only about 30 minutes.

In this chapter you'll find many quick breads that closely resemble cakes: Sour Cream Crumb Ring, Poppy Seed Tea Bread, Apple Coffeecake and Peanut Butter Bread, just to name a few. There also are some quick breads that are similar to yeast breads, like Quick Raisin Bread and Cheesy Whole-Wheat Loaf.

Apricot, blueberries, bananas and cranberries are some of the fruits used to flavor many of our tea breads. If you can wait a day before you serve them, these sweet and moist quick loaves will be more flavorful and easier to slice.

Fast but gentle mixing is essential for tender quick breads. Preheat the oven and have the pans ready prior to mixing the ingredients, because these breads begin to rise as soon as they're mixed. (For more information on making these simple breads, be sure to read Chapter Three.)

For those extra-busy days, there's a pair of homemade mixes that will help you cut corners when making Corn Bread or creamy Spoon Bread and French Crumb Cake. You'll find these mixes used in many other bread recipes throughout this book.

When you want homemade bread with a minimum of effort, look here for more than 40 recipes.

All-purpose Baking Mix

You can make homemade muffins, biscuits, waffles, pancakes and coffeecakes in a jiffy with this basic mix.

10 c. sifted flour
1⅓ c. nonfat dry milk
4 tblsp. baking powder
4 tsp. salt
2 c. shortening

In very large bowl, stir together flour, dry milk, baking powder and salt. With pastry blender, cut in shortening until coarse crumbs form.

Store in airtight container in cool, dry place up to 3 months. Stir before measuring. Makes about 14 c.

Use as directed to make French Crumb Cake (recipe follows) and more.

French Crumb Cake

So easy to make with your own All-purpose Baking Mix, this feather-light breakfast cake tastes as good as any bakery coffeecake.

½ c. packed brown sugar
3 tblsp. flour
1 tsp. ground cinnamon
3 tblsp. butter or regular margarine
2 c. All-purpose Baking Mix
¾ c. sugar
¾ c. milk
1 egg
1 tsp. vanilla
Confectioners' sugar

In small bowl, stir together brown sugar, flour and cinnamon. With pastry blender, cut in butter until coarse crumbs form; set aside.

In large bowl using mixer at medium speed, beat All-purpose Baking Mix, sugar, milk, egg and vanilla 3 minutes. Spread batter in greased 9x9x2" baking pan. Sprinkle with brown sugar mixture.

Bake in 350° oven 30 minutes or until toothpick inserted in

center comes out clean. Cool in pan on rack 15 minutes.
Generously sift confectioners' sugar over top of cake. Serve warm.
Makes 9 servings.

Sour Cream Crumb Ring

*Rich but tender and delicate, this classic quick coffeecake has a
cinnamon-flavored streusel topping.*

> Crumb Topping (recipe follows)
> 2 c. sifted flour
> 1 tsp. baking powder
> 1 tsp. baking soda
> ¼ tsp. salt
> 1 c. sugar
> ½ c. butter or regular margarine
> 2 eggs
> 1 tsp. vanilla
> 1 tsp. lemon juice
> 1 c. dairy sour cream

Prepare Crumb Topping; set aside

Sift together flour, baking powder, baking soda and salt; set
aside.

In large bowl using mixer at medium speed, beat sugar and
butter until light and fluffy. Add eggs, one at a time, beating well
after each addition. Beat in vanilla and lemon juice until well
blended.

Reduce speed to low; beat in dry ingredients alternately with
sour cream until well blended. Spoon batter into well-greased 10"
tube pan. Crumble topping over batter.

Bake in 350° oven 45 to 50 minutes, or until ring is golden
brown and toothpick inserted in center comes out clean. Cool in
pan on rack. Makes 12 to 16 servings.

CRUMB TOPPING: In medium bowl, stir together 1 c. sifted
flour, ½ c. packed brown sugar and 1½ tsp. ground cinnamon.
With fingers, mix in ¼ c. butter or regular margarine, softened,
until mixture is well blended and can be pressed into a ball.

Apple Coffeecake

A crunchy topping of sour cream, sugar, vanilla and walnuts adorns this quick cake.

1½ c. sifted flour
½ c. sugar
2 tsp. baking powder
½ tsp. salt
½ tsp. ground cinnamon
1 c. chopped, peeled apple
1 c. chopped walnuts
½ c. milk
3 tblsp. butter or regular margarine, melted
1 egg
¾ c. dairy sour cream
3 tblsp. sugar
1 tsp. vanilla

Into medium bowl, sift together first 5 ingredients. Stir in apple and ½ c. walnuts; set aside.

In small bowl, mix milk, melted butter and egg until well blended. Add milk mixture to dry ingredients; stir just until moistened. Spread batter in greased 9″ round baking pan; set aside.

In small bowl, stir sour cream, sugar and vanilla until well blended. Spread sour cream mixture over batter. Sprinkle remaining ½ c. walnuts over top.

Bake in 400° oven 30 to 35 minutes, or until cake is golden brown and toothpick inserted in center comes out clean. Cool in pan on rack 10 minutes. Cut into wedges. Serve warm. Makes 6 to 8 servings.

Sugar-top Coffeecake

One of our best-ever coffeecake recipes! It has the same light texture as a yeast coffeecake, but it's easier to make.

1½ c. sifted flour
2 tsp. baking powder
¾ tsp. salt
¼ tsp. baking soda
¾ c. granulated sugar
1 tsp. vanilla
1 egg
1 tblsp. butter or regular margarine, softened
1 c. dairy sour cream
½ c. packed brown sugar
½ tsp. ground cinnamon
2 tblsp. flour
2 tblsp. butter or regular margarine, melted

Sift together flour, baking powder, salt and baking soda; set aside.

In large bowl using mixer at medium speed, beat granulated sugar, vanilla, egg and 1 tblsp. butter until light and fluffy, about 2 minutes. Beat in sour cream until well blended.

Reduce speed to low; beat in dry ingredients until well blended. Pour batter into greased 8x8x2" baking pan.

In small bowl, stir together brown sugar, cinnamon and 2 tblsp. flour. Add 2 tblsp. melted butter; mix until crumbly. Sprinkle crumb mixture over batter.

Bake in 375° oven 25 to 30 minutes, or until cake is browned and toothpick inserted in center comes out clean. Cool in pan on rack. Makes 6 servings.

Colonial Gingerbread

Dark brown, richly spiced, moist and tender, this bread originally was sliced and served warm with butter at lunch or supper. Top with a dollop of whipped cream for dessert.

3 c. sifted flour
2 tsp. baking powder
2 tsp. ground cinnamon
1½ tsp. ground ginger
1 tsp. salt
1 tsp. ground nutmeg
¼ tsp. ground cloves
1 c. shortening
½ c. granulated sugar
½ c. packed brown sugar
2 eggs
1 tsp. baking soda
1 c. boiling water
1 c. molasses

Sift together first 7 ingredients; set aside.

In large bowl using mixer at medium speed, beat shortening, granulated sugar and brown sugar until light and fluffy. Add eggs; beat until well blended.

In small bowl, dissolve baking soda in boiling water. Stir in molasses.

Using mixer at low speed, beat in dry ingredients alternately with molasses mixture until well blended. Pour batter into greased 13x9x2" baking pan.

Bake in 350° oven 45 to 50 minutes or until toothpick inserted in center comes out clean. Cool in pan on rack. Makes 16 servings.

Quick Blueberry Coffeecake

You'll find a blueberry in every bite of this tender cake.

        2 tsp. baking powder
        ½ tsp. salt
        ¾ c. sugar
        1½ c. sifted flour
        ⅔ c. milk
        ¼ c. shortening
        1½ tsp. grated lemon rind
        1 tsp. vanilla
        1 egg
        1 c. fresh or frozen blueberries
        ¼ c. flour
        2 tblsp. sugar
        1 tblsp. butter or regular margarine

Into large bowl, sift together baking powder, salt, ¼ c. sugar and 1½ c. flour. Add milk, shortening, lemon rind and vanilla. Using mixer at medium speed, beat 3 minutes.

Add egg; beat 2 minutes. Pour batter into greased 8x8x2″ baking pan. Sprinkle blueberries evenly over batter; set aside.

In small bowl, stir together ¼ c. flour and 2 tblsp. sugar. With fingers, mix in butter until well blended and mixture forms coarse crumbs. Sprinkle over blueberries.

Bake in 350° oven 45 to 50 minutes, or until cake is lightly browned and toothpick inserted in center comes out clean. Cool in pan on rack. Makes 6 to 9 servings.

Corn Bread Mix

You can make Southern-style pancakes (see Index) and creamy Spoon Bread from this basic mix—as well as traditional corn bread.

        4½ c. yellow corn meal
        4 c. sifted flour
        1½ c. nonfat dry milk
        ¾ c. sugar
        4 tblsp. baking powder
        2 tsp. salt
        1½ c. shortening

Into very large bowl, sift together first 6 ingredients. Sift again to mix well. With pastry blender, cut in shortening until fine crumbs form.

Store in airtight container in cool, dry place up to 3 months. Stir before measuring. Makes about 12½ c.

Use as directed to make Corn Bread and Spoon Bread (recipes follow) and more.

Corn Bread

Made from homemade Corn Bread Mix—just add water and an egg!

1¼ c. water
1 egg
2½ c. Corn Bread Mix

In medium bowl, mix water and egg until well blended. Add Corn Bread Mix; stir just until moistened. Pour batter into greased 8x8x2″ baking pan.

Bake in 425° oven 20 to 25 minutes, or until bread is golden brown and toothpick inserted in center comes out clean. Cut into squares. Serve warm or cold. Makes 9 servings.

Spoon Bread

A favorite in the South, you'll find this corn meal, pudding bread often served with fried chicken.

3½ c. water
2½ c. Corn Bread Mix
3 eggs, separated
Butter or regular margarine

In 3-qt. saucepan over high heat, bring water to a boil. Gradually add Corn Bread Mix. Reduce heat to medium. Cook, stirring constantly, until mixture is thickened and resembles mush. Remove from heat.

Add egg yolks, one at a time, beating with wooden spoon until well blended.

In small bowl using mixer at high speed, beat egg whites until stiff, but not dry, peaks form. Fold beaten egg whites into corn meal mixture.

Pour batter into greased 2-qt. casserole or soufflé dish.

Bake in 325° oven 1 hour, or until spoon bread is golden brown and toothpick inserted in center comes out clean. Spoon into serving dishes and top each serving with a pat of butter. Serve warm. Makes 8 to 10 servings.

Golden Corn Bread

From just one batter, make corn bread, corn muffins or corn sticks.

> 1 c. yellow corn meal
> 1 c. sifted flour
> ¼ c. sugar
> 1 tblsp. baking powder
> 1 tsp. salt
> ¼ c. shortening
> 1 c. milk
> 1 egg

Into large bowl, sift together first 5 ingredients. With pastry blender, cut in shortening until coarse crumbs form.

In small bowl, mix milk and egg until well blended. Add milk mixture to dry ingredients; stir just until moistened. Pour batter into greased 9x9x2″ baking pan.

Bake in 325° oven 20 to 25 minutes, or until bread is golden brown and toothpick inserted in center comes out clean. Cut into squares. Serve warm or cold. Makes 9 servings.

CORN MUFFINS: Prepare batter as directed. Spoon batter into 12 well-greased or paper-lined 2½″ muffin-pan cups, filling two-thirds full. Bake in 425° oven 15 to 20 minutes, or until muffins are golden brown and toothpick inserted in center comes out clean. Remove from pans. Serve warm or cold. Makes 12 muffins.

CORN STICKS: Prepare batter as directed. Place well-greased corn stick pan in 425° oven 3 to 5 minutes or until hot. Spoon half of batter evenly into pan, filling three-quarters full. Bake in 425° oven 12 to 15 minutes or until sticks are golden brown. Remove from pan. Repeat with remaining batter. Serve warm or cold. Makes 14 sticks.

Skillet Mexican Corn Bread

This tastes really good with chili. It's a spicy, cheese-flavored bread that's cooked in a skillet; to serve, cut in wedges.

1 c. sifted flour
1 c. yellow corn meal
1 tblsp. sugar
1 tblsp. baking powder
1 tsp. salt
½ tsp. chili powder
¼ c. shortening
1 c. shredded sharp Cheddar or Monterey Jack cheese
1 (8-oz.) can cream-style corn
1 (4-oz.) can chopped green chilies, drained
½ c. milk
2 eggs

Into medium bowl, sift together first 6 ingredients. With pastry blender, cut in shortening until coarse crumbs form. Stir in cheese; set aside.

In medium bowl, mix corn, chilies, milk and eggs until well blended. Add corn mixture to dry ingredients; stir just until moistened.

Place greased 10″ skillet with oven-safe handle in 425° oven 3 to 5 minutes or until hot. Pour batter into skillet.

Bake 20 minutes, or until bread is golden brown and toothpick inserted in center comes out clean. Cut into wedges. Serve warm. Makes 8 to 10 servings.

Irish Soda Bread

Inherited from Gaelic kitchens, this currant and caraway-studded loaf is brushed with sugar and water for a sweet, crispy crust.

    4 c. sifted flour
    ¼ c. sugar
    1 tsp. salt
    1 tsp. baking powder
    1 tsp. baking soda
    2 tblsp. caraway seed
    ¼ c. butter or regular margarine
    2 c. currants or raisins
    1⅓ c. buttermilk
    1 egg
    1 tblsp. sugar
    1 tblsp. water

Into large bowl, sift together first 5 ingredients. Stir in caraway seed. With pastry blender, cut in butter until coarse crumbs form. Stir in currants.

In small bowl, mix buttermilk and egg until well blended. Add buttermilk mixture to currant mixture; stir just until moistened.

Turn out dough onto lightly floured surface and knead 12 times. Shape into ball and place in greased 2-qt. casserole. With sharp knife, cut a 4" cross, ½" deep, in top of loaf.

Bake in 375° oven 55 minutes, or until bread is golden brown and toothpick inserted in center comes out clean.

Remove from casserole; place on rack. In small bowl, mix together 1 tblsp. sugar and water; immediately brush over hot loaf. Cool completely. Makes 1 loaf.

Millet Quick Bread

Millet is a tiny, round yellow grain that looks like mustard seed. To enhance its flavor, try toasting it before cooking.

    1 c. sifted all-purpose flour
    ¼ c. sugar
    1 tblsp. baking powder
    1 tsp. salt
    1 c. stirred millet flour
    ¼ c. shortening
    1 c. milk
    1 egg
    Sesame seed

Into large bowl, sift together flour, sugar, baking powder and salt. Stir in millet flour until well blended. With pastry blender, cut in shortening until coarse crumbs form.

In small bowl, mix milk and egg until well blended. Add milk mixture to flour-shortening mixture; stir just until moistened. Pour batter into greased 8x8x2" baking pan. Sprinkle with sesame seed.

Bake in 425° oven 20 to 25 minutes, or until bread is golden brown and toothpick inserted in center comes out clean. Cut into squares. Serve warm. Makes 9 servings.

Cheesy Whole-Wheat Loaf

This quick bread has the fine texture of a yeast bread. Cut it into thick slices and serve toasted with soup or stew.

    2 c. stirred whole-wheat flour
    ¾ c. sifted all-purpose flour
    1 tblsp. dried minced onion
    1 tblsp. baking powder
    1½ tsp. salt
    1 tsp. baking soda
    1 c. shredded Swiss cheese
    1½ c. milk
    ⅓ c. vegetable oil
    ¼ c. packed brown sugar
    2 eggs

In large bowl, stir together first 6 ingredients. Stir in cheese; set aside.

In medium bowl, mix milk, oil, brown sugar and eggs until well blended. Add milk mixture to dry ingredients; stir just until moistened. Pour batter into greased and waxed paper-lined 9x5x3″ loaf pan.

Bake in 375° oven 45 minutes. Cover loosely with sheet of foil and bake 15 minutes more, or until loaf is golden brown and toothpick inserted in center comes out clean. Cool in pan 10 minutes. Remove; peel off waxed paper. Cool on rack. Makes 1 loaf.

Whole-Grain Loaf

Three different flours—white, whole-wheat and rye—are mixed with bran to make this rich, dark brown quick bread.

½ c. sifted all-purpose flour
½ c. stirred rye flour
½ c. stirred whole-wheat flour
3 tblsp. sugar
1 tsp. baking powder
1 tsp. baking soda
1 tsp. salt
1 tsp. dill seed (optional)
1 c. buttermilk
½ c. unprocessed bran or high-fiber bran cereal buds
¼ c. vegetable oil
1 egg

In large bowl, stir together first 8 ingredients; set aside.

In medium bowl, pour buttermilk over bran; let stand 5 minutes. Add oil and egg to bran mixture; mix until well blended. Add egg mixture to dry ingredients; stir just until moistened. Pour batter into greased 8½x4½x2½″ loaf pan.

Bake in 375° oven 40 to 45 minutes, or until loaf is golden brown and toothpick inserted in center comes out clean. Cool in pan 10 minutes. Remove; cool on rack at least 30 minutes. Serve warm or cold. Makes 1 loaf.

Gluten-free Bread

Here's a bread for those who are allergic to the gluten protein in wheat flours. It's made with rice flour, flavored with peanut butter and spiced with cinnamon.

2¾ c. stirred rice flour
⅔ c. packed brown sugar
1 tblsp. baking powder
1 tsp. salt
¼ tsp. ground cinnamon
¾ c. peanut butter
1⅔ c. milk
½ c. vegetable oil
1 tsp. vanilla
2 eggs

In large bowl, stir together first 5 ingredients. With pastry blender, cut in peanut butter until coarse crumbs form.

In medium bowl, mix milk, oil, vanilla and eggs until well blended. Add milk mixture to flour-peanut butter mixture; stir just until moistened. Pour batter into greased 9x5x3″ loaf pan. Cover with plastic wrap. Refrigerate 1 hour.

Bake in 375° oven 1 hour, or until loaf is golden brown and toothpick inserted in center comes out clean. Cool in pan 10 minutes. Remove; cool on rack. Makes 1 loaf.

Gluten-free Cheese Bread

Two alternatives for a wheat-allergy diet: a quick savory cheese bread and a sweet fruit loaf.

3 c. stirred rice flour
⅓ c. sugar
1 tblsp. baking powder
1 tsp. salt
1 c. shredded Cheddar cheese
1⅔ c. milk
⅓ c. vegetable oil
2 eggs

In large bowl, stir together rice flour, sugar, baking powder and salt. Stir in cheese; set aside.

In medium bowl, mix milk, oil and eggs until well blended. Add milk mixture to dry ingredients; stir just until moistened. Pour batter into greased and waxed paper-lined 9x5x3" loaf pan. Cover with plastic wrap. Refrigerate 1 hour.

Bake in 375° oven 45 minutes, or until loaf is golden brown and toothpick inserted in center comes out clean. Cool in pan 10 minutes. Remove; peel off waxed paper. Cool on rack. Makes 1 loaf.

GLUTEN-FREE FRUIT BREAD: Increase sugar to ½ c., and substitute ¾ c. raisins, chopped, dried, pitted prunes or chopped, dried apricots for cheese.

Quick Celery-Cheese Loaf

A Pennsylvania woman bakes this golden cheese loaf to sell at a local farmer's market.

> 3 c. sifted flour
> ¼ c. sugar
> 4 tsp. baking powder
> 1 tsp. salt
> ½ c. shortening
> 1 c. shredded sharp Cheddar cheese
> ¼ tsp. celery seed
> 1¼ c. milk
> 2 eggs

Into large bowl, sift together flour, sugar, baking powder and salt. With pastry blender, cut in shortening until coarse crumbs form. Stir in cheese and celery seed; set aside.

In small bowl, mix milk and eggs until well blended. Add milk mixture to dry ingredients; stir just until moistened. Pour batter into greased and waxed paper-lined 9x5x3" loaf pan.

Bake in 350° oven 50 to 60 minutes, or until loaf is golden brown and toothpick inserted in center comes out clean. Cool in pan 10 minutes. Remove; peel off waxed paper. Cool on rack. Makes 1 loaf.

Honey-Zucchini Bread

A North Dakota woman shared this recipe, given to her by her daughter-in-law. For variety, add 1 c. chopped nuts to the batter.

3 c. sifted flour
2 tsp. ground cinnamon
1 tsp. baking soda
1 tsp. salt
¼ tsp. baking powder
3 eggs
1 c. honey
½ c. vegetable oil
2 tsp. vanilla
3 c. shredded zucchini

Into large bowl, sift together first 5 ingredients; set aside.

In medium bowl using wire whisk, beat eggs until foamy. Beat in honey, oil and vanilla until well blended. Stir in zucchini. Add zucchini mixture to flour mixture; stir just until moistened. Pour batter into greased 9x5x3" loaf pan.

Bake in 350° oven 1 hour 15 minutes, or until loaf is golden brown and toothpick inserted in center comes out clean. Cool in pan 10 minutes. Remove; cool on rack. Makes 1 loaf.

Zucchini Nut Bread

One New York reader likes to serve slices of this moist nut bread for dessert along with an assortment of fresh fruit.

3 c. sifted flour
1½ tsp. ground cinnamon
1 tsp. baking soda
1 tsp. salt
¼ tsp. baking powder
2 c. sugar
1 c. vegetable oil
1 tblsp. vanilla
3 eggs
2 c. shredded zucchini
½ c. chopped walnuts

Sift together first 5 ingredients; set aside.

In large bowl using mixer at medium speed, beat sugar, oil, vanilla and eggs until well blended.

Reduce speed to low. Beat in dry ingredients until well blended. Stir in zucchini and walnuts. Pour batter into 2 greased 8½x4½x2½" loaf pans.

Bake in 350° oven 1 hour, or until loaves are browned and toothpick inserted in center comes out clean. Cool in pans 10 minutes. Remove; cool on racks. Makes 2 loaves.

Chocolate-Almond Zucchini Bread

So moist, it almost tastes like a chocolate-nut brownie. This recipe has been preserved thanks to an Ohio farm woman.

3 c. sifted flour
2 c. sugar
1¼ tsp. baking powder
1 tsp. baking soda
1 tsp. salt
1 tsp. ground cinnamon
1 c. chopped blanched almonds
1 c. vegetable oil
1 tsp. vanilla
3 eggs
2 (1-oz.) squares unsweetened chocolate, melted
2 c. shredded zucchini

Into large bowl, sift together first 6 ingredients. Stir in almonds; set aside.

In medium bowl, mix oil, vanilla and eggs until well blended. Stir in melted chocolate until well blended. Stir in zucchini. Stir zucchini mixture into dry ingredients just until moistened. Pour batter into greased 9x5x3" loaf pan.

Bake in 350° oven 1 hour 30 minutes or until toothpick inserted in center comes out clean. Cool in pan 10 minutes. Remove; cool on rack. Makes 1 loaf.

Sweet Potato Nut Bread

Save that last cup of coffee at the bottom of the pot—it's the secret ingredient in this old-fashioned spice bread.

  3⅓ c. sifted flour
  2 tsp. baking soda
  1½ tsp. ground nutmeg
  1 tsp. baking powder
  1 tsp. salt
  1 tsp. ground cinnamon
  1 c. chopped walnuts
  2 c. sugar
  ⅔ c. vegetable oil
  4 eggs
  2 c. mashed, cooked sweet potatoes
  ⅔ c. cold, strong coffee

Into medium bowl, sift together first 6 ingredients. Stir in walnuts; set aside.

In large bowl using mixer at high speed, beat sugar and oil until light. Add eggs, one at a time, beating well after each addition. Add sweet potatoes; beat until well blended.

Reduce speed to low; beat in dry ingredients alternately with coffee until well blended. Pour batter into 2 greased 9x5x3" loaf pans.

Bake in 350° oven 1 hour, or until loaves are golden brown and toothpick inserted in center comes out clean. Cool in pans 10 minutes. Remove; cool on racks.

Wrap each loaf in foil. Let stand, overnight, in cool, dry place before serving. Makes 2 loaves.

Pumpkin Nut Bread

An Oklahoma woman bakes this spicy batter in muffin pans to make individual servings for her Thanksgiving dinner.

3½ c. sifted flour
1½ c. sugar
2 tsp. baking soda
1½ tsp. ground cinnamon
1 tsp. salt
1 tsp. ground allspice
½ tsp. baking powder
½ tsp. ground cloves
1½ c. chopped walnuts
1½ c. golden raisins
1 c. vegetable oil
⅔ c. milk
4 eggs
2 c. mashed, cooked pumpkin

Into large bowl, sift together first 8 ingredients. Stir in walnuts and raisins; set aside.

In medium bowl, with wire whisk, beat oil, milk and eggs until well blended. Beat in pumpkin until well blended. Add pumpkin mixture to dry ingredients; stir just until moistened. Pour batter into 2 greased 9x5x3" loaf pans.

Bake in 350° oven 1 hour, or until loaves are golden brown and toothpick inserted in center comes out clean. Cool in pans 10 minutes. Remove; cool on racks. Makes 2 loaves.

PUMPKIN NUT MUFFINS: Prepare batter as directed. Spoon batter into 30 paper-lined 2½" muffin-pan cups, filling two-thirds full. Bake in 400° oven 20 to 25 minutes, or until muffins are golden brown and toothpick inserted in center comes out clean. Remove from pans. Serve warm or cold. Makes 30 muffins.

Carrot-Pineapple Bread

An Arkansas woman says that her family especially enjoys this bread when she serves it with orange-flavored cream cheese.

3 c. sifted flour
2 tsp. baking soda
1 tsp. salt
1 tsp. ground cinnamon
½ tsp. baking powder
½ tsp. ground nutmeg
1 c. finely chopped walnuts
2 c. sugar
1 c. vegetable oil
2 tsp. vanilla
3 eggs
2 c. shredded carrots
1 (8-oz.) can crushed pineapple, drained

Into large bowl, sift together first 6 ingredients. Stir in walnuts; set aside.

In large bowl using mixer at medium speed, beat sugar, oil, vanilla and eggs 3 minutes. Stir in carrots and drained pineapple.

Add carrot mixture to dry ingredients; stir just until moistened. Pour batter into 2 greased and floured 8½x4½x2½" loaf pans.

Bake in 350° oven 1 hour, or until loaves are golden brown and toothpick inserted in center comes out clean. Cool in pans 10 minutes. Remove; cool on racks. Makes 2 loaves.

Carrot Bread

The Iowa woman who sent us this recipe likes it so much that she used her personal computer to file it permanently on a disk.

> 4 large carrots, cut into 1″ chunks
> 1½ c. sifted flour
> 1 c. sugar
> 1 tsp. baking soda
> 1 tsp. ground cinnamon
> ½ tsp. salt
> ¾ c. vegetable oil
> 2 eggs

In blender container, place one fourth of the carrots; cover. Blend at medium speed until carrots are finely diced. Repeat with remaining carrots. You should have 1½ c. firmly packed carrots; set aside.

Into large bowl, sift together flour, sugar, baking soda, cinnamon and salt; set aside.

In small bowl, mix oil and eggs until well blended; stir in diced carrots. Add carrot mixture to dry ingredients; stir just until moistened. Pour batter into well-greased 8½x4½x2½″ loaf pan.

Bake in 350° oven 1 hour, or until loaf is golden brown and toothpick inserted in center comes out clean. Cool in pan 10 minutes. Remove; cool on rack. Makes 1 loaf.

Gougère

In France these golden cheese rounds are served as appetizers with a glass of dry red wine. They're made like cream puffs and seasoned with mustard, ground red pepper and cheese.

> 1½ c. water
> 9 tblsp. butter or regular margarine
> 1 tsp. salt
> 2 c. sifted flour
> 5 eggs
> ½ lb. Gruyère or Swiss cheese, finely diced
> 1 tblsp. Dijon mustard
> ⅛ tsp. ground red pepper
> 1 egg, beaten

In 3-qt. saucepan over medium heat, bring water, butter and salt to a boil. Remove from heat. With wooden spoon, stir in flour all at once.

Return to heat; stir until mixture forms a ball that leaves side of pan, about 2 minutes. Remove from heat; cool 5 minutes. Add 4 eggs, one at a time, beating well after each addition, until smooth.

Reserve 2 tblsp. cheese; stir remaining cheese, mustard and red pepper into egg-flour mixture until well blended.

Drop by scant ¼ cupfuls, 1″ apart, onto greased large baking sheet. Brush each with beaten egg and sprinkle with reserved cheese.

Bake in 350° oven 40 to 45 minutes or until golden brown. Carefully remove from baking sheet. Cool slightly on rack. Serve warm. Makes 12 (3½″) gougères.

Pull-apart Herb Ring

This ring-shaped bread looks attractive and it's easy to make. Try serving it fresh from the oven next time you have company.

4 c. sifted flour
2 tblsp. baking powder
1 tsp. salt
1 (3-oz.) pkg. cream cheese
¼ c. butter or regular margarine
1¼ c. milk
2 eggs
¾ c. grated Parmesan cheese
2 tblsp. dried minced onion
1 tsp. dried oregano leaves
1 tsp. dried basil leaves
½ tsp. dried marjoram leaves
½ tsp. garlic powder
½ c. butter or regular margarine, melted

Into large bowl, sift together flour, baking powder and salt. With pastry blender, cut in cream cheese and butter until coarse crumbs form.

In small bowl, mix milk and eggs until well blended. Add milk mixture to cream cheese mixture; stir just until mixture forms a soft dough that leaves side of bowl.

Turn out dough onto lightly floured surface. Knead about 15 times. Divide dough into 24 pieces; shape each piece into a ball.

On sheet of waxed paper, mix Parmesan cheese, onion, oregano, basil, marjoram and garlic powder until well blended.

Dip each ball of dough in melted butter, then roll in cheese-herb mixture until well coated. Place balls in two layers in greased 10" fluted tube pan.

Bake in 400° oven 30 to 35 minutes, or until ring is golden brown and toothpick inserted in center comes out clean. Cool in pan 10 minutes. Invert onto serving plate. Serve warm. Makes 12 servings.

Quick Raisin Bread

Wrap any leftover slices in foil to lock in the flavor. Use them for extra-special French toast the next day.

3½ c. sifted flour
⅓ c. sugar
1 tblsp. baking powder
2 tsp. ground cinnamon
1 tsp. salt
¼ c. butter or regular margarine
1 c. raisins
½ tsp. grated lemon rind
1¼ c. milk
1 tsp. vanilla
1 egg

Into large bowl, sift together first 5 ingredients. With pastry blender, cut in butter until coarse crumbs form. Stir in raisins and lemon rind.

In small bowl, mix milk, vanilla and egg until well blended. Add milk mixture to flour mixture; stir just until moistened.

Turn out dough onto lightly floured surface. Knead until smooth and no longer sticky, about 5 minutes. Shape dough into a loaf and place in greased 9x5x3" loaf pan. Diagonally slash loaf, crosswise, 3 times.

Bake in 375° oven 1 hour 10 minutes, or until loaf is golden brown and toothpick inserted in center comes out clean. Cool in pan 10 minutes. Remove; cool on rack. Makes 1 loaf.

Peanut Butter Bread

A real treat for anyone who likes peanut butter cookies.

3 c. sifted flour
1 tblsp. baking powder
1 tsp. salt
¾ tsp. ground cinnamon
⅔ c. packed brown sugar
¾ c. peanut butter
½ c. butter or regular margarine
1⅔ c. milk
1 tsp. vanilla
1 egg

Into large bowl, sift together flour, baking powder, salt and cinnamon. Stir in brown sugar until well blended. With pastry blender, cut in peanut butter and butter until coarse crumbs form.

In small bowl, mix milk, vanilla and egg until well blended. Add milk mixture to flour-peanut butter mixture; stir just until moistened. Pour batter into greased 9x5x3″ loaf pan.

Bake in 375° oven 1 hour. Cover loosely with sheet of foil; bake 15 minutes more, or until loaf is golden brown and toothpick inserted in center comes out clean. Cool in pan 10 minutes. Remove; cool on rack. Makes 1 loaf.

Oven-baked Boston Brown Bread

This whole-wheat bread bakes in the oven in less than an hour, saving a couple of hours of steaming.

1 c. sifted flour
2 tblsp. sugar
1 tsp. baking powder
1 tsp. baking soda
1 tsp. salt
1 c. stirred whole-wheat flour
1 c. yellow corn meal
1 c. raisins
2 c. buttermilk
¾ c. molasses

Into large bowl, sift together first 5 ingredients. Stir in whole-wheat flour, corn meal and raisins; set aside.

In small bowl, mix buttermilk and molasses until well blended. Add buttermilk mixture to dry ingredients; stir just until moistened. Spoon batter into 2 well-greased 1-lb. coffee cans.

Bake in 375° oven 50 minutes, or until loaves are browned and toothpick inserted in center comes out clean. Cool in cans 5 minutes. Remove; cool on racks. Makes 2 loaves.

Brown Sugar Tea Bread

A generous recipe that yields three round loaves studded with nuts and raisins. Great for breakfast—just toast and serve.

2 c. strong coffee
1½ c. raisins
4 c. sifted flour
1 tblsp. ground cinnamon
2 tsp. baking powder
1 tsp. baking soda
½ tsp. salt
2 c. chopped walnuts
2 eggs
1 tsp. vanilla
1½ c. packed brown sugar

In 2-qt. saucepan over high heat, bring coffee to a boil. Remove from heat. Stir in raisins; let stand 20 minutes.

In large bowl, sift together flour, cinnamon, baking powder, baking soda and salt. Stir in walnuts; set aside.

In another large bowl using mixer at medium speed, beat eggs and vanilla 2 minutes or until well blended. Add brown sugar; beat until well blended.

Reduce speed to low; beat in dry ingredients alternately with raisin mixture until well blended. Spoon batter into 3 greased and floured 1-lb. coffee cans, filling two-thirds full.

Bake in 325° oven 65 minutes, or until loaves are dark brown and toothpick inserted in center comes out clean. Cool in cans 15 minutes. Remove; cool on racks.

Wrap each loaf in foil. Let stand, overnight, in cool, dry place before serving. Makes 3 loaves.

Poppy Seed Tea Bread

Lightly dusted with confectioners' sugar, this moist and fine-textured coffee bread is generously laced with poppy seed.

3 c. sifted flour
1½ tsp. baking soda
1 tsp. salt
2 c. sugar
1 c. vegetable oil
3 eggs
1 (13-oz.) can evaporated milk
⅓ c. poppy seed
Confectioners' sugar

Sift together flour, baking soda and salt; set aside.

In large bowl, using mixer at medium speed, beat sugar, oil and eggs 3 minutes. Beat in dry ingredients alternately with evaporated milk until well blended. Stir in poppy seed. Pour batter into ungreased 10" tube pan.

Bake in 325° oven 1 hour 25 minutes, or until bread is golden brown and toothpick inserted in center comes out clean. Cool in pan on rack. Remove; sift confectioners' sugar over top of cake. Makes 12 to 16 servings.

Apple Streusel Tea Loaf

Whenever Winesap, Rome Beauty or Golden Delicious apples are bountiful, bake this loaf and serve it at breakfast or brunch.

2 c. sifted flour
1 tblsp. baking powder
½ tsp. salt
½ c. sugar
½ c. butter or regular margarine
2 c. chopped, peeled apples
½ tsp. grated lemon rind
½ c. milk
1 egg
½ tsp. ground cinnamon
2 tblsp. sugar

Into large bowl, sift together flour, baking powder, salt and ½ c. sugar. With pastry blender, cut in butter until coarse crumbs form. Reserve ½ c. flour-butter mixture. Stir apples and lemon rind into remaining flour-butter mixture.

In small bowl, mix milk and egg until well blended. Add egg mixture to apple mixture; stir just until moistened. Pour batter into greased 9x5x3" loaf pan.

In small bowl, stir ½ c. reserved flour-butter mixture, cinnamon and 2 tblsp. sugar until well blended. Sprinkle crumb-nut mixture over batter. Press down lightly.

Bake in 350° oven 1 hour, or until loaf is golden brown and toothpick inserted in center comes out clean. Cool in pan 10 minutes. Remove; cool on rack. Makes 1 loaf.

Apricot Nut Bread

"Makes superior toast," says a Pennsylvania farm woman. This moist bread is laden with apricots and nuts.

> 1 c. sifted all-purpose flour
> 1 c. stirred whole-wheat flour
> ½ c. packed brown sugar
> 1 tblsp. baking powder
> 1 tsp. grated orange rind
> ½ tsp. salt
> 1 c. chopped walnuts
> ¾ c. chopped, dried apricots
> 1 c. milk
> 2 tblsp. orange-flavored liqueur or orange juice
> 2 tblsp. butter or regular margarine, melted
> 1 egg
> 1 egg yolk

In large bowl, stir together first 8 ingredients; set aside.

In medium bowl, mix milk, liqueur, butter, egg and egg yolk until well blended. Add milk mixture to dry ingredients; stir just until moistened. Pour batter into greased 8½x4½x2½" loaf pan.

Bake in 350° oven 45 to 50 minutes, or until loaf is golden brown and toothpick inserted in center comes out clean. Cool in pan 10 minutes. Remove; cool on rack. Makes 1 loaf.

Pear Bread

One Pennsylvania farm woman says that when she makes this tea bread and serves it with sweet butter, there's never a crumb left!

> 3½ c. sifted flour
> 1 tsp. baking powder
> 1 tsp. salt
> 1 tsp. ground ginger
> ½ tsp. baking soda
> ½ tsp. ground nutmeg
> 2 c. finely chopped, peeled pears
> 2 c. sugar
> ½ c. vegetable oil
> ½ c. butter or regular margarine, melted
> 2 tsp. vanilla
> 4 eggs

Into large bowl, sift together first 6 ingredients. Stir in pears; set aside.

In small bowl, using mixer at high speed, beat sugar, oil, butter and vanilla until well blended. Add eggs, one at a time; beat until thick and lemon-colored.

Add sugar-egg mixture to dry ingredients; stir just until moistened. Spoon batter into 2 greased 8½x4½x2½" loaf pans.

Bake in 350° oven 55 to 60 minutes, or until loaves are golden brown and toothpick inserted in center comes out clean. Cool in pans 10 minutes. Remove; cool on racks.

Wrap each loaf in foil. Let stand, overnight, in cool, dry place before serving. Makes 2 loaves.

Honey-Date Bread

This dark brown loaf is sweet and moist and tastes like fruitcake.
Makes a good gift—especially if you add a little package of Spiced
Cream Cheese Spread.

2 c. diced, pitted dates
⅔ c. packed brown sugar
2 tblsp. shortening
¾ c. boiling water
2 c. sifted flour
1 tsp. baking soda
1 tsp. salt
1 c. chopped pecans
1 tsp. grated orange rind
½ c. honey
¼ c. orange juice
1 tsp. vanilla
1 egg
Spiced Cream Cheese Spread (recipe follows)

In medium bowl, place dates, brown sugar and shortening. Add
boiling water; let stand 10 minutes.

Into large bowl, sift together flour, baking soda and salt. Stir in
pecans and orange rind; set aside.

In small bowl, mix honey, orange juice, vanilla and egg until
well blended. Add honey mixture to date mixture; stir until well
blended.

Add honey-date mixture to dry ingredients; stir just until
moistened. Pour batter into greased 9x5x3" loaf pan.

Bake in 325° oven 60 to 65 minutes, or until loaf is dark brown
and toothpick inserted in center comes out clean. Cool in pan 10
minutes. Remove; cool on rack. Meanwhile, prepare Spiced Cream
Cheese Spread.

Wrap in foil. Let stand, overnight, in cool, dry place before
serving. Serve with Spiced Cream Cheese Spread. Makes 1 loaf.

SPICED CREAM CHEESE SPREAD: In small bowl, mix 1 (3-oz.)
pkg. cream cheese, softened, 2 tsp. packed brown sugar, ½ tsp.
vanilla, ¼ tsp. ground nutmeg, ¼ tsp. ground cinnamon and
¼ tsp. ground cloves until well blended. Cover and refrigerate at
least 2 hours to blend flavors. Makes ⅓ c.

Pineapple Spice Loaf

Crushed pineapple spiced with ginger and nutmeg makes a golden, moist loaf that's good anytime of the year.

2 c. sifted flour
2 tsp. baking powder
1 tsp. salt
½ tsp. baking soda
½ tsp. ground ginger
½ tsp. ground nutmeg
⅓ c. packed brown sugar
⅓ c. vegetable oil
1 tsp. vanilla
2 eggs
1 (8-oz.) can crushed pineapple

Into large bowl, sift together first 6 ingredients. Stir in brown sugar, set aside.

In small bowl, mix oil, vanilla and eggs until well blended. Stir in undrained pineapple. Add to dry ingredients; stir just until moistened. Pour batter into greased 9x5x3" loaf pan.

Bake in 350° oven 55 to 60 minutes, or until loaf is golden brown and toothpick inserted in center comes out clean. Cool in pan 10 minutes. Remove; cool on rack. Makes 1 loaf.

Cranberry-Banana Loaf

A great combination—tart, tangy cranberries teamed with the mild taste of bananas. A Wisconsin farm woman shared this idea.

¾ c. fresh or frozen cranberries, chopped
1 tsp. grated orange rind
1 c. sugar
1¾ c. sifted flour
2 tsp. baking powder
½ tsp. salt
½ tsp. baking soda
⅓ c. vegetable oil
2 eggs
¾ c. mashed, ripe bananas (about 3 small)

In small bowl, stir together cranberries, orange rind and ½ c. sugar; set aside.

Into large bowl, sift together flour, baking powder, salt, baking soda and remaining ½ c. sugar; set aside.

In another small bowl, mix oil and eggs until well blended; stir in bananas. Add banana and cranberry mixtures to dry ingredients; stir just until moistened. Pour batter into greased 9x5x3" loaf pan.

Bake in 350° oven 1 hour, or until loaf is golden brown and toothpick inserted in center comes out clean. Cool in pan 10 minutes. Remove; cool on rack. Makes 1 loaf.

Cranberry Bread

For the holidays, two orange-flavored loaves, lightly spiced with nutmeg. Enjoy one loaf right now and freeze the second.

> 3 c. sifted flour
> 1¼ c. sugar
> 1 tblsp. baking powder
> ¾ tsp. salt
> ¾ tsp. ground nutmeg
> ½ tsp. baking soda
> 2 tsp. grated orange rind
> ½ c. shortening
> 1½ c. chopped, fresh or frozen cranberries
> 1 c. chopped walnuts
> 1¼ c. orange juice
> 2 eggs

Into large bowl, sift together first 6 ingredients. Stir in orange rind. With pastry blender, cut in shortening until coarse crumbs form. Stir in cranberries and walnuts; set aside.

In small bowl, mix orange juice and eggs until well blended. Add orange juice mixture to shortening-flour mixture; stir just until moistened. Pour into 2 greased 8½x4½x2½" loaf pans.

Bake in 350° oven 1 hour 15 minutes, or until loaves are golden brown and toothpick inserted in center comes out clean. Cool in pans 10 minutes. Remove; cool on racks.

Wrap each loaf in foil. Let stand, overnight, in cool, dry place before serving. Makes 2 loaves.

Glazed Lemon Bread

One of our favorites at Farm Journal for many years—a tea bread that's both tart and sweet. It stores well, too.

1½ c. sifted flour
1½ tsp. baking powder
1 tsp. salt
½ c. chopped pecans
⅓ c. butter or regular margarine, melted
2 tsp. grated lemon rind
2 eggs
1 c. sugar
½ c. milk
¼ c. lemon juice
⅓ c. sugar

Into medium bowl, sift together flour, baking powder and salt. Stir in pecans; set aside.

In large bowl, using mixer at medium speed, beat butter, lemon rind, eggs and 1 c. sugar 2 minutes. Reduce speed to low; beat in dry ingredients alternately with milk until well blended. Pour batter into greased 9x5x3" loaf pan.

Bake in 350° oven 50 to 55 minutes, or until loaf is golden brown and toothpick inserted in center comes out clean. Cool in pan 10 minutes.

Meanwhile, in small bowl, stir together lemon juice and ⅓ c. sugar. With toothpick or fork, prick top of loaf. Pour lemon juice mixture over loaf. Cool completely on rack. Remove from pan.

Wrap in foil. Let stand, overnight, in cool, dry place before serving. Makes 1 loaf.

Chocolate Almond Loaf

For chocolate lovers, a rich tea loaf that's made with plain yogurt, studded with almonds and topped with a buttery glaze.

2 c. sifted flour
⅓ c. unsweetened cocoa
1 tsp. baking soda
1 tsp. ground cinnamon
½ tsp. salt
⅔ c. sugar
¼ c. butter or regular margarine
1 tsp. vanilla
1 egg
1 c. plain yogurt
½ c. chopped blanched almonds
Butter-Almond Glaze (recipe follows)

Sift together first 5 ingredients; set aside.

In large bowl, using mixer at medium speed beat sugar and butter until light and fluffy. Add vanilla and egg; beat until well blended.

Reduce speed to low; beat in dry ingredients alternately with yogurt until well blended. Stir in almonds. Pour batter into greased 9x5x3" loaf pan.

Bake in 350° oven 1 hour or until toothpick inserted in center comes out clean. Cool in pan 10 minutes. Remove; cool on rack.

Prepare Butter-Almond Glaze. Drizzle glaze over loaf. Makes 1 loaf.

BUTTER-ALMOND GLAZE: In medium bowl, stir together 2 c. sifted confectioners' sugar, ⅓ c. butter or regular margarine, melted, 5 tsp. water and ¼ tsp. almond extract until glaze is smooth and thin enough to drizzle. If necessary, add more water, ½ tsp. at a time. Use immediately. Makes 1 c.

Banana Nut Bread

You'll surely taste the bananas when you take a bite of this bread. The recipe comes from an Arkansas cook. For dessert, top with a dollop of whipped cream.

> 2 c. sifted flour
> ¾ c. sugar
> 1 tblsp. baking powder
> ½ tsp. salt
> ½ c. quick-cooking oats
> ⅓ c. butter or regular margarine
> ¾ c. chopped walnuts
> ½ c. milk
> ½ tsp. vanilla
> 1 egg
> 1 c. mashed, ripe bananas (about 3 medium)

Into large bowl, sift together flour, sugar, baking powder and salt. Stir in oats. With pastry blender, cut in butter until coarse crumbs form. Stir in walnuts; set aside.

In small bowl, mix milk, vanilla and egg until well blended. Stir in bananas until well blended. Add milk-banana mixture to dry ingredients; stir just until moistened. Pour batter into greased 9x5x3" loaf pan.

Bake in 350° oven 1 hour 15 minutes, or until loaf is golden brown and toothpick inserted in center comes out clean. Cool in pan 10 minutes. Remove; cool on rack.

Wrap in foil. Let stand, overnight, in cool, dry place before serving. Makes 1 loaf.

BANANA-BLUEBERRY BREAD: Add 1 c. fresh or frozen blueberries to milk-banana mixture.

Bishop's Bread

In Vienna, this bread is known as Bischofsbrot, *and served with coffee or tea. There are many versions; ours is made with nuts, cherries and morsels of chocolate—rich and delicious!*

    2 c. sifted flour
    1 tsp. baking powder
    1 tsp. salt
    1 c. halved, pitted dates
    1 c. whole Brazil nuts
    1 c. coarsely chopped walnuts
    ⅔ c. semisweet chocolate pieces
    1 c. halved maraschino cherries
    4 eggs, separated
    1 c. sugar

Into large bowl, sift together flour, baking powder and salt. Add dates, Brazil nuts, walnuts, chocolate pieces and cherries; stir until well coated; set aside.

In another large bowl, using mixer at high speed, beat egg whites just until soft peaks form. Gradually beat in sugar, 1 tblsp. at a time, beating well after each addition until stiff, glossy peaks form.

In small bowl, using mixer at high speed, beat egg yolks until thick and lemon colored.

Gently fold egg yolks into egg whites. Then, gently fold flour mixture into egg white mixture just until moistened. Pour batter into greased and waxed paper-lined 9x5x3" loaf pan.

Bake in 325° oven 1 hour 15 minutes, or until bread is lightly browned and toothpick inserted in center comes out clean. Cool in pan on rack. Remove; peel off waxed paper.

Wrap in foil. Let stand, overnight, in cool, dry place before serving. Makes 1 loaf.

5
Muffins, Biscuits, Crackers and Popovers

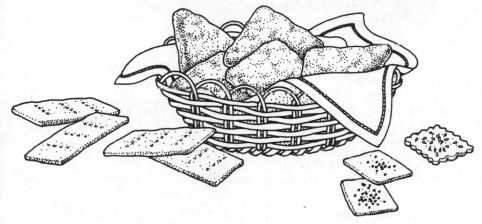

With just a few staple items—flour, milk, oil and eggs—plus 30 minutes or so, you can turn out a baker's dozen of tender and fragrantly delicious muffins. These individual quick breads, once called "gems" or "little muffs," are the easiest and most trouble-free baked goods to make. And there's no limit to the varieties you'll find here—Apple, Bran, Barley, and Nut Muffins, plus ones made in the food processor or baked in the microwave oven.

The basic rule for preparing muffins and biscuits is the same: work fast, but with a gentle touch. Biscuits double in height as they bake and the dough is easily formed into many shapes, such as Buttermilk Biscuit Pinwheels, Cinnamon Biscuit Fan-tans and Double-layer Beaten Biscuits.

Other biscuit-like quick breads are crackers, and they too are not at all difficult to make—the dough is just rolled thinner. Once you've tasted our Graham Crackers, Cheddar Rounds, Sesame Whole-Wheat Wafers and Caraway-Rye Flat Bread, you'll never want to settle for store-bought crackers again!

To keep your homemade crackers oven-fresh, be sure to store them in airtight containers. If they happen to get a little soggy, crackers are easily returned to their original crispness by heating them for about 5 minutes in a 275° oven.

Probably the most unique quick bread of all is the popover, because it is leavened by steam. Recipes for all of these little breads and many more are on the following pages.

Muffins

From this recipe you can make more than ten different muffins. Take your pick and serve them with breakfast, dinner or as snacks.

> 2 c. sifted flour
> ⅓ c. sugar
> 1 tblsp. baking powder
> ½ tsp. salt
> 1 c. milk
> ⅓ c. vegetable oil
> 1 egg

Into large bowl, sift together flour, sugar, baking powder and salt; set aside.

In small bowl, mix milk, oil and egg until well blended. Add milk mixture to dry ingredients; stir just until moistened. Spoon batter into 12 paper-lined 2½" muffin-pan cups, filling two-thirds full.

Bake in 400° oven 25 minutes, or until muffins are golden brown and toothpick inserted in center comes out clean. Remove from pans. Serve warm or cold. Makes 12 muffins.

FOOD PROCESSOR METHOD: Place dry ingredients in processor bowl with metal blade. Cover and process 2 seconds to aerate.

In small bowl, mix milk, oil and egg until well blended. While processor is running, pour milk mixture through feed tube. Process 4 to 5 seconds, just until flour mixture is moistened (batter will be lumpy). Spoon batter into cups and continue as directed.

NUT MUFFINS: Stir ¾ c. chopped peanuts, pecans or walnuts into dry ingredients.

WHEAT GERM MUFFINS: Use only 1½ c. sifted flour and stir ½ c. wheat germ into dry ingredients.

APPLE MUFFINS: Increase sugar to ⅔ c. Stir 1 tsp. ground cinnamon into dry ingredients. Then stir in 1 c. chopped, peeled apple.

APRICOT MUFFINS: Increase sugar to ⅔ c. Stir ¾ tsp. ground cinnamon into dry ingredients. Then stir in ⅔ c. chopped, dried apricots. Add ½ tsp. vanilla to milk mixture.

BLUEBERRY MUFFINS: Increase sugar to ⅔ c. Stir ¼ tsp. ground cinnamon into dry ingredients. Then stir in 1 c. fresh or frozen blueberries. Add ½ tsp. vanilla to milk mixture.

CRANBERRY MUFFINS: Increase sugar to ¾ c. Stir 1 tsp. grated orange rind and ⅛ tsp. ground nutmeg into dry ingredients. Then stir in 1 c. fresh or frozen cranberries, chopped. Add ½ tsp. vanilla to milk mixture.

RAISIN OR DATE MUFFINS: Stir ¾ tsp. ground cinnamon into dry ingredients. Then stir in ⅔ c. raisins or ⅔ c. chopped, pitted dates. Add ½ tsp. vanilla to milk mixture.

SURPRISE MUFFINS: Use only 1½ c. sifted flour and stir ½ c. wheat germ into dry ingredients.
   Fill muffin-pan cups one-half full with batter. Spoon 1 to 2 tsp. jelly into center of batter in each cup. Cover with remaining batter. Bake as directed.

CHEESE OR BACON MUFFINS: Use only 2 tblsp. sugar and stir 1 c. shredded sharp Cheddar cheese or 8 slices bacon, diced, cooked and drained, into dry ingredients.

Whole-Wheat Muffins

A Montana woman's recipe for sweet wheat muffins. They're just as good two days later, if they last that long!

> 1 c. sifted all-purpose flour
> 1 tblsp. baking powder
> ½ tsp. salt
> 1 c. stirred whole-wheat flour
> ¼ c. packed brown sugar
> ¾ c. milk
> ½ c. vegetable oil
> 1 egg

   Into large bowl, sift together all-purpose flour, baking powder and salt. Stir in whole-wheat flour and brown sugar; set aside.
   In small bowl, mix milk, oil and egg until well blended. Add milk mixture to dry ingredients; stir just until moistened. Spoon

batter into 12 paper-lined 2½″ muffin-pan cups, filling two-thirds full.

Bake in 400° oven 25 minutes, or until muffins are golden brown and toothpick inserted in center comes out clean. Remove from pans. Serve warm or cold. Makes 12 muffins.

Quick Blueberry Muffins

Tender and light and studded with blueberries—these muffins are so easy to make that you can enjoy them often.

> 2¼ c. All-purpose Baking Mix (see Index)
> 1 c. fresh or frozen blueberries
> ½ c. sugar
> ⅔ c. water
> 1 egg

In large bowl, gently stir together All-purpose Baking Mix, blueberries and sugar; set aside.

In small bowl, mix water and egg until well blended. Add egg mixture to blueberry mixture; stir just until moistened. Spoon batter into 12 paper-lined 2½″ muffin-pan cups, filling two-thirds full.

Bake in 425° oven 20 minutes, or until muffins are golden brown and toothpick inserted in center comes out clean. Remove from pans. Serve warm or cold. Makes 12 muffins.

Bran Muffins

Plain or fruited, these whole-grain muffins are rich in B vitamins. If you wish, you can substitute an equal amount of unprocessed bran for the cereal.

1½ c. high-fiber bran cereal buds
1¼ c. milk
1½ c. sifted flour
⅓ c. granulated sugar
1 tblsp. baking powder
1 tsp. salt
¼ c. vegetable oil
1 egg

In medium bowl, stir together cereal buds and milk. Let stand 5 minutes.

Meanwhile, into large bowl, sift together flour, sugar, baking powder and salt; set aside.

In small bowl, mix oil and egg until well blended. Add egg mixture to cereal mixture; mix well. Add cereal-egg mixture to dry ingredients; stir just until moistened. Spoon batter into 12 paper-lined 2½" muffin-pan cups, filling two-thirds full.

Bake in 400° oven 20 to 25 minutes, or until muffins are browned and toothpick inserted in center comes out clean. Remove from pans. Serve warm. Makes 12 muffins.

UNPROCESSED BRAN MUFFINS: Substitute 1½ c. unprocessed bran for high-fiber cereal buds. Substitute ⅓ c. packed brown sugar for granulated sugar. Stir brown sugar into dry ingredients.

PINEAPPLE-BRAN MUFFINS: Stir ¾ c. well-drained crushed pineapple into cereal-egg mixture.

APPLE-BRAN MUFFINS: Stir 1 c. chopped, peeled apples into dry ingredients.

Corn Meal-Bran Muffins

Moist and crunchy, with lots of fiber. For fresh muffins in 10 minutes, use the microwave.

> 1¼ c. high-fiber bran cereal buds
> 1¼ c. milk
> ½ c. sifted all-purpose flour
> 1 tblsp. baking powder
> ½ tsp. salt
> ¾ c. stirred whole-wheat flour
> ⅓ c. yellow corn meal
> ⅓ c. packed brown sugar
> ⅓ c. vegetable oil
> 1 egg

In small bowl, stir together cereal buds and milk. Let stand 5 minutes.

Meanwhile, into large bowl, sift together all-purpose flour, baking powder and salt. Stir in whole-wheat flour, corn meal and brown sugar; set aside.

In another small bowl, mix oil and egg until well blended. Stir egg mixture into cereal mixture until well blended. Add cereal-egg mixture to dry ingredients; stir just until moistened. Spoon batter into 12 paper-lined 2½" muffin-pan cups, filling two-thirds full.

Bake in 400° oven 20 minutes, or until muffins are browned and toothpick inserted in center comes out clean. Remove from pans. Serve warm. Makes 12 muffins.

MICROWAVE METHOD: Prepare batter as directed.

Spoon half of the batter into 7 double paper-lined 6-oz. glass custard cups, filling one-half full. Sprinkle with ¼ c. wheat germ.

Arrange custard cups in a circle in microwave oven. Microwave at high setting (100% power) 1 minute 30 seconds. Rearrange muffins.

Microwave at high setting 1 minute 30 seconds to 2 minutes more, or until toothpick inserted in center comes out clean. Remove muffins from custard cups. Repeat with remaining batter and ¼ c. wheat germ. Makes 14 muffins.

Oatmeal-Raisin Muffins

The inviting aroma of homemade muffins baking can lure even the most reluctant family member to breakfast on a winter morning.

Cinnamon Crumb Topping (recipe follows)
1 c. sifted flour
1 tblsp. baking powder
1 tsp. salt
½ tsp. ground cinnamon
¼ tsp. ground nutmeg
¾ c. milk
½ c. vegetable oil
⅓ c. packed brown sugar
1 egg
1 c. quick-cooking oats
½ c. raisins

Prepare Cinnamon Crumb Topping; set aside.

Into large bowl, sift together next 5 ingredients.

In small bowl, mix milk, oil, brown sugar and egg until well blended. Stir in oats and raisins until well mixed. Add oat mixture to dry ingredients; stir just until moistened. Spoon batter into 12 paper-lined 3″ muffin-pan cups, filling two-thirds full. Sprinkle topping over each muffin.

Bake in 400° oven 20 minutes, or until muffins are browned and toothpick inserted in center comes out clean. Remove from pans. Serve warm or cold. Makes 12 muffins.

CINNAMON CRUMB TOPPING: In small bowl, stir together 6 tblsp. flour, 3 tblsp. packed brown sugar and 1½ tsp. ground cinnamon. With pastry blender, cut in 3 tblsp. butter or regular margarine until coarse crumbs form.

MICROWAVE METHOD: Prepare batter and topping as directed.

Spoon half of the batter into 6 double paper-lined 6-oz. glass custard cups, filling two-thirds full. Sprinkle with half of the topping.

Arrange custard cups in a circle in microwave oven. Microwave at high setting (100% power) 1 minute. Rearrange muffins.

Microwave at high setting 1 minute 45 seconds more, or until toothpick inserted in center comes out clean. Remove muffins from custard cups. Repeat with remaining batter and topping.

Rice Flour Muffins

Stir the batter briefly—just 10 to 12 strokes—to keep the texture light and tender. These muffins bake to a golden brown.

1¾ c. stirred rice flour
⅓ c. sugar
1 tblsp. baking powder
½ tsp. salt
1 c. milk
⅓ c. vegetable oil
2 eggs

In medium bowl, stir together rice flour, sugar, baking powder and salt; set aside.

In small bowl, mix milk, oil and eggs until well blended. Add milk mixture to dry ingredients; stir just until moistened. Spoon batter into 12 greased 2½″ muffin-pan cups, filling two-thirds full. Refrigerate 1 hour.

Bake in 400° oven 20 to 25 minutes, or until muffins are golden brown and toothpick inserted in center comes out clean. Remove from pans. Serve warm or cold. Makes 12 muffins.

Barley Muffins

Honey is used to sweeten these whole-grain muffins. They're made with whole-wheat flour, barley flour and yogurt.

1½ c. stirred whole-wheat flour
1 c. stirred barley flour
1½ tsp. baking powder
1 tsp. salt
½ tsp. baking soda
2 tblsp. sesame seed
¼ c. shortening
1½ c. plain yogurt
¼ c. honey
2 eggs

In large bowl, stir together first 6 ingredients. With pastry blender, cut in shortening until coarse crumbs form.

In medium bowl, mix yogurt, honey and eggs until well blended. Add yogurt mixture to dry ingredients; stir just until moistened. Spoon batter into 12 greased 3″ muffin-pan cups, filling three-fourths full.

Bake in 400° oven 20 to 25 minutes, or until muffins are golden brown and toothpick inserted in center comes out clean. Remove from pans. Serve warm or cold. Makes 12 muffins.

Baking Powder Biscuits

You can use butter, margarine or lard in place of the shortening for these biscuits. Don't have a round biscuit cutter? Just use the top of a jelly jar, or cut the dough into squares or diamonds.

2 c. sifted all-purpose flour
1 tblsp. baking powder
2 tsp. sugar
½ tsp. salt
⅓ c. shortening
⅔ c. milk

Into large bowl, sift together flour, baking powder, sugar and salt. With pastry blender, cut in shortening until coarse crumbs form.

Add milk to shortening-flour mixture; with fork, stir until mixture forms a soft dough that leaves side of bowl.

Turn out dough onto lightly floured surface and knead 10 times. With floured rolling pin, roll out dough to ½″ thickness. Cut dough with floured 2½″ round biscuit cutter and place, 1″ apart, on ungreased baking sheet.

Bake in 450° oven 10 to 12 minutes or until golden brown. Serve immediately. Makes 10 to 12 biscuits.

DROP BISCUITS: Increase milk to 1 c. With fork, stir dough until well mixed (do not knead).

Drop dough by rounded tablespoonfuls, 1″ apart, onto greased large baking sheets. Bake as directed. Makes 18 biscuits.

BUTTERMILK BISCUITS: Stir ¼ tsp. baking soda into dry ingredients and substitute ⅔ c. buttermilk for milk.

WHOLE-WHEAT BISCUITS: Use only 1 c. all-purpose flour. Stir 1 c. stirred whole-wheat flour into dry ingredients.

CHEESE BISCUITS: Stir 1 c. shredded Cheddar cheese and ¼ c. chopped green or yellow onion (optional) into shortening-flour mixture.

BACON BISCUITS: Stir 8 slices bacon, diced, cooked and drained, into shortening-flour mixture.

BUTTERSCOTCH BISCUITS: Prepare and knead dough as directed. Cut dough with floured 2" round biscuit cutter and set aside.

In small bowl, stir ½ c. packed brown sugar, ¼ c. butter or regular margarine, melted, and 1 tblsp. water until smooth.

Spoon 2 tsp. sugar mixture into 12 well-greased 2½" muffin-pan cups. Place dough circles on top of sugar mixture.

Bake in 425° oven 15 to 18 minutes or until golden brown. Immediately invert onto sheet of waxed paper.

CINNAMON BISCUIT PINWHEELS: Prepare and knead dough as directed. With floured rolling pin, roll out dough into a 16x6" rectangle.

In small bowl, stir together ½ c. sugar, ⅓ c. butter or regular margarine, softened, and 1½ tsp. ground cinnamon. Spread mixture over dough.

Starting with one long side, roll up dough, jelly-roll fashion; pinch seam to seal. Cut roll into 1" slices. Place slices, cut-side down, in 16 greased 2½" muffin-pan cups; brush tops with melted butter or regular margarine.

Bake in 400° oven 15 to 20 minutes or until golden brown. Remove from pans. Makes 16 pinwheels.

TEXAS BISCUIT PINWHEELS: Prepare and knead dough as directed, stirring ½ c. shredded sharp Cheddar cheese into shortening-flour mixture.

With floured rolling pin, roll out dough into an 18x9" rectangle. Sprinkle dough with ½ c. shredded Cheddar cheese and ¾ tsp. chili powder.

Starting with one long side, roll up dough, jelly-roll fashion; pinch seam to seal. Cut roll into 1" slices. Place slices, cut-side down, 1" apart, on greased large baking sheet.

Bake in 450° oven 12 minutes or until golden brown. Makes 18 pinwheels.

Quick Rolled Biscuits

Just add water to your own All-purpose Baking Mix and you'll have piping-hot biscuits in less than 15 minutes.

> 2¼ c. All-purpose Baking Mix (see Index)
> ½ c. water

In bowl with fork, stir All-purpose Baking Mix and water until mixture forms a soft dough that leaves side of bowl.

Turn out dough onto lightly floured surface and knead 10 times. With floured rolling pin, roll out dough to ¾" thickness. Cut dough with floured 2" round biscuit cutter and place, 1" apart, on greased baking sheet.

Bake in 450° oven 10 to 12 minutes or until golden brown. Serve immediately. Makes 10 biscuits.

QUICK DROP BISCUITS: Use only 2 c. All-purpose Baking Mix. With fork, stir dough until well mixed (do not knead).

Drop dough by heaping tablespoonfuls, 1" apart, onto greased baking sheet. Bake as directed.

Freezer Biscuits

Once you've prepared the dough, you can keep these biscuits in the freezer for several months before you pop them into the oven.

> 2 c. sifted flour
> 1 tblsp. baking powder
> 2 tsp. sugar
> 1 tsp. salt
> ⅔ c. shortening
> ½ c. milk

Into large bowl, sift together flour, baking powder, sugar and salt. With pastry blender, cut in shortening until coarse crumbs form.

Add milk to shortening-flour mixture; with fork, stir until mixture forms a soft dough that leaves side of bowl.

Turn out dough onto lightly floured surface and knead 10 times. With floured rolling pin, roll out dough to ½" thickness. Cut dough with floured 2½" round biscuit cutter and place on ungreased baking sheet.

Freeze biscuits until firm, about 2 hours. Remove biscuits from baking sheet and wrap in heavy-duty foil or place in heavy freezer-storage bags. Freeze up to 3 months.

To bake: Place frozen biscuits, 1" apart, on greased baking sheet. Bake in 400° oven 25 minutes or until golden brown. Serve immediately. Makes 10 biscuits.

Whole-Wheat Buttermilk Biscuits

These light-as-a-feather yeast biscuits are from a Michigan farm woman, who serves them with her homemade crab apple butter.

> 1 pkg. active dry yeast
> ¼ tsp. sugar
> 3 tblsp. warm water (105 to 115°)
> 4 c. sifted all-purpose flour
> 1 tblsp. baking powder
> 1 tsp. salt
> 1 tsp. baking soda
> ¼ c. sugar
> 1 c. stirred whole-wheat flour
> 1 c. shortening
> 2 c. buttermilk

In small bowl, sprinkle yeast and ¼ tsp. sugar over warm water; stir until dissolved. Set aside.

Into large bowl, sift together all-purpose flour, baking powder, salt, baking soda and ¼ c. sugar. Stir in whole-wheat flour. With pastry blender, cut in shortening until coarse crumbs form.

Add yeast mixture and buttermilk to shortening-flour mixture; with fork, stir until mixture forms a soft dough that leaves side of bowl.

Turn out dough onto lightly floured surface and knead 10 times. With floured rolling pin, roll out dough to ¾" thickness. Cut dough with floured 2½" round biscuit cutter and place, 1" apart, on ungreased baking sheets.

Bake in 350° oven 25 minutes or until golden brown. Serve immediately. Makes 24 biscuits.

Wheat Germ Biscuits

More substantial than most biscuits, these have a nutlike flavor and a flaky, but firm texture.

> 1½ c. sifted flour
> 1 tblsp. baking powder
> ¾ tsp. salt
> ½ c. wheat germ
> ½ c. shortening
> ½ c. milk

Into large bowl, sift together flour, baking powder and salt. Stir in wheat germ. With pastry blender, cut in shortening until coarse crumbs form.

Add milk to shortening-flour mixture; with fork, stir until mixture forms a soft dough that leaves side of bowl.

Turn out dough onto lightly floured surface and knead 15 to 20 times. With floured rolling pin, roll out dough to ½" thickness. Cut dough with floured 2" round biscuit cutter and place, 1" apart, on ungreased large baking sheet.

Bake in 450° oven 12 to 15 minutes or until golden brown. Serve immediately. Makes 16 biscuits.

Corn Meal Biscuits

You can still make these biscuits even if you don't keep buttermilk on hand. Simply place 1½ tsp. vinegar in a 1-c. glass measure. Add enough milk to make ½ c. and use this in place of the buttermilk.

> 1⅓ c. sifted flour
> 1 tsp. sugar
> 1 tsp. baking powder
> ½ tsp. salt
> ¼ tsp. baking soda
> ⅓ c. white or yellow corn meal
> ⅓ c. shortening
> ½ c. buttermilk
> 1½ tblsp. butter or regular margarine, melted

Into large bowl, sift together first 5 ingredients. Stir in corn meal. With pastry blender, cut in shortening until coarse crumbs form.

Add buttermilk to shortening-flour mixture; with fork, stir until mixture forms a soft dough that leaves side of bowl.

Turn out dough onto lightly floured surface and knead 10 times. With lightly floured rolling pin, roll out dough to ½" thickness. Cut dough with floured 2½" round biscuit cutter and place, 1" apart, on ungreased baking sheet. Brush tops with melted butter.

Bake in 450° oven 12 to 15 minutes or until golden brown. Serve immediately. Makes 8 biscuits.

Garden Biscuits

Bits of carrot and parsley add a dash of color to these tender biscuits. The recipe comes from a Missouri farm woman.

> 2 c. sifted flour
> 4 tsp. baking powder
> 2 tsp. sugar
> ½ tsp. salt
> ½ tsp. cream of tartar
> ½ c. shortening
> ⅓ c. finely chopped carrot
> 2 tblsp. finely chopped green onions
> 2 tblsp. finely chopped parsley
> ⅔ c. milk

Into large bowl, sift together first 5 ingredients. With pastry blender, cut in shortening until coarse crumbs form. Stir in carrot, green onions and parsley.

Add milk to shortening-flour mixture; with fork, stir until mixture forms a soft dough that leaves the side of bowl.

Turn out dough onto lightly floured surface and knead 10 times. With floured rolling pin, roll out dough to ½" thickness. Cut dough with floured 2½" round biscuit cutter and place, 1" apart, on ungreased baking sheet.

Bake in 450° oven 10 to 12 minutes or until golden brown. Serve immediately. Makes 12 biscuits.

Crescent Cloud Biscuits

To make a ring-shaped loaf, arrange the crescent-shaped biscuits in a circle on a baking sheet with their sides touching.

> 2 c. sifted flour
> 4 tsp. baking powder
> 1 tblsp. sugar
> ½ tsp. salt
> ½ c. shortening
> ½ c. milk
> 1 egg
> 1 egg white, slightly beaten

Into large bowl, sift together flour, baking powder, sugar and salt. With pastry blender, cut in shortening until coarse crumbs form.

In small bowl, mix milk and egg until well blended. Add milk mixture to shortening-flour mixture; with fork, stir until mixture forms a soft dough that leaves side of bowl.

Turn out dough onto lightly floured surface and knead 20 times. With floured rolling pin, roll out dough into a 12" circle. Cut dough into 12 wedges. Roll up wedges toward point; curve ends. Place crescents, 1" apart, on ungreased baking sheet; brush with egg white.

Bake in 450° oven 10 to 12 minutes or until golden brown. Serve immediately. Makes 12 crescents.

Sourdough Biscuits

These are light biscuits with a tangy flavor. Be sure to make the starter the day before you make the biscuits.

> 2⅔ c. sifted flour
> 1 tsp. salt
> 1 tsp. baking powder
> ½ tsp. baking soda
> ½ c. butter or regular margarine
> 1 c. Sourdough Starter (see Index)
> ½ c. buttermilk
> 2 tblsp. butter or regular margarine, melted

Into large bowl, sift together flour, salt, baking powder and baking soda. With pastry blender, cut in ½ c. butter until coarse crumbs form.

In small bowl, mix Sourdough Starter and buttermilk until well blended. Add buttermilk mixture to butter-flour mixture; with fork, stir until mixture forms a soft dough that leaves side of bowl.

Turn out dough onto well-floured surface and knead until no longer sticky, about 30 seconds. With floured rolling pin, roll out dough to ½" thickness. Cut dough with floured 2½" round biscuit cutter and place, 1" apart, on greased large baking sheet.

Cover with towel and let stand in warm place 30 minutes. Brush biscuit rounds with 2 tblsp. melted butter.

Bake in 425° oven 12 to 15 minutes or until golden brown. Serve immediately. Makes 12 biscuits.

Crackling Biscuits

Cracklings—crisp, fried morsels of salt pork—add lots of zip. These biscuits make good toppings for casseroles: cut them a little larger (3") and bake just 10 minutes; then place them on top of the casserole and continue baking about 15 minutes more.

⅓ c. finely diced salt pork
2 c. sifted flour
2 tsp. baking powder
½ tsp. salt
⅓ c. butter or regular margarine
⅔ c. water
1 egg yolk
1 tsp. water

In 7" skillet over medium heat, cook salt pork 6 to 8 minutes or until golden brown. Remove with slotted spoon; drain on paper towels.

Into large bowl, sift together flour, baking powder and salt. With pastry blender, cut in butter until coarse crumbs form. Stir in cooked salt pork until well blended.

Add ⅔ c. water to butter-flour mixture; with fork, stir until mixture forms a soft dough that leaves side of bowl.

Turn out dough onto lightly floured surface and knead 10 times.

With floured rolling pin, roll out dough to ³/₈″ thickness. Cut dough with floured 2″ round biscuit cutter and place, 1″ apart, on ungreased baking sheets.

In small bowl, mix egg yolk and 1 tsp. water until well blended. Brush biscuit rounds with egg yolk mixture.

Bake in 375° oven 25 minutes or until golden brown. Serve immediately. Makes 18 biscuits.

Beaten Biscuits

A Southern specialty since the Civil War, these biscuits once were made by beating the dough with a rolling pin for 20 to 45 minutes, usually to the rhythm of a spiritual. In this updated recipe, the dough is "beaten" in the food processor for only two minutes. Today these biscuits may be served as sandwiches with country ham, tuna salad or egg salad.

> 3 c. sifted flour
> ½ tsp. sugar
> ½ tsp. salt
> ¾ c. cold butter or regular margarine
> ¾ c. very cold milk

Place flour, sugar and salt in processor bowl with metal blade. Cover and process 2 seconds to aerate.

Cut butter into 10 pieces and distribute evenly over dry ingredients. Process 15 to 20 seconds, or until mixture resembles corn meal.

While processor is running, pour milk through feed tube in a steady stream. Process until mixture forms a ball; continue processing for 2 minutes.

Carefully turn out dough onto lightly floured surface. With floured rolling pin, roll out dough to ¼″ thickness. Cut dough with floured 1½″ round biscuit cutter and place, 1″ apart, on ungreased baking sheets. With fork, prick each biscuit several times.

Bake in 350° oven 25 minutes or until golden brown. Serve warm or cold. Store in airtight container up to 4 days. Makes 6 doz. biscuits.

DOUBLE-LAYER BEATEN BISCUITS: Prepare dough as directed.

With floured rolling pin, roll out dough to ⅛" thickness. Fold dough in half. Cut dough with floured 1½" round biscuit cutter and place, 1" apart, on ungreased baking sheets. Bake in 350° oven 25 minutes.

Carefully split apart each hot biscuit; place on baking sheets, split-side up. Bake 2 to 3 minutes more, or until biscuits are crisp and golden brown. Serve warm or cold. Makes 12 doz. biscuits.

Cinnamon Biscuit Fan-tans

Called fan-tans because as the cinnamon-coated dough layers bake, they spread to form a shape that resembles a fan.

> 2 c. sifted flour
> 4 tsp. baking powder
> ½ tsp. cream of tartar
> ½ tsp. salt
> 3 tblsp. sugar
> ½ c. shortening
> ⅔ c. milk
> 2 tblsp. butter or regular margarine, melted
> ½ c. sugar
> 1 tblsp. ground cinnamon

Into large bowl, sift together flour, baking powder, cream of tartar, salt and 3 tblsp. sugar. With pastry blender, cut in shortening until coarse crumbs form.

Add milk to shortening-flour mixture; with fork, stir until mixture forms a soft dough that leaves side of bowl.

Turn out dough onto lightly floured surface and knead 20 times. With floured rolling pin, roll out dough into a 12x10" rectangle. Brush with melted butter. In small bowl, stir together ½ c. sugar and cinnamon; sprinkle evenly over dough.

Cut dough lengthwise into 5 (12x2") strips. Stack strips in one stack. Cut stacked dough, crosswise, into 12 (1") pieces. Place pieces, cut-side down, in 12 well-greased 2½" muffin-pan cups.

Bake in 425° oven 15 minutes or until golden brown. Serve immediately. Makes 12 fan-tans.

Buttermilk Biscuit Pinwheels

A cheese filling forms the pinwheel pattern in these hearty rolls, and a sprinkling of chopped onion adds extra flavor.

2 tblsp. butter or regular margarine
¼ c. finely chopped onion
2 tblsp. chopped fresh parsley
2 drops hot pepper sauce
2 c. sifted flour
2 tsp. sugar
2 tsp. baking powder
½ tsp. salt
¼ tsp. baking soda
½ c. shortening
1 c. buttermilk
½ c. shredded Swiss or Cheddar cheese

In 10" skillet over medium heat, melt butter. Add onion, parsley and hot pepper sauce; cook 5 minutes, or until onion is tender. Remove from heat; set aside.

Into large bowl, sift together flour, sugar, baking powder, salt and baking soda. With pastry blender, cut in shortening until coarse crumbs form.

Add buttermilk to shortening-flour mixture; with fork, stir until mixture forms a soft dough that leaves side of bowl.

Turn out dough onto lightly floured surface and knead 20 times. With floured rolling pin, roll out dough into a 12x9" rectangle. Spread onion mixture over dough; sprinkle with cheese. Starting with one long side, roll up dough, jelly-roll fashion; pinch seam to seal.

Cut roll into 1" slices. Place slices, cut-side down, in greased 9" round baking pan.

Bake in 450° oven 25 minutes or until golden brown. Remove from pan. Serve immediately. Makes 12 pinwheels.

Scones

Here's a Scottish recipe for tender, slightly sweet biscuits.
Serve these flaky triangles warm with breakfast, lunch or dinner.

> 1¾ c. sifted flour
> 2½ tsp. baking powder
> ½ tsp. salt
> 1 tblsp. sugar
> 5 tblsp. butter
> 2 eggs, slightly beaten
> ⅓ c. milk or heavy cream
> Sugar

Into large bowl, sift together flour, baking powder, salt and 1 tblsp. sugar. With pastry blender, cut in butter until coarse crumbs form.

Reserve 2 tblsp. beaten egg. In small bowl, mix remaining egg and milk until well blended. Add milk mixture to butter-flour mixture; with fork, stir until mixture forms a soft dough that leaves side of bowl.

On lightly floured surface with floured rolling pin, roll out dough into a 15x3" rectangle. Cut rectangle into 5 (3") squares; then diagonally cut each square in half. Place triangles, 1" apart, on greased baking sheet; brush each one with reserved beaten egg and sprinkle with sugar.

Bake in 425° oven 10 to 12 minutes or until golden brown. Serve immediately. Makes 10 scones.

FOOD PROCESSOR METHOD: Place flour, baking powder, salt and 1 tblsp. sugar in processor bowl with metal blade. Cover and process 2 seconds to aerate. Cut butter into 5 pieces and distribute evenly over dry ingredients. Process 10 seconds or until coarse crumbs form.

Reserve 2 tblsp. beaten egg. In small bowl, mix remaining egg and milk until well blended. While processor is running, pour egg-milk mixture through feed tube. Process 4 to 5 seconds, just until mixture forms a soft dough that leaves side of bowl. Roll out and bake as directed.

RAISIN OR CURRANT SCONES: Stir ½ c. raisins or currants into butter-flour mixture.

SOUR CREAM SCONES: Increase sugar to 2 tblsp. and substitute ½ c. dairy sour cream for milk.

OATMEAL SCONES: Use only 1¼ c. flour and stir ½ c. quick-cooking oats into dry ingredients. Use only ¼ c. milk.

Naan

In India, this flat bread is baked on the walls of clay ovens. For a peppery flavor, add 1 tsp. cracked pepper to the dry ingredients.

>   4 c. sifted flour
>   1 tblsp. sugar
>   1 tblsp. baking powder
>   ½ tsp. salt
>   ¼ tsp. baking soda
>   2 eggs
>   ¾ c. plus 2 tblsp. milk
>   Vegetable oil

Into large bowl, sift together first 5 ingredients; set aside.

In small bowl, mix eggs and milk until well blended. Gradually stir egg mixture into dry ingredigents until a stiff dough forms.

Turn out dough onto lightly floured surface and knead until smooth, about 8 minutes. Divide dough into 12 pieces. Shape each piece into a ball. Place balls, 1″ apart, on greased baking sheet. Brush with oil. Cover with damp towel and let rest in warm place 1 hour.

With oiled hands, pat and stretch each ball into a teardrop shape, 9″ long and 4″ wide at widest part. Place, ½″ apart, on greased large baking sheets.

Broil, 1 baking sheet at a time, 3″ from source of heat, about 2 minutes on each side, or until breads are golden brown and slightly puffy. Serve warm. Makes 12 naans.

To Reheat: Wrap in a single layer in foil. Heat in 350° oven until hot, about 10 minutes.

Graham Crackers

These crisp, thin, cinnamon-and ginger-flavored crackers are better than store-bought. (Be sure to save some for the kids!)

1¼ c. sifted all-purpose flour
1¼ c. stirred whole-wheat flour
½ c. wheat germ
1 tsp. baking powder
1 tsp. ground cinnamon
½ tsp. baking soda
½ tsp. ground ginger
¼ tsp. salt
½ c. packed brown sugar
½ c. shortening
1 tsp. vanilla
½ c. milk

In medium bowl, stir together first 8 ingredients; set aside.

In large bowl using mixer at medium speed, beat brown sugar, shortening and vanilla until light and fluffy.

Reduce speed to low; beat in dry ingredients alternately with milk until well blended. Wrap dough in plastic wrap. Refrigerate until dough is easy to handle, at least 4 hours.

Divide dough into thirds. On lightly floured surface with floured rolling pin, roll out a third into a 12" square. (Keep remaining dough refrigerated.) Cut square into 8 (6x3") rectangles.

Place rectangles, 1" apart, on greased baking sheets. Score each rectangle with blunt side of knife to make 4 sections (do not cut all the way through dough). With fork, prick each rectangle several times. Repeat with remaining dough.

Bake in 350° oven 8 to 10 minutes or until golden brown. Remove from baking sheets. Cool on racks. Store in airtight container up to 2 weeks. Makes 24 crackers.

Cheddar Rounds

Crisp, buttery crackers, perfect as appetizers. If you make the dough and freeze it, you can have a hot snack with 20 minutes notice.

2 c. sifted flour
½ tsp. salt
⅛ tsp. ground red pepper
⅔ c. butter or regular margarine
1 c. shredded sharp Cheddar cheese
5 to 7 tblsp. iced water
Pecan halves

Into large bowl, sift together flour, salt and red pepper. With pastry blender, cut in butter until coarse crumbs form. Stir in cheese.

Sprinkle iced water over cheese mixture, 1 tblsp. at a time, tossing with fork until dough forms. Press dough into a ball. (You may have to work dough lightly with fingers until dough forms a ball.) Wrap in plastic wrap; refrigerate until dough is easy to handle, at least 30 minutes.

Divide dough in half. On floured surface with floured rolling pin, roll out a half to ¼" thickness. (Keep remaining dough refrigerated.) Cut dough with floured 2" round biscuit cutter.

Place rounds, 1" apart, on greased baking sheets. Press a pecan half in center of each round. Repeat with remaining dough.

Bake in 350° oven 15 minutes or until golden brown. Remove from baking sheets. Cool slightly on racks. Serve warm. Store in airtight container up to 2 days. Makes about 3½ doz. rounds.

To Freeze and Bake Later: Prepare Cheddar Rounds, but do not bake. Freeze rounds on baking sheets until firm, about 2 hours. Remove rounds from baking sheets and wrap in heavy-duty foil or place in heavy freezer-storage bags. Freeze up to 3 months.

To bake: Place, 1" apart, on greased baking sheets. Bake in 350° oven 18 to 20 minutes or until golden brown.

Health Crackers

One of our favorites. Made with oats and wheat germ, these crackers are flavorful, crisp and good for you, too!

3 c. quick-cooking oats
2¼ c. sifted flour
1 c. wheat germ
3 tblsp. sugar
1 tsp. salt
1 c. water
¾ c. vegetable oil

In large bowl, stir together first 5 ingredients. Add water and oil; with fork, stir until mixture forms a soft dough that leaves side of bowl.

Divide dough into fourths. On lightly floured surface with floured rolling pin, roll out a fourth into a 12x10″ rectangle. (Keep remaining dough covered.) Roll dough loosely around rolling pin and unroll onto greased baking sheet.

Cut into 30 (2″) squares. Repeat with remaining dough.

Bake in 350° oven 15 to 20 minutes or until golden brown. Remove from baking sheets. Cool on racks. Store in airtight container up to 5 days. Makes 10 doz. crackers.

Oyster Crackers

For the classic accompaniment to soups, especially chowders, add these bite-size nuggets to each serving.

1⅔ c. sifted cake flour
1 c. sifted all-purpose flour
1 tsp. salt
½ c. shortening
1 pkg. active dry yeast
¼ tsp. sugar
¼ c. warm water (105 to 115°)

Place cake flour, all-purpose flour and salt in food processor bowl with metal blade. Cover and process 2 seconds to aerate.

Divide shortening into 10 pieces and distribute evenly over dry ingredients. Process 15 to 20 seconds, or until fine crumbs form.

In small bowl, sprinkle yeast and sugar over warm water; stir until dissolved.

While processor is running, pour yeast mixture through feed tube in a steady stream. Process until mixture forms a ball; continue processing for 2 minutes.

Carefully turn out dough onto lightly floured surface. With floured rolling pin, roll out dough as thin as possible into a rectangle. Fold each long side to center; then fold each end to center to form a smaller rectangle. Repeat rolling and folding twice more, adding flour to surface as necessary to keep dough from sticking.

Roll out dough into an 8x6" rectangle. Cut rectangle into 48 (1") squares. Place squares, 1" apart, on greased large baking sheet. With fork, prick each square once.

Bake in 375° oven 20 to 25 minutes or until lightly browned. Immediately remove from baking sheet. Cool on racks. Store in airtight container up to 1 week. Makes 4 doz. crackers.

Sesame Whole-Wheat Wafers

Especially good topped with a sharp Cheddar spread, these crisp, wheaty crackers have a strong sesame flavor.

1 ¾ c. stirred whole-wheat flour
½ c. toasted sesame seed
¼ c. wheat germ
½ tsp. salt
1 pkg. active dry yeast
¼ tsp. sugar
¾ c. warm water (105 to 115°)
¼ c. vegetable oil
Onion or garlic salt

In medium bowl, stir together flour, sesame seed, wheat germ and salt; set aside.

In small bowl, sprinkle yeast and sugar over warm water; stir until dissolved.

Add yeast mixture and oil to dry ingredients; with fork, stir until mixture forms a soft dough that leaves side of bowl. Knead in bowl until smooth, about 1 minute.

Divide dough in half. On lightly floured surface with floured rolling pin, roll out each half into a 14x10" rectangle. Roll dough loosely around rolling pin and unroll onto greased baking sheets.

Cut each rectangle into 35 (2″) squares. Cover with towel and let rise in warm place until doubled, about 30 minutes. Sprinkle with onion or garlic salt.

Bake in 375° oven 18 to 20 minutes or until browned. Remove from baking sheets. Cool on racks. Store in airtight container up to 2 weeks. Makes about 5 doz. crackers.

Corn Meal Crackers

Spicy golden triangles—great with guacamole or anytime you might serve corn chips. For nachos, sprinkle with Monterey Jack or Cheddar cheese and broil briefly.

> ¾ c. yellow corn meal
> ¾ c. sifted flour
> 1 tsp. salt
> 1 tsp. baking powder
> ½ tsp. chili powder
> ½ c. milk
> ¼ c. butter or regular margarine, melted
> ½ tsp. Worcestershire sauce
> Seasoned salt

In medium bowl, stir together first 5 ingredients. Add milk, melted butter and Worcestershire sauce to corn meal mixture; with fork, stir until mixture forms a soft dough that leaves side of bowl.

Divide dough in half. On heavily floured surface with floured rolling pin, roll out each half into a 12″ square. Roll dough loosely around rolling pin and unroll onto greased large baking sheets.

Cut each square into 16 (3″) squares; then cut each smaller square diagonally in half to form triangles. Sprinkle with seasoned salt, if you wish.

Bake in 350° oven 10 to 15 minutes or until golden brown. Remove from baking sheets. Cool on racks. Store in airtight container up to 1 week. Makes about 5 doz. crackers.

Low-Sodium Whole-Grain Crackers

For people on sodium-restricted diets, commercially made crackers are off-limits. There is only 1 mg sodium per cracker, but lots of flavor and fiber, too!

2 c. stirred whole-wheat flour
1½ c. quick-cooking oats
½ c. wheat germ
3 tblsp. sugar
2 tblsp. sesame seed
⅔ c. water
½ c. vegetable oil

In medium bowl, stir together first 5 ingredients. Add water and oil. Using rubber spatula, stir until mixture forms a soft dough that leaves side of bowl. Press dough into a ball. Divide dough in half.

On lightly floured surface, roll out each half into a 14" square. Cut each square into 16 (3½") squares, then cut each smaller square diagonally in half to form triangles. Place triangles, ½" apart, on ungreased baking sheets.

Bake in 350° oven 18 minutes or until golden brown. Remove from baking sheets. Cool on racks. Store in airtight container up to 1 week. Makes about 5 doz. crackers.

Whole-Wheat Flat Bread

An Illinois farm woman lets her children help make these thin, whole-grain crackers. Sometimes she sprinkles them with sugar before baking.

2 c. quick-cooking oats
2 c. stirred whole-wheat flour
2 tblsp. sugar
1 tsp. salt
⅔ c. water
½ c. butter or regular margarine, melted
Sugar (optional)

In large bowl, stir together oats, flour, sugar and salt. Add water and butter to oat mixture; with rubber spatula, stir until mixture forms a soft dough that leaves side of bowl. Work dough lightly with fingers until dough forms a ball.

Divide dough into thirds. On lightly floured surface with floured rolling pin, roll out a third into a 12x10″ rectangle. (Keep remaining dough covered.) Roll dough loosely around rolling pin and unroll onto greased baking sheet. Cut rectangle into 16 (3x2½″) rectangles. Sprinkle with additional sugar if you wish. Repeat with remaining dough.

Bake in 350° oven 22 to 24 minutes or until golden brown. Remove from baking sheets. Cool on racks. Store in airtight container up to 1 week. Makes 4 doz. crackers.

Caraway-Rye Flat Bread

Scandinavian cooks make many versions of crisp flat bread, depending upon the flour used—barley, oat, rye, graham or whole-wheat. Before winter begins, they often make a big batch of dough, roll it into circles and cut a hole in the center of each circle. Then the baked breads are strung on lines and stored, like beads on a string.

> 1¼ c. stirred whole-wheat flour
> 1¼ c. stirred rye flour
> 2 tblsp. sugar
> 1 tsp. baking powder
> 1 tsp. salt
> ½ tsp. dry mustard
> ½ c. shortening
> ½ c. iced water
> 1 egg white, slightly beaten
> Caraway seed
> Salt

In large bowl, stir together first 6 ingredients. With pastry blender, cut in shortening until coarse crumbs form.

Sprinkle iced water over crumb mixture, 1 tblsp. at a time, tossing with fork until dough forms. Press dough into a ball. (You may have to work dough lightly with fingers until dough forms a ball.)

Divide dough into thirds. On lightly floured surface with floured rolling pin, roll out each third into a 12x10″ rectangle. Roll dough loosely around rolling pin and unroll onto greased baking sheets.

Cut each rectangle into 16 (3x2½") rectangles. With fork, prick each rectangle several times. Brush each with egg white. Sprinkle with caraway seed and additional salt.

Bake in 375° oven 10 to 12 minutes or until browned. Remove from baking sheets. Cool on racks. Store in airtight container up to 3 weeks. Makes 4 doz. flat breads.

Popovers

The high heat of the oven makes this light batter rise into fragile shells that "pop over" the sides of the pan. Resist the temptation to peek as they bake—one small draft of air will make them collapse.

> 1 c. sifted all-purpose flour
> ½ tsp. salt
> 1 c. milk
> 1 tblsp. butter or regular margarine, melted
> 2 eggs

Preheat 12 well-greased 2½" muffin-pan cups in 375° oven 5 minutes.

In large bowl using mixer at medium speed, beat flour, salt, milk and melted butter until well blended. Add eggs, one at a time, to flour mixture, beating until well blended. Do not over beat.

Pour batter into hot muffin-pan cups, filling two-thirds full.

Bake in 375° oven 50 minutes. With knife, make a slit in each popover. Bake 5 minutes more, or until popovers are golden brown and crisp. Remove from pans. Serve immediately. Makes 12 popovers.

WHOLE-WHEAT POPOVERS: Substitute ¼ c. stirred whole-wheat flour for ¼ c. all-purpose flour. Increase eggs to 3.

JUMBO POPOVERS: Prepare batter as directed. Generously grease 6 (6-oz.) jumbo-size popover cups. Preheat popover cups in 350° oven 5 minutes. Fill cups one-half full. Bake in 350° oven 45 minutes. With knife, make a slit in each popover. Bake 5 minutes more, or until golden brown and crisp. Remove from pans. Serve immediately. Makes 6 popovers.

6
Basics of Yeast Breads

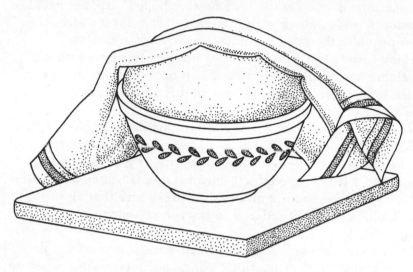

Something about the aroma of freshly baked bread gives you a supreme sense of well-being, especially if you've nurtured the bread from a formless mass of dough into a well-shaped loaf.

If you've never made yeast bread, just the thought of making one loaf may seem like an arduous, time-consuming task. Although it does take a little longer to prepare yeast breads than quick breads, it doesn't have to be difficult.

Making yeast bread is easy, especially if you follow our step-by-step recipe. You'll find additional helpful information in the section called *Yeast Bread Tips.* Once you've mastered these basics, we have more recipes for you to try.

Whole-Wheat Bread, rye bread, Brown-and-Serve Rolls plus more than 50 additional yeast bread recipes are in Chapter Seven. Besides Hot Cross Buns and other sweet rolls, in Chapter Eight there's a versatile Sweet Dough that you can use to make more than a baker's dozen different sweet breads and rolls.

If you're an experienced baker, then Chapter Nine is especially for you. There you'll find recipes for Brioche, Danish pastries and Croissants. And for those who don't want to knead dough, there's a whole selection of batter breads in Chapter Ten.

No matter what kind of yeast breads you make, the first step begins with dissolving the yeast. In this book we've used two of the most common methods for mixing yeast into batters and doughs—the Conventional Method and the Rapidmix Method.

CONVENTIONAL METHOD

Active dry yeast is sprinkled over warm water that ranges in temperature from 105 to 115°. This mixture is stirred until the yeast is *completely* dissolved.

Sometimes a small amount of sugar, about ½ tsp. per package of yeast, is added along with the yeast to the warm water. The sugar provides the yeast with an energy boost and starts it working faster. The dissolved yeast mixture is mixed with the remaining ingredients and about a cup or so of flour to make a batter. (The exact amount of flour that is added depends on the type of bread you are making.)

We like to use a mixer for beating in this first addition of flour, because it's easier. But, if you don't have a mixer, all of the mixing can be done with a wooden spoon—it just takes a little longer and a little more effort. This mixture is beaten at medium or high speed for about 2 minutes, to make sure that all of the ingredients are well mixed and to start the development of the gluten.

If you have a mixer that's capable of kneading yeast doughs, you can add the rest of the flour using your mixer. Otherwise use a wooden spoon to stir the additional flour into the batter.

Working with a cup of flour at a time, gradually stir the flour into the batter, mixing well after each addition. The flour is added gradually to the batter because it makes mixing the dough easier.

Stir in *only* enough of the additional flour to make a soft dough that leaves the side of the bowl. You may or may not have a cup or so of flour left over. That's okay, because the important endpoint is that you have a soft dough, not how much flour you add. Some of the leftover flour will be added during kneading.

Note that when this method is used in our recipes, warm water is used for dissolving the yeast, *not milk.* Because milk tends to coat the yeast granules and prevents the granules from dissolving completely, milk is added after the yeast has been dissolved in water.

A variation of the Conventional Method is called the sponge method. Though it's not used as frequently today as it was in the past, the sponge method is still a viable way to make yeast bread. You'll see this method used in our recipe for Sourdough White Bread in Chapter Seven.

In the sponge method, yeast is dissolved in warm water. Sugar, liquid and part of the flour are stirred into the dissolved yeast. It is then allowed to rise forming an airy, foamy mixture that resembles a sponge. The sponge is then stirred down and the remaining ingredients are added before kneading.

RAPIDMIX METHOD

In this method the necessity of first dissolving the yeast in warm water is eliminated. You'll find detailed directions for this method in the step-by-step recipe in this chapter.

The undissolved active dry yeast is stirred into some of the dry ingredients. The liquid ingredients are heated to 120 to 130°. (If shortening, butter or margarine is heated with the liquid, it's not necessary for it to melt completely.)

Using the mixer, this very warm liquid mixture is gradually beaten into the dry ingredients containing the yeast. The thin batter that results should be beaten until the yeast is completely dissolved. If the yeast granules are still visible after beating 2 minutes, continue beating until all of the yeast granules are dissolved.

The temperature of the liquids used here is warmer than the water used to directly dissolve the yeast in the Conventional Method. It is possible to use higher-temperature liquids without killing the yeast *only* because the yeast has been combined with the dry ingredients and does not come in direct contact with the warmer liquids.

Additional flour is then added and the mixture is beaten another 2 minutes using the mixer. During this second beating period, the gluten begins to form, which can actually shorten the kneading time.

Using a wooden spoon, the additional flour is stirred into the batter, a cup at a time, just as the flour is added in the Conventional Method.

If you're an experienced bread maker, you'll notice that the dough made by the Rapidmix Method feels and handles a little differently when kneaded than dough made by the Conventional Method. You will also notice that the dough rises faster, since all of the ingredients are warmer from the start.

What you do to your dough next—whether or not it's made by the Conventional or Rapidmix methods—determines what your bread will look like.

KNEADING

Kneading is an important step in most yeast bread recipes. The dough is folded and stretched again and again to develop the strands of gluten that will form the bread's structure. The average time for kneading most doughs ranges from 5 to 10 minutes.

A range is given in most recipes because the actual time can vary depending on the nature of the dough and just how vigorously you knead. Whereas it is almost impossible to overknead dough, it is important that you do not underknead it.

As kneading progresses, the rough mass of dough becomes less sticky, firmer and easier to handle. It will begin to spring back each time it is pushed down with the heels of your hands. It's important to knead the dough long enough to thoroughly mix the ingredients.

If, toward the end of the kneading time you decide that the dough is too soft and more flour must be added, be sure to extend the kneading time so that *all* of the flour is completely mixed into the dough.

When the dough has been kneaded sufficiently it will be smooth, elastic, and will have a satiny sheen. Tiny bubbles or blisters will be visible just under the surface of the dough, and your hand held lightly on the dough for 30 seconds should not stick.

Different types of bread dough will feel differently when kneaded. For instance, doughs made with whole-wheat flour feel heavier and stickier than those made with all-purpose flour. Doughs made with rye flour feel softer and will have a finer texture.

Not all yeast bread recipes require kneading. Batters for batter breads are vigorously beaten to help develop the gluten. Some shortcut recipes keep the kneading to a minimum and others skip it entirely. The baked breads from these no-knead recipes will have a rough, irregular top crust and a larger, more open texture on the inside than kneaded yeast breads.

RISING

The kneaded dough is placed in a greased large bowl, covered with a towel and set in a warm place to rise.

During rising, the yeast begins to grow by feeding on the sugars and starches in the dough. As it feeds, the yeast releases small bubbles of carbon dioxide gas. The gas is trapped in the dough by the network of gluten developed during kneading. As the yeast produces more and more gas, the dough begins to rise.

The rising time depends to a large extent on the temperature of the dough and the temperature of the place where it is set to rise. However some doughs, especially the richer ones containing a higher proportion of fat, generally will take longer to rise.

Doughs are usually allowed to rise until they have doubled in size. Test for doubling by quickly pressing two fingers about ½" into the top of the dough. If the impression remains, you'll know that the dough has risen enough. If not, cover the dough and let it rise a little longer.

Low-gluten flours, such as rye or soy, are often used in

combination with all-purpose and/or whole-wheat flour to make different flavored breads. Because rye and soy flours contain little or no gluten, the doughs made with them will not rise so much as doughs made with only wheat flours. The recipes will tell you to let these doughs rise until *almost* doubled.

As a general rule yeast breads are not made with more than 50% low-gluten flours. This helps to ensure that these bread doughs contain enough gluten-producing proteins so that they'll rise adequately.

After the dough has risen it is punched down by plunging your fist deep into the center of the dough. This action collapses the cell structure; releasing the carbon dioxide gas that has been produced by the yeast, and brings the yeast in contact with a fresh food supply. The dough can then rise again after shaping without overstretching and injuring the gluten. The cell structure that forms during the second rising will be stronger and finer.

SHAPING

The step-by-step instructions for Basic Yeast Bread in this chapter show just one of the many ways to shape dough into a loaf. There are probably as many ways to do this as there are bakers, and you may wish to experiment with different shaping methods until you find one that you prefer. Here's just one way that a yeast dough can be shaped.

After the dough is punched down, it is usually allowed to rest about 10 minutes. This relaxes the gluten, making the dough easier to handle and shape.

The dough is then flattened with a rolling pin and/or with your hands into a rectangle to press out excess gas that would otherwise form large air holes in the loaf.

The dough is then tightly rolled up and the seams and ends are sealed before it is placed in the greased loaf pan. Some bakers will place the dough, seam-side up in the pan and then roll it over so the seam is down. This will lightly grease the top of the dough and help prevent it from drying out during the final rising period.

It is important to use as little flour as possible when shaping the loaf to avoid streaks of flour in the bread.

FINAL RISING

After shaping, the dough is again allowed to rise. You may notice that it usually takes a little less time for the dough to rise the second time. Test the risen dough by *lightly* pressing the top edge of the loaf with your finger. If the impression remains then the dough is ready to bake.

FINISHING TOUCHES

There are many ways you can enhance the appearance, texture and taste of the crusts of your yeast breads. Glazes, sometimes called "washes," or just plain water can be brushed over the loaves or rolls before baking to make the crusts shiny or dull, tender or crisp, sweet or salty. It depends on the nature of the mixture used. To apply these finishing touches to your loaves, use a pastry brush.

Ordinary tap water can be brushed or lightly sprayed over the loaves or rolls before or during baking for a crisp, lightly browned crust. Keep a plant mister handy to spray the water quickly and evenly over the loaves. If you like a crisp crust with a slightly salty flavor, then add ½ tsp. salt to ¼ c. water and use this to mist the dough.

Another way to produce a crisp crust is with steam. Just place a pan of hot water in the oven on the rack below the bread during baking. Or, take a hint from a smart Montana farm wife. She simply tosses a couple of ice cubes on the bottom of the oven when she puts the bread in to bake. The ice cubes produce steam as they melt; they don't leave a mess since the water evaporates; and there's no pan of boiling water to juggle to the sink after the bread baking is finished.

A beaten egg or egg yolk mixed with 1 tblsp. water, milk or cream can be brushed over the risen dough for a shiny, richly browned finish on your baked breads. An egg white beaten with 1 tblsp. water will give your crust a shiny, golden brown appearance, a shade or two lighter than one on which whole egg or egg yolk is used. Any one of these egg washes is often used before the bread dough is sprinkled with coarse salt, poppy, caraway or sesame seed, nuts or sugar. The egg mixture will act like glue, helping the nuts, etc., adhere to the crust when baked.

Honey, molasses, dark corn syrup or maple syrup can be mixed with a little water so it's thin enough to brush over the risen dough without tearing it. Any of these mixtures will give your bread a rich brown color when baked and also impart a slightly sweet flavor to the crust.

Brush the dough with milk before baking for a lovely, tender, golden brown crust. Or, for an old-fashioned effect, use a sharp knife or razor blade to slash the tops of loaves or rolls. Then dust them with flour and pop them into the oven.

Many breads are brushed with solid shortening or butter as soon as they come from the oven. The heat of the bread will melt the shortening on contact, so you don't have to bother with melting the shortening beforehand. The result is a soft, tender crust with a satiny sheen.

After the bread has cooled, store it in a plastic bag if you want the crust to soften or to remain soft. For loaves or rolls with crisp crusts, skip the plastic bag and use a paper one instead.

BAKING

Begin preheating your oven at least 15 minutes before you are ready to start baking. It is best to use an oven thermometer so that you are sure your oven temperature is accurate.

During the first 10 minutes of baking, the dough will continue to rise, but at an accelerated rate. This is due to the continued fermentation of the yeast and to the rapid expansion of the gases in the dough caused by the heat from the oven. This rapid spurt of rising at the beginning of baking is referred to as *oven spring*. It will cease when the temperature of the dough becomes hot enough to kill the yeast. The structure will then begin to set and a crust will start to form as the surface of the bread dries.

When the bread is completely baked, it will sound hollow when tapped. Immediately remove the baked loaf from the pan and cool it on a rack away from drafts. When you remove the loaf from its pan, you may notice an even wide line, sometimes a break, along both sides of the top crust. This is called *shredding* and occurs naturally during oven spring when the strands of gluten are rapidly stretched.

Step-by-Step Yeast Bread

Coarse, crusty and flavorful, or light, tender and delicate—it's a matter of personal preference as to what type of bread you like to serve and eat at home.

But when it comes to the traditional, classic loaf of white yeast bread, every baker will agree that the loaf should have an evenly rounded top without any bumps or bulges. The crust should be crisp, yet tender. The shredding, if it occurs, should be even. Inside, the loaf should be uniform in color without light or dark streaks. The texture should be uniformly small-grained and the crumb moist and tender.

Here's how to make two loaves of white bread.

    2 pkg. active dry yeast
    2 tblsp. sugar
    1½ tsp. salt
    5⅓ to 6⅓ c. sifted flour
    1 c. milk
    1 c. water
    2 tblsp. shortening

Step 1: In large bowl, stir together the yeast, sugar, salt and 2 c. flour. Set aside.

Step 2: In 2-qt. saucepan over low heat, heat milk, water and shortening until *very warm* (120 to 130°). It's not necessary for the shortening to melt completely. Use a yeast thermometer to check the temperature of the liquids. The temperature of the liquids must be hot enough (at least 120°) to dissolve the yeast in the flour mixture, but not so hot (over 130°) as to kill the yeast in the flour mixture.

Step 3: Using mixer at low speed, gradually beat the very warm milk mixture into the yeast mixture until it's well blended. Increase the speed to medium; beat 2 minutes. It's important that all of the yeast granules are dissolved. If necessary, beat a little longer until all of the yeast granules are no longer visible.

Step 4: Add 1 c. flour. Increase speed to high; beat 2 minutes more. Beating this thick batter starts the development of the gluten in the flour, which will later form the structure for the bread.

Step 5: Stir in enough additional flour to make a soft dough that leaves the side of the bowl and can be easily handled. As stirring becomes more difficult, you may wish to finish adding and mixing in the flour with your hands. The dough will be sticky and have a rough, uneven appearance. The amount of flour that you add will vary slightly depending on the humidity, and the brand of flour used. However there should be some flour left to be used when kneading.

Step 6: Turn out the dough onto a lightly floured, wooden board, counter top or pastry cloth. Lightly flour your hands. Shape the dough into a ball and flatten the dough slightly. You are now ready to begin kneading the dough.

Step 7: Kneading the dough is very important. Besides evenly mixing the flour into the dough, kneading further develops the gluten, making the dough elastic. To knead, begin by folding the dough toward you.

Step 8: With your fingers curved over the top of the dough, use the heels of your hands to push the dough down and away from you.

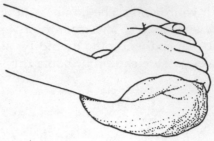

Step 9: Give the dough a quarter turn.

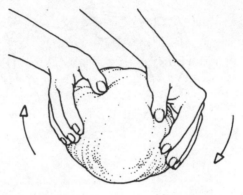

Step 10: Repeat this process (Steps 7 through 9) using a rhythmic, rocking motion, until the dough is smooth and elastic, and blisters appear just under the surface. This will take about 5 to 10 minutes, depending on how vigorously you knead. It will be necessary to occasionally dust the kneading surface and your hands with flour to keep the dough from sticking, but try to use as little flour as possible. You will find that the dough will stick less as the kneading progresses.

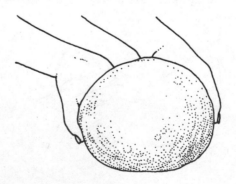

Step 11: Place the kneaded dough in a greased large bowl and turn over the dough so that the top is greased. This will help prevent a crust from forming on the top of the dough that is exposed to the air.

Step 12: Cover the bowl with a clean towel and let the dough rise in a warm (85°), draft-free place until doubled, about 45 minutes. A good way to do this is by placing the dough in a cold oven with a large pan filled with hot water on the rack beneath the dough, or place a wire rack over a large pan filled two-thirds full with hot water and then place the covered bowl of dough on the rack. Too high a temperature will kill the yeast, so don't be tempted to put the bowl of dough in a hot oven or on top of a radiator. Check the temperature of the water periodically and as it cools replace it with more hot water.

Step 13: The time it takes for the dough to double will depend on the temperature as well as the amount and type of ingredients used in each recipe. Test the dough to see if it has doubled by quickly pressing two fingers about ½" into the top of the dough. If the dough feels light and an impression remains, then the dough has risen sufficiently.

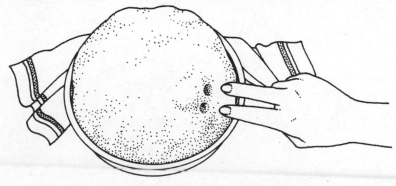

Step 14: The dough is then punched down by plunging your fist deep into the center of the risen dough. This action releases the carbon dioxide gas produced by the growing yeast. So when the yeast dough rises again, the bread will have a finer, more uniform texture and its structure will be stronger.

Step 15: Gather the edges of the dough and press them into the center, forming a ball.

Step 16: Turn out the dough onto a lightly floured surface. With a sharp knife cut the dough in half and shape each dough half into a smooth ball.

Step 17: Cover the balls of dough with a towel and let them rest 10 minutes. The resting period allows the gluten in the dough to relax, making it easier for the dough to be rolled and shaped.

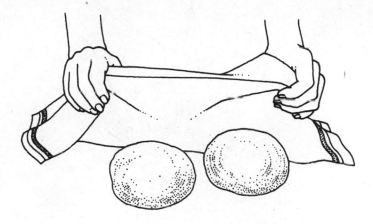

Step 18: With a lightly floured rolling pin, roll out each dough half into a 12x8″ rectangle. Using the sides of your hands and working from the center of a rectangle out to the ends, firmly press out any air bubbles. Repeat with the remaining rectangle.

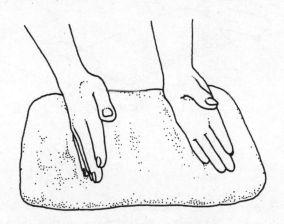

Step 19: Starting at one narrow side, tightly roll up one rectangle jelly-roll fashion, sealing the dough at each turn with your fingertips. Repeat with remaining rectangle.

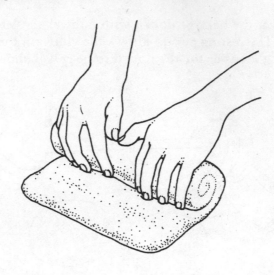

Step 20: Turn roll, seam-side down. Seal the ends by pressing down with the sides of your hands and tucking under the ends of the roll. Repeat with remaining roll.

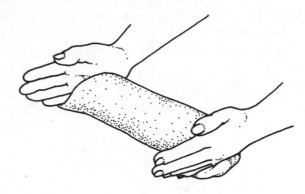

Step 21: Place rolls, seam-side down, in 2 greased 8½x4½x2½" dull or dark metal loaf pans. Metal pans with a dull or dark finish will absorb the heat more readily so that the bottoms and sides of the loaves will brown, forming a crust which helps support the structure of the bread.

Step 22: Cover with a towel and let the loaves rise in a warm (85°) place until doubled, about 45 minutes. The loaves are doubled when an imprint remains after lightly touching the loaf at the corner of each pan.

Step 23: After the final rising, you may wish to slash the top of each loaf with a *very* sharp knife. Professional bakers will often use a single-edge razor blade for this purpose. Because a razor has a thinner, sharper edge than most kitchen knives, it is easier to slash the dough without tearing it.

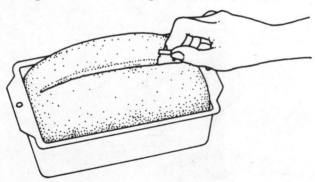

Step 24: Bake in preheated 400° oven 35 minutes, or until the loaves are golden brown and sound hollow when tapped with your fingertips. When baking, the loaves should be placed so that the tops of the pans are in the center of the oven, allowing the heat to evenly circulate around the loaves.

It's a good idea to check the loaves after half of the baking time. If the loaves are browning too quickly, loosely cover them with sheets of foil to prevent overbrowning. If they are browning unevenly, rotate the pans from back to front and from left to right.

Step 25: Immediately remove loaves from pans. Place each loaf on its side and let cool on racks away from drafts. It is important to take the loaves out of the pans before cooling to prevent the bottoms and sides from becoming soggy.

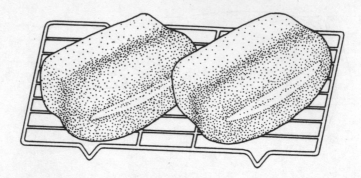

Step 26: Although it is easier to slice a loaf of bread after it has cooled completely, many yeast breads taste even better when eaten slightly warm. The best way to slice bread, especially a warm loaf, is to first turn the loaf on its side. Then, with a sharp, wavy-edge knife, use a sawing motion to cut the loaf into slices.

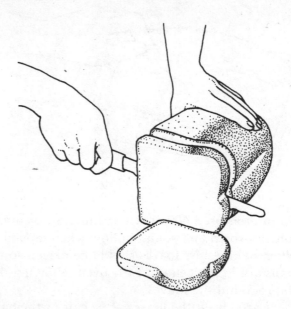

Yeast Bread Tips

The single most important thing to remember when making yeast breads is temperature. To begin with, all of your ingredients, unless otherwise specified in the recipe, should be at room temperature. This includes eggs and yeast, if you keep yeast stored in the refrigerator. It even helps if your mixing bowls are slightly warm when you're ready to use them.

Use a yeast or candy thermometer to check the temperature of the liquid before using it in the recipe. Refer to the recipe for the correct liquid temperature—105 to 115° for the Conventional Method, and 120 to 130° for the Rapidmix Method. Liquids that are too hot will kill the yeast, and liquids that are too cold will shock or numb the yeast, preventing it from dissolving properly.

The optimal temperature at which yeast doughs and yeast batters should rise is 85°. Don't risk killing the yeast by putting the dough or batter in a hot oven or on top of a radiator. If the rising temperature is too cool, there is no harm done, but it will take longer for the dough or batter to double.

The importance of the correct oven temperature for baking bread cannot be stressed enough. We seriously recommend that you invest in an oven thermometer and not rely solely on your oven's temperature setting.

Here are the answers to some of the most commonly asked questions about preparing and baking yeast bread.

My yeast dough didn't rise—why?

You may have forgotten to add the yeast or you may have killed the yeast either by using too hot a liquid to dissolve the yeast or by putting the dough in too warm a place to rise.

You can salvage the dough in one of two ways. One way is to make a second batch of dough. This time be sure to use the correct temperature for the liquid to dissolve the yeast.

Then knead the two batches of dough together. Be sure to knead thoroughly so the two batches are well mixed and then let the dough rise as directed. It may take slightly longer to rise, but there will be enough live yeast cells for both batches of dough.

The second way to salvage the dough is to dissolve the required amount of yeast in a small amount of warm (105 to 115°) water. Sprinkle some of the yeast mixture over the dough. Begin kneading, gradually adding the remaining yeast mixture and a small amount of flour to compensate for the extra liquid. Continue kneading until the new yeast is thoroughly mixed in and the dough is smooth and elastic. Let the dough rise as directed.

My yeast dough is very firm and doesn't seem to have any elasticity left now that I have finished kneading it—why?

You've added too much flour to the dough. The dough can be salvaged by kneading a small amount of water into the dough. It should feel softer and more elastic.

I shaped my yeast dough into round loaves and placed them on a baking sheet to rise. They didn't hold their shape but spread out instead—why?

Not enough flour was kneaded into the dough. You can salvage the dough by kneading in a small amount of flour. Be sure to knead the dough thoroughly so the flour is mixed in completely. Reshape the dough into loaves and let it rise as directed.

My yeast dough has risen much too high in the pan—why?

You may have let the dough rise too long or the pan may be too small. If it has overrisen and you bake it, the dough will collapse. Instead, punch down the dough, reshape it and let it rise again just until it has doubled.

   If the pan is too small, reshape the dough as above, but place it in a larger pan before letting it rise. The reverse is true if the dough has risen sufficiently but is very low in the pan. Reshape the dough but place it in a smaller pan.

   As a general rule of thumb, use enough dough to fill the pan two-thirds full. However in the case of a batter bread, the pan should be filled only one-half full.

The top of my yeast loaf is golden brown but the sides and bottom are very pale—why?

This often happens when the bread is baked in a shiny aluminum pan. This type of pan tends to reflect the heat rather than absorb it, thus preventing the bottom and sides of the loaf from browning. Simply remove the loaf from the pan and return it to the oven, placing it directly on the oven rack. Bake about 5 minutes longer, or until the bottom and sides are golden brown.

My yeast loaf is very moist and gummy—why?

Most likely the loaf was underbaked. Check for doneness before the loaf cools. If it does not sound hollow when tapped, then immediately return it to the oven and finish baking.

My yeast loaf is small and hard—why?

This can happen if the yeast in the dough was killed, or the dough was not allowed to rise long enough before baking.

My yeast loaf is flat and has a heavy, compact texture even though it rose nicely before baking—why?

The dough was definitely allowed to rise too long. This causes the gluten to overstretch and collapse during baking.

The shape of my yeast loaves is uneven—why?

Too low an oven temperature can cause the bread to rise unevenly while baking. Or, your oven may have hot spots, which can cause the bread to rise unevenly when baked—so it's a good idea to rotate the pans (from back to front and left to right) halfway through the baking time. If you're baking on both oven racks, rotate the loaves from top to bottom.

Uneven shaping of the dough, or dough that is too soft or too stiff or underkneaded, can also result in a poorly shaped, baked loaf. However, batter breads, because of their very soft batter-like dough, and unkneaded bread doughs when baked will have a characteristic irregular-shaped top crust.

The top crust separated from my yeast loaf—why?

This is called shelling and it happens when the top surface of the dough dries out during the final rising. To prevent this, lightly brush the top of the dough with vegetable oil, or cover the dough with a slightly damp towel or a sheet of plastic wrap during the final rising. A too-low oven temperature can also cause shelling.

My yeast loaf has a dense, moist layer near the bottom—why?

Too much flour was added at the end of the kneading process. If you decide that your dough is too soft and more flour must be added, be sure to extend the kneading time so that all the flour is completely incorporated into the dough.

My yeast loaf has a strong yeast flavor—why?

Using too much yeast or yeast that is old can cause your bread to have a strong, unpleasant yeast flavor. As a general rule, use 1 pkg. yeast for every 3 to 4 c. flour. Don't try to speed things up by doubling the amount of yeast in the recipe. Check the date on the yeast package. If it has expired, it's best not to use the yeast.

7
Breads and Rolls

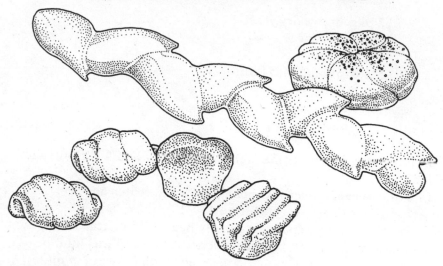

Gone forever are the days when all of our bread was homemade. Our grandmothers spent many hours, sometimes even days, preparing the family's bread. But today, many time-conscious cooks are making bread with a minimum of effort. They have discovered just how flexible making bread can be.

There are mixers that will knead yeast dough in only a few minutes—all you do is shape the dough. Then while it rises and bakes, you're free to do other tasks. Most of the 50 or so yeast doughs in this chapter, including recipes for Best-ever White Bread, German Pumpernickel and Honey-Wheat Buns, can be easily made using a mixer equipped with dough hooks.

The food processor can be used to make and knead French Bread and Pizza Dough. Both can be prepared with whole-wheat flour, and the Pizza Dough can also be refrigerated overnight.

Using quick-rise yeast in the dough or letting yeast dough rise in your microwave are two more ways to save time when preparing yeast bread. Or, try the one-step No-knead Dinner Rolls—complete with directions for make-ahead Brown-and-Serve Dinner Rolls. For freezing yeast dough, just follow the recipe for Freezer White Bread.

For those who have the time, make loaves from homemade Sourdough Starter. Triticale, Polenta and Millet Breads, plus Kaiser Rolls, Bread Sticks and Sesame-Onion Bow Ties are all recipes that you'll find on the following pages.

Best-ever White Bread

*You can shape the dough in the usual way, or into braided loaves.
The dough can also rise in your refrigerator overnight.*

> 2 pkg. active dry yeast
> 2 tblsp. sugar
> 1½ tsp. salt
> 5⅓ to 6⅓ c. sifted flour
> 1 c. milk
> 1 c. water
> 2 tblsp. shortening

In large bowl, stir together yeast, sugar, salt and 2 c. flour; set aside.

In 2-qt. saucepan over low heat, heat milk, water and shortening until very warm (120 to 130°).

Using mixer at low speed, gradually beat milk mixture into yeast mixture until well blended. Increase speed to medium; beat 2 minutes. Add 1 c. flour. Increase speed to high; beat 2 minutes.

Stir in enough additional flour to make a soft dough. Turn out dough onto lightly floured surface. Knead until smooth and elastic, about 8 to 10 minutes.

Place in greased large bowl, turning over dough so that top is greased. Cover with towel and let rise in warm place until doubled, about 45 minutes.

Punch down dough. Cover and let rise again, until almost doubled, about 30 minutes.

Punch down dough. Divide dough in half. Cover and let rest 10 minutes.

With lightly floured rolling pin, roll out each half into a 16x6" rectangle. Starting with one short side, roll up each rectangle, jelly-roll fashion. Pinch seams and ends to seal. Place each roll, seam-side down, in greased 8½x4½x2½" loaf pan.

Cover and let rise until doubled, about 45 minutes.

Bake in 400° oven 35 minutes, or until loaves are golden brown and sound hollow when tapped. Immediately remove from pans. Cool on racks. Makes 2 loaves.

BRAIDED BEST-EVER WHITE BREAD: Prepare dough and let rise as directed. Divide each dough half into thirds. Roll each third into a 10"-long rope. For each loaf, braid 3 ropes; pinch ends together. Place each braid in greased loaf pan, tucking ends under. Let rise and bake as directed.

COOLRISE BEST-EVER WHITE BREAD: Prepare and knead dough as directed. Cover with towel and let rest 20 minutes.

Divide dough in half. On lightly floured surface with floured rolling pin, roll out each dough half into a 16x6" rectangle.

Starting with one short side, roll up each rectangle, jelly-roll fashion; pinch seams and ends to seal. Place each roll, seam-side down, in greased 8½x4½x2½" loaf pan. Brush loaves with vegetable oil.

Cover tightly with plastic wrap. Refrigerate 2 to 24 hours.

About 15 minutes before baking, uncover loaves. Preheat oven to 400°. Puncture any air bubbles with toothpick.

Bake 35 minutes, or until loaves are golden brown and sound hollow when tapped. Immediately remove from pans. Cool on racks.

Rich White Bread

Eggs and milk make this white bread rich, soft and moist.

> 2 pkg. active dry yeast
> 2 tblsp. sugar
> 1½ tsp. salt
> 5¼ to 6¼ c. sifted flour
> 1½ c. milk
> 2 tblsp. butter or regular margarine
> 2 eggs

In large bowl, stir together yeast, sugar, salt and 2 c. flour; set aside.

In 2-qt. saucepan over low heat, heat milk and butter until very warm (120 to 130°).

Using mixer at low speed, gradually beat milk mixture into yeast mixture until well blended. Increase speed to medium; beat 2 minutes. Add eggs and 1 c. flour. Increase speed to high; beat 2 minutes more.

Stir in enough additional flour to make a soft dough. Turn out dough onto lightly floured surface. Knead until smooth and elastic, about 8 to 10 minutes.

Place in greased large bowl, turning over dough so that top is greased. Cover with towel and let rise in warm place until doubled, about 1 hour.

Punch down dough. Cover and let rise again until almost doubled, about 30 minutes.

Punch down dough. Divide dough in half. Cover and let rest 10 minutes.

With lightly floured rolling pin, roll out each half into a 16x6" rectangle. Starting with one short side, roll up each rectangle, jelly-roll fashion; pinch seams and ends to seal. Place each roll, seam-side down, in greased 9x5x3" loaf pan.

Cover and let rise until doubled, about 45 minutes.

Bake in 400° oven 30 to 40 minutes, or until loaves are dark golden brown and sound hollow when tapped. Immediately remove from pans. Cool on racks. Makes 2 loaves.

Shortcut White Bread

Just right for smaller families—makes a single loaf. The dough has only one rising.

> 1 pkg. active dry yeast
> 1 tblsp. sugar
> 1 c. warm water (105 to 115°)
> ⅓ c. nonfat dry milk
> 1 tblsp. butter or regular margarine, melted
> ½ tsp. salt
> 2½ to 3 c. sifted flour
> 1 egg white, slightly beaten
> Sesame seed

In large bowl, sprinkle yeast and sugar over warm water; stir until dissolved. Add dry milk, melted butter, salt and 1¼ c. flour.

Using mixer at low speed, beat until well blended. Increase speed to medium; beat 3 minutes.

Stir in enough additional flour to make a soft dough. Turn out dough onto lightly floured surface. Knead until smooth and elastic, about 5 to 8 minutes. Cover with towel and let rest 20 minutes.

Shape dough into a loaf and place in greased 8½x4½x2½" loaf pan. Cover and let rise in warm place until doubled, about 1 hour.

Brush loaf with slightly beaten egg white; sprinkle with sesame seed.

Bake in 375° oven 35 minutes, or until loaf is golden brown and sounds hollow when tapped. Immediately remove from pan. Cool on rack. Makes 1 loaf.

Freezer White Bread

Makes four loaves of white or whole-wheat dough. Keep them in your freezer until needed—then just thaw and bake. You'll notice that this dough has more yeast and salt than most, but resist the temptation to reduce these amounts. They're necessary because the dough is frozen before it's baked.

    4 pkg. active dry yeast
    ⅔ c. nonfat dry milk
    ½ c. sugar
    4 tsp. salt
    11½ to 12½ c. sifted all-purpose flour
    4 c. water
    ¼ c. butter or regular margarine

In large bowl, stir together yeast, dry milk, sugar, salt and 4 c. flour; set aside.

In 2-qt. saucepan over low heat, heat water and butter until very warm (120 to 130°).

Using mixer at low speed, gradually beat water mixture into yeast mixture until well blended. Increase speed to medium; beat 2 minutes. Add 1½ c. flour. Increase speed to high; beat 2 minutes more.

Stir in enough additional flour to make a moderately soft dough. Turn out dough onto lightly floured surface. Knead until smooth and elastic, about 10 minutes. Cover with towel and let rest 15 minutes.

Divide dough into fourths. Shape each fourth into a round loaf, about 6½" wide. Place loaves on opposite corners of 2 greased large baking sheets.

Or, with lightly floured rolling pin, roll out each fourth into a 12x8" rectangle. Starting with one short side, roll up each rectangle, jelly-roll fashion; pinch seam and ends to seal. Place each roll, seam-side down, in greased 9x5x3" loaf pan.

Cover with plastic wrap. Freeze until firm, about 2 hours.

Remove from baking sheets or pans. Rewrap loaves with plastic wrap or place in individual plastic bags. Freeze up to 4 weeks.

To thaw: Unwrap breads. Place rounds on greased baking sheets or loaves in greased 9x5x3" loaf pans. Cover loosely with waxed paper. Let stand at room temperature until thawed, 2 to 3 hours. Remove waxed paper; cover with towel. Let rise in warm place until doubled, about 2 hours.

Bake in 375° oven 35 minutes, or until loaves are golden brown and sound hollow when tapped. Immediately remove from sheet(s) or pan(s). Cool on rack(s). Makes 4 loaves.

FREEZER WHOLE-WHEAT BREAD: Substitute 6 c. stirred whole-wheat flour for 6 c. all-purpose flour.

In large bowl, stir together 5½ c. sifted all-purpose flour and 6 c. stirred whole-wheat flour. Measure and use this flour mixture in place of all-purpose flour as directed.

Cornell Formula Bread

Developed by Dr. Clive McCay at Cornell University, this formula of adding soy flour, nonfat dry milk and wheat germ to flour can be used in most baking recipes to increase protein, iron and B vitamins in home-baked goods. The proportions are: In 1-c. measure, place 1 tblsp. stirred soy flour, 1 tblsp. nonfat dry milk and 1 tsp. wheat germ. Add enough all-purpose flour to make 1 c.

> 2 tblsp. stirred soy flour
> 2 tsp. wheat germ
> 2 tblsp. nonfat dry milk
> 2½ to 3 c. sifted all-purpose flour
> 1 pkg. active dry yeast
> 1 tblsp. sugar
> 1 c. warm water (105 to 115°)
> 1 tblsp. butter or regular margarine, melted
> ½ tsp. salt
> ⅓ c. nonfat dry milk

In small bowl, stir together soy flour, wheat germ, 2 tblsp. dry milk and 2 c. all-purpose flour; set aside.

In large bowl, sprinkle yeast and sugar over warm water; stir until dissolved. Add melted butter, salt, ⅓ c. dry milk and 1¼ c.

soy flour mixture. Using mixer at low speed, beat until well blended. Increase speed to medium; beat 3 minutes.

Stir in remaining soy flour mixture and enough additional all-purpose flour to make a soft dough. Turn out dough onto lightly floured surface. Knead until smooth and elastic, about 3 to 5 minutes. Cover with towel and let rest 20 minutes.

With floured rolling pin, roll out dough into a 16x6" rectangle. Starting with one short side, roll up rectangle, jelly-roll fashion; pinch seam and ends to seal. Place roll, seam-side down, in greased 8½x4½x2½" loaf pan.

Cover and let rise in warm place until doubled, about 1 hour.

Bake in 375° oven 35 minutes, or until loaf is golden brown and sounds hollow when tapped. Immediately remove from pan. Cool on rack. Makes 1 loaf.

Triticale Bread

Doughs made with triticale flour have a more delicate structure than those made with rye or whole-wheat, so knead with a light hand. The rising may be a bit longer than usual, too. (For more information on triticale flour, see Index.)

> 1 pkg. active dry yeast
> 2 tsp. sugar
> 1½ tsp. salt
> 3½ to 4½ c. sifted all-purpose flour
> 2 c. stirred triticale flour
> 2 c. milk
> ¼ c. vegetable oil
> ¼ c. honey
> 1 egg
> 1 tblsp. butter or regular margarine, melted

In large bowl, stir together yeast, sugar, salt, 1 c. all-purpose flour and 1 c. triticale flour; set aside.

In 2-qt. saucepan over low heat, heat milk, oil and honey until very warm (120 to 130°).

Using mixer at low speed, gradually beat milk mixture into yeast mixture until well blended. Increase speed to medium; beat 2 minutes. Add egg and 1 c. all-purpose flour. Increase speed to high; beat 2 minutes more.

Stir in remaining 1 c. triticale flour and enough additional all-purpose flour to make a moderately soft dough. Cover with towel; let rise in warm place until doubled, about 1 hour 30 minutes.

Punch down dough. Using dough hook attachment, beat 2 minutes, or, on lightly greased surface with greased hands (dough will be sticky), knead lightly until smooth, about 1 to 2 minutes.

Divide dough in half. Shape each dough half into a loaf. Place each loaf in greased 8½x4½x2½" loaf pan.

Cover and let rise until doubled, about 1 hour.

Bake in 375° oven 30 minutes. Cover loosely with foil; bake 15 minutes more, or until loaves are browned and sound hollow when tapped. Immediately remove from pans. Brush tops of hot loaves with melted butter. Cool on racks. Makes 2 loaves.

Polenta Bread

A dairy farmer from New York created this recipe for a corn-meal-flavored bread and sells it in his family's bakery.

½ c. yellow corn meal
2 c. boiling water
1 c. very warm milk (120 to 130°)
2 tblsp. shortening
2 pkg. active dry yeast
¼ c. packed brown sugar
2 tsp. salt
6½ to 7½ c. sifted flour
Shortening

In medium bowl, gradually stir corn meal into boiling water; let stand 5 minutes, stirring occasionally. Stir in warm milk and 2 tblsp. shortening; cool until very warm (120 to 130°).

In large bowl, stir together yeast, brown sugar, salt and 2 c. flour.

Using mixer at low speed, gradually beat very warm corn meal mixture into yeast mixture. Increase speed to medium; beat 2 minutes. Add 1½ c. flour; beat 2 minutes more.

Stir in enough additional flour to make a soft dough. Turn out dough onto lightly floured surface. Knead until smooth and elastic, about 8 minutes (dough will be slightly sticky).

Place in greased large bowl, turning over dough so that top is greased. Cover with towel and let rise in warm place until doubled, about 50 minutes.

Punch down dough. Turn out dough onto lightly floured surface. Knead until no longer sticky, about 30 seconds. Divide dough in half. Cover and let rest 10 minutes.

Shape each half into a loaf. Place each loaf in greased 9x5x3" loaf pan.

Cover and let rise until doubled, about 35 minutes.

Bake in 375° oven 35 to 40 minutes, or until loaves are golden brown and sound hollow when tapped. Immediately remove from pans. Brush tops of loaves with shortening. Cool on racks. Makes 2 loaves.

Italian Bread

Lots of kneading is essential to develop the texture so characteristic of good Italian bread!

> 2 pkg. active dry yeast
> 2½ c. warm water (105 to 115°)
> 1½ tsp. salt
> 7¼ to 7¾ c. sifted flour
> Yellow corn meal
> 1 egg white
> 1 tblsp. water

In large bowl, sprinkle yeast over 2½ c. warm water; stir until dissolved. Add salt and 3 c. flour.

Using mixer at low speed, beat until well blended. Increase speed to medium; beat 2 minutes.

Stir in 3½ c. flour to make a soft dough. Turn out dough onto lightly floured surface. Working in remaining ¾ to 1¼ c. flour, knead until smooth and very elastic, about 20 to 25 minutes. Do not underknead.

Place in greased large bowl, turning over dough so that top is greased. Cover with towel and let rise in warm place until doubled, about 1 hour 15 minutes.

Punch down dough. Cover and let rise again until doubled, about 1 hour.

Punch down dough. Divide in half. Cover; let rest 10 minutes.

On lightly floured surface, flatten a half into an oval, about 13x6". Fold in half lengthwise; repeat flattening and folding dough once more. Pinch seam to seal. With palms of hands, roll dough into a 15"-long loaf. Repeat with remaining dough.

Grease a large baking sheet and sprinkle with corn meal. Place loaves, seam-side down and 3" apart, on prepared baking sheet. Cover and let rise until doubled, about 45 minutes.

Diagonally slash each loaf, crosswise about ¼"-deep, 3 times. In small bowl, mix together egg white and 1 tblsp. water. Brush loaves with some egg white mixture; reserve remaining egg white mixture.

On lowest rack in 375° oven, place large shallow roasting pan filled with 1" boiling water. Bake loaves on middle rack of oven 20 minutes.

Brush loaves with remaining egg white mixture. Bake 15 to 20 minutes more, or until loaves are golden brown and sound hollow when tapped. Immediately remove from baking sheet. Cool on racks. Makes 2 loaves.

French Bread

To ensure crisp, golden brown crusts, brush the loaves with water before baking or mist them with a water-filled atomizer.

> 2 pkg. active dry yeast
> 1 tblsp. sugar
> 2½ c. warm water (105 to 115°)
> 1 tblsp. shortening
> 1½ tsp. salt
> 7 to 7¾ c. sifted flour
> Yellow corn meal

In large bowl, sprinkle yeast and sugar over warm water; stir until dissolved. Add shortening, salt and 3 c. flour.

Using mixer at low speed, beat until well blended. Increase speed to medium; beat 2 minutes.

Stir in enough additional flour to make a moderately stiff dough. Turn out dough onto lightly floured surface. Knead until smooth and elastic, about 10 minutes.

Place in greased large bowl, turning over dough so that top is greased. Cover with towel and let rise in warm place until doubled, about 45 minutes to 1 hour.

Punch down dough. Divide dough into fourths. Cover and let rest 10 minutes.

On lightly floured surface, flatten a fourth into an oval, about 12x4". Fold in half lengthwise; repeat flattening and folding dough once more. Pinch seam to seal. With palms of hands, roll dough into a 15"-long loaf. Repeat with remaining dough.

Grease 2 large baking sheets and sprinkle each with corn meal. Place loaves, seam-side down and 3" apart, on prepared baking sheets. Cover and let rise until doubled, about 30 to 45 minutes.

Diagonally slash each loaf, crosswise about ¼"-deep, 3 times. Brush or mist loaves with water.

On lowest rack in 400° oven, place large shallow roasting pan filled with 1" boiling water. Bake loaves on middle rack of oven 15 minutes.

Brush or mist loaves with water; remove pan of water from oven. Bake 10 minutes more, or until loaves are golden brown and sound hollow when tapped. Immediately remove from baking sheets. Cool on racks. Makes 4 loaves.

EPI: Prepare dough, shape into loaves and let rise as for French Bread, but do not slash tops. With scissors, make deep V-shaped cuts in top of each loaf, 2 to 3" apart. Alternately pull V-shapes to the right and then to the left. Brush or mist loaves with water and bake as directed.

KAISER ROLLS: Prepare dough and let rise as for French Bread. Punch down dough and divide into 12 pieces. Roll each piece into a 22"-long rope. Gently tie each piece into a knot. Bring ends up and over top of each knot, tucking ends into center of each knot.

Grease 2 large baking sheets and sprinkle each roll with corn meal. Place rolls, 2" apart, on prepared baking sheets. Cover and let rise until doubled, about 30 minutes. Brush or mist rolls with water.

On lowest rack in 400° oven, place large, shallow roasting pan filled with 1" boiling water. Bake rolls on middle rack of oven 15 minutes.

Brush or mist rolls with water; remove pan of water from oven. Bake 5 to 10 minutes more, or until rolls are golden brown and sound hollow when tapped. Immediately remove from baking sheets. Cool on racks. Makes 12 rolls.

Processor French Bread

It's a cinch to make French bread, especially when the food processor does all of the kneading. We Americans like to slice the bread, but the French are more apt to break off a piece at a time. Delicious either way!

> 1 pkg. active dry yeast
> 2 tsp. sugar
> ¼ c. warm water (105 to 115°)
> 3 c. sifted all-purpose flour
> 1 tsp. salt
> 4 tsp. butter or regular margarine
> ½ to ¾ c. warm water (105 to 115°)
> Yellow corn meal

In small bowl, sprinkle yeast and sugar over ¼ c. warm water; stir until dissolved.

In processor bowl with metal blade, place flour and salt. Cut butter into 4 pieces and distribute evenly over flour. Cover and process 10 seconds or until fine crumbs form.

Add yeast mixture; process 10 seconds or until well blended. While processor is running, slowly pour about ½ c. warm water through feed tube, process just until dough leaves side of bowl. Process 15 seconds more. Let rest 1 to 2 minutes.

While processor is running, slowly pour enough additional water through feed tube, to make a dough that is smooth and shiny, but not sticky. Process 10 seconds more.

Turn out dough; shape into a ball. Place in greased large bowl, turning over dough so that top is greased. Cover with towel and let rise in warm place until doubled, about 1 hour.

Punch down dough. Divide dough in half. Cover and let rest 5 minutes.

On lightly floured surface with palms of hands, roll each half into a 12"-long loaf.

Grease a large baking sheet and sprinkle with corn meal. Place loaves, 3" apart, on prepared baking sheet. Cover and let rise until doubled, about 45 minutes.

Diagonally slash each loaf, crosswise about ¼"-deep, 3 times. Brush or mist loaves with water.

Bake in 425° oven 15 minutes. Brush or mist loaves with water. Bake 10 to 15 minutes more, or until loaves are golden brown and sound hollow when tapped. Immediately remove from baking sheet. Cool on racks. Makes 2 loaves.

WHOLE-WHEAT PROCESSOR FRENCH BREAD: Substitute
1½ c. stirred whole-wheat flour for 1½ c. sifted all-purpose flour.

Sourdough Starter

In the past fresh yeast was hard to find, so pioneers carried a bread starter similar to this one as they crossed the plains of America. With this starter you can make bread, rolls, biscuits and pancakes—all of which will have a slightly tangy taste.

> 2 pkg. active dry yeast
> 2 tblsp. sugar
> 4 c. warm water (105 to 115°)
> 4 c. unsifted flour

In large glass, stoneware or plastic bowl, sprinkle yeast and sugar over ½ c. warm water; stir until dissolved. (Do not use metal utensils, since prolonged contact with metal will drastically reduce the purity and change the taste of the starter.)

Add remaining 3½ c. warm water alternately with flour, stirring well after each addition. Cover loosely with plastic wrap. Let stand in warm place (85°) for 6 to 24 hours.

The starter is ready to use in any of the sourdough recipes (see Index). It will look bubbly and a clear liquid will rise to the top. Stir the starter before measuring.

After removing the required amount of starter, pour remaining starter into stoneware crock, glass jar or plastic container. Cover loosely and refrigerate. (Do not cover tightly. As the starter stands it ferments. The fermentation produces a harmless gas and if covered tightly, the container might burst.) The starter can be stored indefinitely in the refrigerator.

Replenish starter at least once a week by stirring in ½ c. warm water and ½ c. unsifted flour. Cover with towel and let stand at room temperature overnight. The next morning, stir down starter. Cover loosely and refrigerate. Makes 5⅓ c.

Use as directed to make Sourdough White Bread, Sourdough French Bread (recipes follow) and more.

Sourdough White Bread

Makes three large loaves of light-textured sourdough bread.

1 c. Sourdough Starter
2 c. warm water (105 to 115°)
2½ c. sifted flour
1 pkg. active dry yeast
¼ c. warm water (105 to 115°)
1 c. milk
3 tblsp. sugar
2 tsp. salt
3 tblsp. butter or regular margarine
8½ to 9½ c. sifted flour
1 tblsp. butter or regular margarine, melted

In large glass, stoneware or plastic bowl, using wooden spoon, stir together Sourdough Starter, 2 c. warm water and 2½ c. flour until well blended. Cover loosely with plastic wrap. Let stand in warm place (85°) at least 12 hours.

In small bowl, sprinkle yeast over ¼ c. warm water; stir until dissolved.

In 2-qt. saucepan over low heat, heat milk, sugar, salt and 3 tblsp. butter until warm (105 to 115°). Remove from heat; stir in yeast mixture.

Stir yeast-milk mixture into starter mixture. Stir in 2½ c. flour until well blended. Cover loosely with plastic wrap. Let rise in warm place until almost doubled, about 45 minutes to 1 hour.

Stir down batter. Gradually stir in enough additional flour to make a soft dough. Turn out dough onto lightly floured surface. Knead until smooth and elastic, about 5 to 7 minutes.

Divide dough into thirds. Cover and let rest 10 minutes.

Shape each third into a loaf. Place each loaf in greased 8½x4½x2½" loaf pan. Cover and let rise until doubled, about 45 minutes to 1 hour.

Bake in 375° oven 40 minutes, or until loaves are golden brown and sound hollow when tapped. Immediately remove from pans. Brush tops of hot loaves with melted butter. Cool on racks. Makes 3 loaves.

Sourdough French Bread

The older the Sourdough Starter is, the more pronounced flavor it will have in these crusty, French-style loaves or rolls.

> 1 c. Sourdough Starter
> 1 c. warm water (105 to 115°)
> 1½ c. sifted flour
> 2 tsp. salt
> ⅔ c. warm water (105 to 115°)
> 4½ to 5½ c. sifted flour
> Yellow corn meal

In large glass, stoneware or plastic bowl, using wooden spoon, stir together Sourdough Starter and 1 c. warm water. Gradually stir in 1½ c. flour until well blended. Cover loosely with plastic wrap. Let stand in warm place (85°) at least 12 hours.

Stir in salt, ⅔ c. warm water and enough additional flour to make a soft dough. Turn out dough onto lightly floured surface. Knead until smooth and elastic, about 5 to 7 minutes.

Place in greased large bowl, turning over dough so that top is greased. Cover with towel and let rise in warm place until doubled, about 1 hour 30 minutes.

Punch down dough. Turn out dough onto lightly floured surface and knead until no longer sticky, about 30 seconds. Divide dough in half. Cover and let rest 5 minutes.

Flatten each half into an oval, about 12x4". Fold in half lengthwise; repeat flattening and folding dough once more. Pinch seam to seal. With palms of hands, roll each half into a 14"-long loaf.

Grease a large baking sheet and sprinkle with corn meal. Place loaves, seam-side down and 3" apart, on prepared baking sheet. Cover with towel and let rise until doubled, about 50 minutes to 1 hour.

Using very sharp knife or razor held almost parallel to top of loaf, cut a lengthwise slash in top of each loaf. Brush or mist loaves thoroughly with water.

On lowest rack in 400° oven, place large shallow roasting pan filled with 1" boiling water. Bake loaves on middle rack of oven 10 minutes.

Brush or mist loaves with water; remove pan of water from oven. Bake 25 minutes more, or until loaves are golden brown and sound hollow when tapped. Immediately remove from baking sheet. Cool on racks. Makes 2 loaves.

SOURDOUGH FRENCH ROLLS: Prepare and let dough rise as directed. Punch down dough. Cover and let rest 5 minutes.

On lightly floured surface, roll out dough into a 16" square. Cut into 16 (4") squares. Fold each square in half. Pinch seams to seal.

Grease 2 large baking sheets and sprinkle each with corn meal. Place rolls, seam-side down and 2" apart, on prepared baking sheets. Cover and let rise until doubled, about 40 to 50 minutes.

Using sharp knife or razor held almost parallel to top of roll, cut a lengthwise slash in top of each roll. Brush or mist rolls with water.

On lowest rack in 400° oven, place large shallow roasting pan filled with 1" boiling water. Bake rolls on middle rack of oven 10 minutes.

Brush or mist rolls with water; remove pan of water from oven. Bake 15 minutes more, or until rolls are browned and sound hollow when tapped. Makes 16 rolls.

Salt-rising Bread

Named because the starter was placed in a bed of rock salt to keep it warm while it fermented. Use whole-grain corn meal, which contains the corn germ—without this vital ingredient the starter won't ferment. This bread presents a challenge for even the most experienced baker, so read about Starters in Chapter One before you begin.

> 3 c. boiling water
> 2 tblsp. sugar
> ¼ c. whole-grain corn meal
> 2 pkg. active dry yeast
> ½ c. warm water (105 to 115°)
> 1 c. milk
> ¼ c. butter or regular margarine
> 2 tsp. salt
> ¼ tsp. ground ginger
> 2 tblsp. sugar
> 11½ to 12½ c. sifted flour
> Shortening

In large glass or stoneware bowl, using wooden spoon, stir 3 c. boiling water and 2 tblsp. sugar into corn meal until well blended.

Cover tightly with plastic wrap. Let stand in warm place (85°) 24 hours.

In small bowl, sprinkle yeast over ½ c. warm water; stir until dissolved.

In 2-qt. saucepan over low heat, heat milk, butter, salt, ginger and 2 tblsp. sugar until warm (105 to 115°). Remove from heat. Stir in yeast mixture.

Stir yeast-milk mixture into starter mixture. Stir in 4 c. flour until well blended. Cover loosely with plastic wrap. Let rise in warm place until almost doubled, about 1 hour.

Stir down batter. Gradually stir in enough additional flour to make a soft dough. Turn out dough onto lightly floured surface. Knead until smooth and elastic, about 10 minutes.

Divide dough into thirds. Cover and let rest 10 minutes.

Shape each third into a loaf. Place each loaf in greased 8½x4½x2½" loaf pan.

Cover with towel and let rise until doubled, about 45 minutes to 1 hour.

Bake in 375° oven 40 minutes, or until loaves are golden brown and sound hollow when tapped. Immediately remove from pans. Brush tops of hot loaves with shortening. Cool on racks. Makes 3 loaves.

Whole-Wheat Bread

Healthful hamburger and frankfurter rolls can be made from this dough—directions for shaping follow.

> 3 c. stirred whole-wheat flour
> 2 to 3 c. sifted all-purpose flour
> 2 pkg. active dry yeast
> 2 tsp. salt
> ½ c. wheat germ
> 2¼ c. milk
> ⅓ c. packed dark brown sugar
> ⅓ c. shortening

Stir together whole-wheat flour and 2 c. all-purpose flour; set aside.

In large bowl, stir together yeast, salt, wheat germ and 3 c. whole-wheat flour mixture; set aside.

In 2-qt. saucepan over low heat, heat milk, brown sugar and shortening until very warm (120 to 130°).

Using mixer at low speed, gradually beat milk mixture into yeast mixture until well blended. Increase speed to medium; beat 2 minutes. Add 1 c. whole-wheat flour mixture. Increase speed to high; beat 2 minutes more.

Stir in remaining 1 c. whole-wheat flour mixture and enough additional all-purpose flour to make a stiff dough. Turn out dough onto lightly floured surface. Knead until smooth and elastic, about 10 minutes.

Place in greased large bowl, turning over dough so that top is greased. Cover with towel and let rise in warm place until doubled, about 1 hour.

Punch down dough. Divide dough in half. Cover and let rest 10 minutes.

On lightly floured surface with lightly floured rolling pin, roll out each half into a 16x8" rectangle.

Starting with one short side, roll up each rectangle, jelly-roll fashion; pinch seam and ends to seal. Place each roll, seam-side down, in greased 9x5x3" loaf pan.

Cover and let rise until doubled, about 45 minutes.

Bake in 400° oven 30 to 35 minutes, or until loaves are dark golden brown and sound hollow when tapped. Immediately remove from pans. Cool on racks. Makes 2 loaves.

WHOLE-WHEAT HAMBURGER ROLLS: Divide dough into fourths. Divide each fourth into 5 pieces. Shape each piece into a ball. Place balls, 3" apart, on greased large baking sheets. Flatten each ball slightly to make 3¼" circle.

Cover and let rise until doubled, about 45 minutes.

Bake in 350° oven 18 minutes, or until rolls are golden brown and sound hollow when tapped. Immediately remove from baking sheets. Cool on racks. Makes 20 rolls.

WHOLE-WHEAT FRANKFURTER ROLLS: Divide dough into fourths. On lightly floured surface with lightly floured rolling pin, roll out each fourth into a 7½x4" rectangle. Cut each rectangle into 5 (4x1½") strips. Roll each strip to form a 5½"-long rope. Place ropes, 3" apart, on greased large baking sheets.

Cover and let rise until doubled, about 45 minutes.

Bake in 350° oven 18 minutes, or until rolls are golden brown and sound hollow when tapped. Immediately remove from baking sheets. Cool on racks. Makes 20 rolls.

Wheat Germ Bread

Has a nutty flavor and also provides iron, protein, B vitamins.

> 2 pkg. active dry yeast
> 1 c. wheat germ
> 1½ tsp. salt
> 2 c. stirred whole-wheat flour
> 2½ to 3½ c. sifted all-purpose flour
> 2¼ c. milk
> ¼ c. honey
> ¼ c. shortening
> 1 tblsp. butter or regular margarine, melted
> Sesame seed

In large bowl, stir together yeast, wheat germ, salt, 1 c. whole-wheat flour and 1 c. all-purpose flour; set aside.

In 2-qt. saucepan over low heat, heat milk, honey and shortening until very warm (120 to 130°).

Using mixer at low speed, gradually beat milk mixture into yeast mixture until well blended. Increase speed to medium; beat 2 minutes. Add remaining 1 c. whole-wheat flour; beat 2 minutes more.

Stir in enough additional all-purpose flour to make a moderately soft dough. Turn out dough onto lightly floured surface. Knead until smooth and elastic, about 10 minutes.

Place in greased large bowl, turning over dough so that top is greased. Cover with towel and let rise in warm place until doubled, about 1 hour.

Punch down dough. Cover and let rise again until doubled, about 30 minutes.

Punch down dough. Divide dough in half. Cover and let rest 10 minutes.

Shape each half into a loaf. Place each loaf in greased 8½x4½x2½" loaf pan.

Cover and let rise until doubled, about 1 hour.

Brush each loaf with melted butter; sprinkle with sesame seed.

Bake in 400° oven 20 minutes. Cover loosely with foil; bake 15 to 20 minutes more, or until loaves are golden brown and sound hollow when tapped. Immediately remove from pans. Cool on racks. Makes 2 loaves.

Dark Raisin Bread

Because these molasses-flavored loaves are made exclusively with whole-wheat flour, they have a denser texture than most.

2 pkg. active dry yeast
1 tsp. salt
7 to 8 c. stirred whole-wheat flour
2 c. milk
½ c. water
½ c. packed brown sugar
⅓ c. shortening
½ c. molasses
1 c. raisins

In large bowl, stir together yeast, salt and 2 c. whole-wheat flour; set aside.

In 2-qt. saucepan over low heat, heat milk, water, brown sugar and shortening until very warm (120 to 130°).

Using mixer at low speed, gradually beat milk mixture into yeast mixture until well blended. Increase speed to medium; beat 2 minutes. Add molasses and 2 c. flour. Increase speed to high; beat 2 minutes more.

Stir in raisins and enough additional flour to make a moderately stiff dough. Turn out dough onto lightly floured surface. Knead until smooth and elastic, about 10 minutes.

Place in greased large bowl, turning over dough so that top is greased. Cover with towel and let rise in warm place until doubled, about 1 hour.

Punch down dough. Divide dough in half. Cover and let rest 10 minutes.

Shape each half into a loaf. Place each loaf in greased 9x5x3" loaf pan.

Cover and let rise until doubled, about 45 minutes.

Bake in 375° oven 35 minutes. Cover loosely with foil; bake 15 to 20 minutes more, or until loaves are dark brown and sound hollow when tapped. Immediately remove from pans. Cool on racks. Makes 2 loaves.

Whole-Wheat Molasses Bread

For sweeter loaves, substitute an equal amount of honey for the molasses. This recipe comes from a Wisconsin farm wife.

        5 c. stirred whole-wheat flour
        3½ to 4½ c. sifted all-purpose flour
        2 pkg. active dry yeast
        2 tsp. salt
        3¼ c. milk
        ⅓ c. molasses
        ¼ c. shortening

Stir together whole-wheat flour and 3½ c. all-purpose flour; set aside.

In large bowl, stir together yeast, salt and 4 c. whole-wheat flour mixture; set aside.

In 2-qt. saucepan over low heat, heat milk, molasses and shortening until very warm (120 to 130°).

Using mixer at low speed, gradually beat milk mixture into yeast mixture until well blended. Increase speed to medium; beat 2 minutes. Add 1½ c. whole-wheat flour mixture. Increase speed to high; beat 2 minutes more.

Stir in remaining 3 c. whole-wheat flour mixture and enough additional all-purpose flour to make a moderately soft dough. Turn out dough onto lightly floured surface. Knead until smooth an elastic, about 10 minutes.

Place in greased large bowl, turning over dough so that top is greased. Cover with towel and let rise in warm place until doubled, about 1 hour.

Punch down dough. Divide dough in half. Cover and let rest 10 minutes.

On lightly floured surface with lightly floured rolling pin, roll out each half into a 16x8" rectangle.

Starting with one short side, roll up each rectangle, jelly-roll fashion; pinch seam and ends to seal. Place each roll, seam-side down, in greased 9x5x3" loaf pan.

Cover and let rise until doubled, about 45 minutes.

Bake in 400° oven 25 minutes. Cover loosely with foil; bake 10 to 15 minutes more, or until loaves are golden brown and sound hollow when tapped. Immediately remove from pans. Cool on racks. Makes 2 loaves.

Cracked Wheat Bread

Made from wheat berries, cracked wheat is available in coarse, medium and fine grinds. Nutritionally, it's high in iron, fiber, protein, B vitamins and minerals.

2 pkg. active dry yeast
2 tsp. salt
1 c. stirred whole-wheat flour
4½ to 5½ c. sifted all-purpose flour
2¼ c. milk
¼ c. molasses
2 tblsp. shortening
1 c. cracked wheat

In large bowl, stir together yeast, salt, whole-wheat flour and 1½ c. all-purpose flour; set aside.

In 2-qt. saucepan over low heat, heat milk, molasses and shortening until very warm (120 to 130°).

Using mixer at low speed, gradually beat milk mixture into yeast mixture until well blended. Increase speed to medium; beat 2 minutes.

Stir in cracked wheat and enough additional all-purpose flour to make a stiff dough. Turn out dough onto lightly floured surface. Knead until smooth and elastic, about 5 minutes.

Place in greased large bowl, turning over dough so that top is greased. Cover with towel and let rise in warm place until doubled, about 1 hour.

Punch down dough. Divide dough in half. Cover and let rest 10 minutes.

On lightly floured surface with lightly floured rolling pin, roll out each half into a 16x8" rectangle.

Starting with one short side, roll up each rectangle, jelly-roll fashion. Pinch seam and ends to seal. Place each roll, seam-side down, in greased 9x5x3" loaf pan.

Cover and let rise until doubled, about 45 minutes.

Bake in 400° oven 40 minutes, or until loaves are golden brown and sound hollow when tapped. Immediately remove from pans. Cool on racks. Makes 2 loaves.

Sprouted Wheat Bread

Homemade from start to finish! The wheat berries take about five days to sprout; afterward, just stir them into the wheat dough.

½ c. wheat berries
2 c. warm water (105 to 115°)
3 c. stirred whole-wheat flour
2½ to 3½ c. sifted all-purpose flour
2 pkg. active dry yeast
2 tsp. salt
2 c. milk
⅓ c. honey
¼ c. shortening
1 tsp. molasses
1 tblsp. water

About 5 days before making bread: place wheat berries in 1-qt. jar. Add 2 c. warm water to cover. Place cheesecloth over jar; secure with rubber band. Let soak at room temperature for at least 12 hours.

With cheesecloth in place, drain and rinse berries with warm running water. Drain again.

Set jar at 45° angle in warm, dark place until sprouts emerge, and are about 1" long, rinsing sprouts twice a day, and allowing them to drain at a 45° angle. Rinse under cold running water; drain on paper towels. (You should have 2½ c. sprouted berries.)

Stir together whole-wheat flour and 2½ c. all-purpose flour.

In large bowl, stir together yeast, salt and 3 c. whole-wheat flour mixture; set aside.

In 2-qt saucepan over low heat, heat milk, honey and shortening until very warm (120 to 130°).

Using mixer at low speed, gradually beat milk mixture into yeast mixture until well blended. Increase speed to medium; beat 2 minutes.

Stir in sprouted wheat berries, remaining 2½ c. whole-wheat flour mixture and enough additional all-purpose flour to make a stiff dough. Turn out dough onto lightly floured surface. Knead until smooth and elastic, about 8 minutes.

Place in greased large bowl, turning over dough so that top is greased. Cover with towel and let rise in warm place until doubled, about 1 hour.

Punch down dough. Divide dough in half. Cover and let rest 10 minutes.

On lightly floured surface with floured rolling pin, roll out each half into a 16x8" rectangle.

Starting with one short side, roll up each rectangle, jelly-roll fashion; pinch seam and ends to seal. Place each roll, seam-side down, in greased 9x5x3" loaf pan.

Cover and let rise until doubled, about 1 hour.

In small bowl, mix together molasses and 1 tblsp. water. Brush each loaf with molasses mixture.

Bake in 375° oven 45 minutes, or until loaves are dark brown and sound hollow when tapped. Immediately remove from pans. Cool on racks. Makes 2 loaves.

Soy Wheat Loaf

High in protein and iron, this one-loaf recipe is made with a mix of three flours—all-purpose, whole-wheat and soy.

    1½ c. stirred whole-wheat flour
    1 c. stirred soy flour
    1 pkg. active dry yeast
    ¼ c. sugar
    2 tsp. salt
    1¼ to 1¾ c. sifted all-purpose flour
    1¼ c. milk
    ¼ c. butter or regular margarine
    1 egg

In medium bowl, stir together whole-wheat flour and soy flour; set aside.

In large bowl, stir together yeast, sugar, salt, 1 c. whole-wheat flour mixture and 1 c. all-purpose flour; set aside.

In 2-qt. saucepan over low heat, heat milk and butter until very warm (120 to 130°).

Using mixer at low speed, gradually beat milk mixture into yeast mixture until well blended. Increase speed to medium; beat 2 minutes. Add egg and 1 c. whole-wheat flour mixture; beat 2 minutes more.

Stir in remaining ½ c. whole-wheat flour mixture and enough additional all-purpose flour to make a moderately stiff dough. Turn out dough onto lightly floured surface. Knead until smooth and elastic, about 5 to 8 minutes.

Place in greased medium bowl, turning over dough so that top is greased. Cover with towel and let rise in warm place until almost doubled, 30 minutes.

Punch down dough. Turn out dough onto lightly floured surface. Knead 1 minute. Repeat rising and kneading 2 times.

Punch down dough. Shape into loaf. Place loaf in greased 9x5x3" loaf pan.

Cover and let rise until doubled, about 1 hour.

Bake in 375° oven 30 minutes. Cover loosely with foil; bake 15 minutes more, or until loaf is dark brown and sounds hollow when tapped. Immediately remove from pan. Cool on rack. Makes 1 loaf.

Whole-Wheat Rye Bread

Plenty of flavor and fiber in these loaves—the result of corn meal and mashed potatoes added to the whole-wheat and rye flours.

¾ c. yellow corn meal
2¾ c. water
2 c. cold mashed potatoes
¼ c. dark molasses
3 tblsp. caraway seed (optional)
2 tblsp. shortening
1 tblsp. salt
2 pkg. active dry yeast
½ c. warm water (105 to 115°)
5 c. stirred rye flour
5 to 5¾ c. stirred whole-wheat flour

In 3-qt. saucepan, stir together corn meal and 2¾ c. water. Cook over medium heat, stirring constantly, until mixture boils. Boil, stirring constantly, until thick, about 2 minutes.

Pour into a large bowl. Stir in cold mashed potatoes, molasses, caraway seed, shortening and salt. Let stand to cool until warm (105 to 115°).

In small bowl, sprinkle yeast over ½ c. warm water; stir until dissolved. Add yeast mixture to corn meal-potato mixture; stir well until well blended.

Gradually stir in rye flour and enough whole-wheat flour to make a stiff dough, using hands to mix dough as stirring becomes difficult. Turn out dough onto lightly whole-wheat floured surface. Knead until smooth and elastic and dough is no longer sticky, about 10 minutes.

Place in greased large bowl, turning over dough so that top is greased. Cover with towel and let rise in warm place until almost doubled, about 1 hour.

Punch down dough. Turn out dough onto lightly floured surface; knead 1 minute. Divide dough into thirds. Cover and let rest 5 minutes.

Shape each third into a round loaf. Place loaves, 4″ apart, on greased large baking sheets.

Cover and let rise until almost doubled, about 45 minutes.

Bake in 375° oven 30 to 35 minutes, or until loaves are browned and sound hollow when tapped. Immediately remove from baking sheets. Cool on racks. Makes 3 loaves.

Swedish Limpa

In Sweden, "limpa" means a loaf of bread of any kind. Swedish-Americans think of it as a rye bread flavored with orange rind.

> 2 pkg. active dry yeast
> ¼ c. packed brown sugar
> 1¾ c. warm water (105 to 115°)
> ¼ c. molasses
> 2 tblsp. caraway seed
> 2 tblsp. grated orange rind
> 2 tblsp. shortening
> 2 tsp. salt
> 2½ c. stirred rye flour
> 2¾ to 3½ c. sifted all-purpose flour
> 1 egg white
> 1 tblsp. water

In large bowl, sprinkle yeast and brown sugar over warm water; stir until dissolved. Add molasses, caraway seed, orange rind, shortening, salt and rye flour.

Using mixer at low speed, beat until well blended. Increase speed to medium; beat 2 minutes.

Stir in enough additional all-purpose flour to make a moderately stiff dough. Turn out dough onto lightly floured surface. Knead until smooth and elastic, about 5 minutes.

Place in greased large bowl, turning over dough so that top is greased. Cover with towel and let rise in warm place until almost doubled, about 45 minutes to 1 hour.

Punch down dough. Divide dough in half. Cover and let rest 10 minutes.

Shape each half into a round or oval loaf. Place loaves, 4" apart, on greased large baking sheet.

Cover and let rise until doubled, about 45 minutes to 1 hour.

In small bowl, mix together egg white and 1 tblsp. water. Brush each loaf with egg white mixture.

Bake in 375° oven 25 to 30 minutes, or until loaves are browned and sound hollow when tapped. If necessary, cover loaves with foil during last 15 minutes of baking time to prevent overbrowning. Immediately remove from baking sheet. Cool on racks. Makes 2 loaves.

Jewish Sour Rye Bread

One Pennsylvania woman treasures this recipe from an old neighborhood bakery. These oval, crisp-crusted loaves are made with rye flour starter that takes about three days to ferment.

2 pkg. active dry yeast
1½ c. warm water (105 to 115°)
2 c. stirred rye flour
1 tblsp. sugar
¼ c. warm water (105 to 115°)
1 c. beer (room temperature)
1 egg
2 tblsp. shortening
2 tsp. salt
2 tblsp. caraway seed
6½ to 7 c. sifted all-purpose flour
1 egg white
1 tblsp. water
Caraway seed

In medium glass, plastic or stoneware bowl, sprinkle 1 pkg. yeast over 1½ c. warm water; stir until dissolved. Stir in rye flour until well blended. Cover tightly with plastic wrap and rubber band. Let stand at room temperature for 72 hours.

In large bowl, sprinkle remaining pkg. yeast and sugar over ¼ c. warm water; stir until dissolved. Add beer, egg, shortening, salt, 2 tblsp. caraway seed, 2 c. all-purpose flour and rye mixture.

Using mixer at low speed, beat until well blended. Increase speed to medium; beat 2 minutes. Add 1 c. all-purpose flour. Increase speed to high; beat 2 minutes more.

Stir in enough additional flour to make a soft dough. Turn out dough onto lightly floured surface. Knead until smooth and elastic, about 6 to 8 minutes.

Place in greased large bowl, turning over dough so that top is greased. Cover with towel and let rise in warm place until doubled, about 1 hour.

Punch down dough. Divide dough in half. Cover and let rest 5 minutes.

Shape each half into an oval. Place, 4″ apart, on greased large baking sheet. Cover and let rise until doubled, about 45 minutes.

Diagonally slash each loaf, crosswise, 3 times. In small bowl, mix together egg white and 1 tblsp. water. Brush each loaf with egg white mixture; sprinkle with additional caraway seed.

Bake in 375° oven 30 to 40 minutes, or until loaves are browned and sound hollow when tapped. Immediately remove from baking sheet. Cool on racks. To retain crisp crusts, store loaves in paper bag. Makes 2 loaves.

German Pumpernickel

An Oklahoma woman's recipe that combines rye flour, molasses, cocoa and caraway seed in two dark, hearty loaves.

2 pkg. active dry yeast
¼ c. unsweetened cocoa
2 tblsp. sugar
1 tblsp. caraway seed
1½ tsp. salt
3 c. stirred rye flour
2 c. water
¼ c. molasses
¼ c. butter or regular margarine
3 to 3½ c. sifted all-purpose flour
Shortening

In large bowl, stir together yeast, cocoa, sugar, caraway seed, salt and 2 c. rye flour; set aside.

In 2-qt. saucepan over low heat, heat water, molasses and butter until very warm (120 to 130°).

Using mixer at low speed, gradually beat molasses mixture into yeast mixture until well blended. Increase speed to medium; beat 2 minutes. Add remaining 1 c. rye flour. Increase speed to high; beat 2 minutes more.

Stir in enough all-purpose flour to make a soft dough. Turn out dough onto lightly floured surface. Knead until smooth and elastic, about 5 minutes.

Place in greased large bowl, turning over dough so that top is greased. Cover with towel and let rise in warm place until almost doubled, about 45 minutes to 1 hour.

Punch down dough. Divide dough in half. Cover and let rest 5 minutes.

Shape each half into a round loaf. Place, 4" apart, on greased large baking sheet.

Cover and let rise until almost doubled, 45 minutes to 1 hour. Diagonally slash each loaf, crosswise, 3 times.

Bake in 375° oven 20 minutes. Cover loosely with foil; bake 15 minutes more or until loaves sound hollow when tapped. Immediately remove from baking sheet. Brush tops of hot loaves with shortening. Cool on racks. Makes 2 loaves.

Dark Pumpernickel

Coffee and cocoa add flavor and color to this unique whole-grain bread, made with buckwheat, rye and whole-wheat flours.

2 pkg. active dry yeast
3 tblsp. unsweetened cocoa
2 tblsp. packed brown sugar
2 tsp. salt
2 tsp. instant coffee granules
2½ c. stirred rye flour
2 c. water
⅓ c. molasses
3 tblsp. shortening
½ c. stirred buckwheat flour
3 to 3⅓ c. stirred whole-wheat flour
1 egg white
1 tblsp. water

In large bowl stir together yeast, cocoa, brown sugar, salt, coffee granules and 2 c. rye flour; set aside.

In 2-qt. saucepan over low heat, heat water, molasses and shortening until very warm (120 to 130°).

Using mixer at low speed, gradually beat molasses mixture into yeast mixture until well blended. Increase speed to medium; beat 2 minutes. Add buckwheat flour and remaining ½ c. rye flour; beat 2 minutes more.

Stir in enough whole-wheat flour to make a moderately stiff dough. Turn out dough onto lightly whole-wheat floured surface. Knead in enough additional whole-wheat flour until dough is smooth and elastic and no longer sticky, about 5 minutes.

Place in greased large bowl, turning over dough so that top is greased. Cover with towel and let rise in warm place until almost doubled, about 45 minutes to 1 hour.

Punch down dough. Divide dough in half. Cover and let rest 10 minutes.

Shape each half into a round or oval loaf. Place loaves, 4″ apart, on greased large baking sheet.

Cover and let rise until almost doubled, about 30 to 45 minutes.

In small bowl, mix together egg white and 1 tblsp. water. Brush each loaf with egg white mixture.

Bake in 375° oven 35 to 40 minutes, or until loaves are browned and sound hollow when tapped. Immediately remove from baking sheet. Cool on racks. Makes 2 loaves.

Old-fashioned Oatmeal Bread

Before baking, brush these loaves with a mix of dark corn syrup and water; then sprinkle them with oats to give them a handsome crust.

2 pkg. active dry yeast
2 tsp. salt
2 c. old-fashioned oats
6 to 7 c. sifted flour
2½ c. milk
¼ c. packed brown sugar
2 tblsp. butter or regular margarine
1 tblsp. dark corn syrup
1 tblsp. water
Old-fashioned oats

In large bowl, stir together yeast, salt, 2 c. oats and 2½ c. flour; set aside.

In 2-qt. saucepan over low heat, heat milk, brown sugar and butter until very warm (120 to 130°).

Using mixer at low speed, gradually beat milk mixture into yeast mixture until well blended. Increase speed to medium; beat 2 minutes.

Stir in enough additional flour to make a soft dough. Turn out dough onto lightly floured surface. Knead until smooth and elastic, about 5 to 8 minutes.

Place in greased large bowl, turning over dough so that top is greased. Cover with towel and let rise in warm place until doubled, about 1 hour.

Punch down dough. Cover and let rise again until almost doubled, about 30 minutes.

Punch down dough. Divide dough in half. Cover and let rest 5 minutes.

Shape each half into a loaf. Place each loaf in greased 9x5x3" loaf pan.

Cover and let rise until doubled, about 45 minutes.

In small bowl, mix together corn syrup and 1 tblsp. water. Brush each loaf with corn syrup mixture; sprinkle with oats.

Bake in 375° oven 40 to 45 minutes, or until loaves are golden brown and sound hollow when tapped. Immediately remove from pans. Cool on racks. Makes 2 loaves.

Cereal Bread

With a mix of three cereals—bran, shredded wheat and oats—these loaves are good sources of fiber, iron and B vitamins.

2 c. warm milk (105 to 115°)
1 c. high fiber bran cereal buds
1 c. crushed shredded wheat cereal
2 pkg. active dry yeast
1 tblsp. sugar
½ c. warm water (105 to 115°)
½ c. quick-cooking oats
⅓ c. molasses
¼ c. vegetable oil
1½ tsp. salt
5½ to 6½ c. sifted flour

In medium bowl, pour warm milk over bran cereal and wheat cereal; let stand 5 minutes.

In large bowl, sprinkle yeast and sugar over warm water; stir until dissolved. Add cereal mixture, oats, molasses, oil, salt and 2 c. flour.

Using mixer at low speed, beat until well blended. Increase speed to medium; beat 2 minutes. Add 1 c. flour; beat 2 minutes more.

Stir in enough additional flour to make a moderately soft dough. Turn out dough onto lightly floured surface. Knead until smooth and elastic, about 10 minutes.

Place in greased large bowl, turning over dough so that top is greased. Cover with towel and let rise in warm place until doubled, about 1 hour 30 minutes.

Punch down dough. Divide dough in half. Cover and let rest 5 minutes.

On lightly floured surface with lightly floured rolling pin, roll out each half into a 14x8″ rectangle.

Starting with one short side, roll up rectangles; jelly-roll fashion; pinch seams and ends to seal. Place each roll, seam-side down, in greased 9x5x3″ loaf pan.

Cover and let rise until doubled, about 1 hour.

Bake in 375° oven 40 to 45 minutes, or until loaves are dark brown and sound hollow when tapped. Immediately remove from pans. Cool on racks. Makes 2 loaves.

Pilgrim's Bread

A blue ribbon winner for one Iowa woman—a bread made with corn meal, whole-wheat, rye and all-purpose flours.

2 c. water
⅓ c. honey
⅔ c. yellow corn meal
¼ c. vegetable oil
1 c. stirred whole-wheat flour
1 c. stirred rye flour
2 pkg. active dry yeast
2 tsp. sugar
½ c. warm water (105 to 115°)
2½ tsp. salt
3¼ to 4¼ c. sifted all-purpose flour

In 2-qt. saucepan over high heat, bring 2 c. water and honey to a boil. Reduce heat to medium. With wire whisk, gradually beat in corn meal until smooth.

Cook, stirring constantly, until mixture boils and thickens, about 1 minute. Remove from heat. Stir in oil. Let stand to cool until warm (105 to 115°).

In small bowl, stir together whole-wheat flour and rye flour; set aside.

In large bowl, sprinkle yeast and sugar over ½ c. warm water; stir until dissolved. Add salt, corn meal mixture, ½ c. whole-wheat flour mixture and 1 c. all-purpose flour. Using mixer at low speed, beat until well blended. Increase speed to medium; beat 2 minutes.

Stir in remaining 1½ c. whole-wheat flour mixture and enough additional all-purpose flour to make a moderately soft dough. Turn out dough onto lightly floured surface. Knead until smooth and elastic, about 15 minutes.

Place in greased large bowl, turning over dough so that is top greased. Cover with towel and let rise in warm place until doubled, about 1 hour.

Punch down dough. Divide dough in half. Cover and let rest 5 minutes.

Shape each half into a loaf. Place each loaf in greased 9x5x3" loaf pan. Cover and let rise until doubled, about 45 minutes.

Bake in 375° oven 45 minutes, or until loaves are golden brown and sound hollow when tapped. Immediately remove from pans. Cool on racks. Makes 2 loaves.

Indian Bread

Once, cooks had to grind raisins by hand; now your blender or food processor will do the job.

3 c. stirred whole-wheat flour
1½ c. stirred rye flour
2 pkg. active dry yeast
2 tsp. salt
2 to 3 c. sifted all-purpose flour
⅓ c. packed brown sugar
¼ c. raisins
¼ c. honey
2¼ c. milk
⅓ c. shortening
Yellow corn meal

In medium bowl, stir together whole-wheat flour and rye flour; set aside.

In large bowl, stir together yeast, salt, 2 c. whole-wheat flour mixture and 1 c. all-purpose flour; set aside.

In blender container or food processor with metal blade, place brown sugar, raisins, honey and ½ c. milk; cover. Blend or process 10 to 15 seconds or until raisins are ground. Pour blended mixture into 2-qt. saucepan. Add shortening and remaining 1¾ c. milk. Over low heat, heat mixture until very warm (120 to 130°).

Using mixer at low speed, gradually beat milk mixture into yeast mixture until well blended. Increase speed to medium; beat 2 minutes. Add 1 c. whole-wheat flour mixture; beat 2 minutes.

Stir in remaining 1½ c. whole-wheat flour mixture and enough additional all-purpose flour to make a moderately stiff dough. Turn out dough onto lightly floured surface. Knead until smooth and elastic, about 10 minutes.

Place in greased large bowl, turning over dough so that top is greased. Cover with towel and let rise in warm place until doubled, about 1 hour 30 minutes.

Punch down dough. Divide dough in half. Cover and let rest 10 minutes. Shape each half into a round loaf.

Grease a large baking sheet and sprinkle with corn meal. Place loaves, 6" apart, on prepared baking sheet.

Cover and let rise until doubled, about 1 hour.

Bake in 375° oven 30 to 35 minutes, or until loaves are dark brown and sound hollow when tapped. Immediately remove from baking sheet. Cool on racks. Makes 2 loaves.

Golden Pumpkin-Raisin Bread

The flavor of pumpkin pie in a yeast bread—a great holiday treat!

2 pkg. active dry yeast
½ c. sugar
⅔ c. warm water (105 to 115°)
1 (16-oz.) can solid-pack pumpkin
¼ c. vegetable oil
2 tsp. salt
2 tsp. ground cinnamon
1½ tsp. ground ginger
½ tsp. ground nutmeg
6¼ to 7¼ c. sifted flour
2 eggs
1½ c. raisins

In large bowl, sprinkle yeast and sugar over warm water; stir until dissolved. Add pumpkin, oil, salt, cinnamon, ginger, nutmeg and 1½ c. flour.

Using mixer at low speed, beat until well blended. Increase speed to medium; beat 2 minutes. Add eggs and 1 c. flour; beat 2 minutes more.

Stir in raisins and enough additional flour to make a moderately soft dough. Turn out dough onto lightly floured surface. Knead until smooth and elastic, about 5 to 8 minutes.

Place in greased large bowl, turning over dough so that top is greased. Cover with towel and let rise in warm place until doubled, about 1 hour.

Punch down dough. Divide dough in half. Cover and let rest 10 minutes.

Shape each half into a loaf. Place each loaf in greased 9x5x3" loaf pan.

Cover and let rise until doubled, about 45 minutes.

Bake in 375° oven 35 to 40 minutes, or until loaves are dark golden brown and sound hollow when tapped. Immediately remove from pans. Cool on racks. Makes 2 loaves.

Melissa's Dairy Bread

Twice this bread has won blue ribbons for an Indiana woman. It's made with milk, eggs, Cheddar cheese and cottage cheese.

> 2 pkg. active dry yeast
> ⅓ c. sugar
> 1 tsp. salt
> 8½ to 9½ c. sifted flour
> 1⅔ c. milk
> 1 c. water
> 1 c. cream-style, small-curd cottage cheese
> ¼ c. butter or regular margarine
> 2 eggs
> 3 c. shredded sharp Cheddar cheese

In large bowl, stir together yeast, sugar, salt and 2½ c. flour; set aside.

In 2-qt. saucepan over low heat, heat milk, water, cottage cheese and butter until very warm (120 to 130°).

Using mixer at low speed, gradually beat milk mixture into yeast mixture until well blended. Increase speed to medium; beat 2 minutes. Add eggs and 2 c. flour. Increase speed to high; beat 2 minutes more.

Stir in Cheddar cheese and enough additional flour to make a moderately soft dough. Turn out dough onto lightly floured surface. Knead until smooth and elastic, about 10 minutes.

Place in greased large bowl, turning over dough so that top is greased. Cover with towel and let rise in warm place until doubled, about 1 hour.

Punch down dough. Divide dough into thirds. Cover and let rest 15 minutes.

Shape each third into a loaf. Place each loaf in greased 8½x4½x2½" loaf pan.

Cover and let rise until doubled, about 40 minutes.

Bake in 375° oven 35 minutes. Cover loosely with foil; bake 10 to 15 minutes more, or until loaves are dark brown and sound hollow when tapped. Immediately remove from pans. Cool on racks. Makes 3 loaves.

Millet Bread

High in iron and fiber, the millet gives these loaves a nutty flavor. Cook millet just as you do barley: simmer one part grain in three parts water until the grain absorbs the water, about 45 minutes.

3 c. water
¼ c. butter or regular margarine
1½ tsp. salt
1 c. millet
2 pkg. active dry yeast
¼ c. sugar
1¼ c. warm water (105 to 115°)
3 c. stirred whole-wheat flour
4½ to 5½ c. sifted all-purpose flour

In 2-qt. saucepan over high heat, bring water, butter and salt to a boil. Add millet. Reduce heat to low. Cover and simmer until all water is absorbed, about 45 minutes. Remove from heat; let stand to cool until warm (105 to 115°).

In large bowl, sprinkle yeast and sugar over warm water; stir until dissolved. Add 1 c. whole-wheat flour, 1 c. all-purpose flour and millet mixture.

Using mixer at low speed, beat until well blended. Increase speed to medium; beat 2 minutes. Add 1 c. whole-wheat flour; beat 2 minutes more.

Stir in remaining 1 c. whole-wheat flour and enough additional all-purpose flour to make a moderately soft dough. Turn out dough onto lightly floured surface. Knead until smooth and elastic, about 10 minutes.

Place in greased large bowl, turning over dough so that top is greased. Cover with towel and let rise in warm place until doubled, about 1 hour.

Punch down dough. Divide dough in half. Cover and let rest 5 minutes.

On lightly floured surface, roll out each half into 14x7" rectangle.

Starting with one short side, roll up each rectangle, jelly- roll fashion; pinch seam and ends to seal. Place each roll, seam-side down, in greased 9x5x3" loaf pan.

Cover and let rise until doubled, about 45 minutes.

Bake in 375° oven 50 to 55 minutes, or until loaves are golden brown and sound hollow when tapped. Immediately remove from pans. Cool on racks Makes 2 loaves.

Pizza Dough

You can make this versatile dough with white or whole-wheat flour.
Knead it by hand, or let the food processor do the job for you.

>1 pkg. active dry yeast
>1 tsp. sugar
>1 c. warm water (105 to 115°)
>2 tblsp. vegetable oil
>1 tsp. salt
>3 to 3¼ c. sifted all-purpose flour

In large bowl, sprinkle yeast and sugar over warm water; stir until dissolved. Stir in oil, salt and enough flour to make a soft dough.

Turn out dough onto lightly floured surface. Knead until smooth and elastic, about 5 minutes.

Place in greased large bowl, turning over dough so that top is greased. Cover with towel and let rise in warm place until almost doubled, about 30 minutes.

Punch down dough; turn out onto lightly floured surface. Knead until no longer sticky, about 30 seconds. Cover and let rest 5 minutes.

Use as directed to make All-American Pizza, Deep-dish Pizza, Broccoli and Spinach Pizza, and Calzones (recipes follow).

WHOLE-WHEAT PIZZA DOUGH: Add 1½ c. stirred whole-wheat flour to liquid ingredients. Use only 1½ to 1¾ c. sifted all-purpose flour to make a soft dough.

FOOD PROCESSOR METHOD: In small bowl, sprinkle yeast and sugar over warm water; stir until dissolved.

Place salt and 3 c. sifted all-purpose flour (or, 1½ c. sifted all-purpose flour and 1½ c. stirred whole-wheat flour) in processor bowl with metal blade.

While processor is running, pour yeast mixture through feed tube. Process until soft dough forms that leaves side of bowl, about 45 seconds.

Add oil; process 1 minute. If dough sticks to side of bowl, add additional flour, 1 tblsp. at a time, processing 10 seconds after each addition.

COOLRISE PIZZA DOUGH: Prepare and knead dough as directed. Cover with plastic wrap and refrigerate 2 to 24 hours. Punch down dough; turn out onto lightly floured surface. Knead until no longer sticky, about 30 seconds. Cover and let rest 5 minutes.

All-American Pizza

Make the dough first thing in the morning or even the night before and let it rise in the refrigerator.

> 1 recipe Pizza Dough
> 1½ c. prepared pizza sauce or thick spaghetti sauce
> 1 tsp. dried oregano leaves
> ½ tsp. dried basil leaves
> 3 c. shredded mozzarella cheese (12 oz.)
> ⅓ c. grated Parmesan cheese
> Toppings: Choose from sliced pepperoni,
>   mushrooms, onions, pitted olives, green or red
>   sweet peppers, cooked sausage, ham or ground beef.

Prepare Pizza Dough. Let rise and punch down dough as directed. Divide dough in half. Pat and stretch each half into a greased 12″ round pizza pan.

Spread each crust with sauce and then sprinkle with oregano, basil, mozzarella cheese, Parmesan cheese and desired toppings.

Bake, on lowest rack, in 400° oven 20 minutes or until bottoms of crusts are browned. Cut into wedges. Serve hot. Makes 2 pizzas.

To Freeze and Serve Later: Prepare Pizza Dough; divide in half. Pat and stretch each half into a greased 12″ round pizza pan.

Bake in 400° oven 8 to 10 minutes, or until crusts are set but not browned. Remove from pans; cool on racks.

Brush each crust with 1 tsp. oil. Top each as directed.

Place each crust on a sheet of foil and freeze until firm. Wrap frozen pizzas in foil and store in freezer up to 1 month.

Unwrap frozen pizzas. Bake on a sheet of foil on lowest rack in 425° oven 15 minutes or until bottoms of crusts are browned.

Deep-dish Pizza

For a thicker, chewier crust, try this deep-dish version of the classic pizza. These pizzas are baked in cake pans.

    1 recipe Pizza Dough
    1 c. prepared pizza sauce or thick spaghetti sauce
    ½ tsp. dried oregano leaves
    ¼ tsp. dried basil leaves
    1⅓ c. shredded mozzarella cheese
    3 tblsp. grated Parmesan cheese
    Toppings: Choose from sliced pepperoni,
        mushrooms, onions, pitted olives, green or red sweet
        peppers, or cooked sausage, ham or ground beef.

Prepare Pizza Dough. Let rise and punch down dough as directed.

Divide dough in half. Pat and stretch each half into bottom and up side of a greased 9″ round baking pan.

Spread each crust with sauce and then sprinkle with oregano, basil, mozzarella cheese, Parmesan cheese and desired toppings.

Bake, on lowest rack, in 425° oven 15 to 20 minutes, or until edges and bottoms of crusts are browned. Cool in pans on racks 10 minutes before serving. Cut into wedges. Makes 2 pizzas.

Broccoli and Spinach Pizza

If you fancy the flavor of quiche, be sure to try this golden-crusted open pie with creamy cottage cheese and lots of vegetables.

    1 recipe Pizza Dough
    1 (10-oz.) pkg. frozen, chopped spinach, thawed
    1 (8- or 10-oz.) pkg. frozen broccoli spears, thawed
    1 (16-oz.) container small-curd cottage cheese,
        or 1 (15-oz.) container ricotta cheese
    ½ c. grated Parmesan cheese
    1 egg
    1 tsp. dried oregano leaves
    ½ tsp. garlic salt
    2 c. shredded Cheddar cheese (8 oz.)

Prepare Pizza Dough. Let rise and punch down dough as directed.

Divide dough in half. Pat and stretch each half into a greased 12" round pizza pan; set aside.

In sieve, drain spinach, pressing out as much liquid as possible. Coarsely chop broccoli spears and drain well on paper towels; set aside.

In bowl, mix cottage cheese, Parmesan cheese, egg, oregano and garlic salt until well blended. Spread evenly over each crust. Sprinkle each with spinach, broccoli and then Cheddar cheese.

Bake, on lowest rack, in 400° oven 20 minutes or until bottoms of crusts are browned. Cut into wedges. Serve hot.
Makes 2 pizzas.

Calzones

For a robust, Italian-style sandwich, wrap Pizza Dough around salami and provolone cheese.

1 recipe Pizza Dough
8 oz. provolone cheese, shredded
6 oz. sliced hard salami, coarsely chopped
1 tsp. dried oregano leaves
¼ tsp. pepper
1 tblsp. vegetable oil

Prepare Pizza Dough. Let rise and punch down dough as directed.

Divide dough into 6 pieces. On lightly floured surface with floured rolling pin, roll out each piece into a 7" circle.

On half of each circle, place one-sixth of the cheese and salami. Sprinkle with oregano and pepper. Fold each circle in half over filling. Fold under edges ½" and pinch together to seal. Place, 3" apart, on greased baking sheets.

Cover and let rest 15 minutes. Brush tops with oil.

Bake in 425° oven 15 to 20 minutes or until golden brown. Cool on racks 5 minutes before serving. Makes 6 calzones.

Rich Hot Rolls

With this egg-rich dough, you can make Cloverleaf, Parker House, Fan-tans, Crescents, Rosettes and even Brown-and-Serve rolls.

2 pkg. active dry yeast
½ tsp. sugar
½ c. warm water (105 to 115°)
¾ c. milk
½ c. shortening
1 tsp. salt
2 eggs
¼ c. sugar
4¼ to 4¾ c. sifted flour

In large bowl, sprinkle yeast and ½ tsp. sugar over warm water; stir until dissolved. Add milk, shortening, salt, eggs, ¼ c. sugar and 1½ c. flour.

Using mixer at low speed, beat until well blended. Increase speed to medium, beat 2 minutes. Add 1 c. flour; beat 2 minutes more.

Stir in enough additional flour to make a soft dough. Turn out dough onto lightly floured surface. Knead until smooth and elastic, about 5 minutes.

Place in greased large bowl, turning over dough so that top is greased. Cover with towel and let rise in warm place until doubled, about 1 hour.

Punch down dough. Divide dough in half. Cover and let rest 10 minutes.

Cut or roll dough into the shape of your choice, using the following directions. (If you want your rolls to be crusty, brush with 3 tblsp. melted butter after shaping and let them rise, uncovered.)

Cover and let rise until doubled, about 30 minutes.

Bake in 375° oven 15 to 20 minutes or until golden brown. (If you want the crust to be soft, brush with 3 tblsp. shortening or softened butter immediately after baking.) Immediately remove from pans or baking sheets. Serve warm. Makes 24 rolls.

PAN ROLLS: Cut each dough half into 12 pieces. Shape each piece of dough into a ball. Place balls in rows in 2 greased 8x8x2" baking pans.

DINNER ROLLS: Cut each dough half into 12 pieces. Shape each piece of dough into an oval. (Do not brush with butter.) Place, 2" apart, on greased baking sheets.
   Cover and let rise until doubled, about 40 minutes.
   In small bowl, mix together 1 egg white and 1 tblsp. water. Brush rolls with egg white mixture; sprinkle with 2 tsp. poppy seed, caraway seed or coarse salt. Bake as directed.

CRUSTY ROLLS: Cut each dough half into 12 pieces. Shape each piece into an oval. Place, 2" apart, on greased baking sheets. Cut one lengthwise slash in top of each roll, ½"-deep. Dust lightly with flour. (Do not brush with shortening or butter after baking.)

CLOVERLEAF ROLLS: Cut each dough half into 36 pieces. Shape each piece into a ball. Place 3 balls in each of 24 greased 2½" muffin-pan cups.

QUICK CLOVERLEAF ROLLS: Cut each dough half into 12 pieces. Shape each piece into a ball. Place balls in 24 greased 2½" muffin-pan cups. With kitchen scissors cut each ball almost in half, then in quarters, cutting almost to bottoms of balls.

KNOT OR ROSETTE ROLLS: Cut each dough half into 12 pieces. Roll each piece into a 12"-long rope. Gently tie each rope in a knot. (To make rosettes, tuck ends under knot.) Place, 2" apart, on greased baking sheets.

SNAIL ROLLS: Cut each dough half into 12 pieces. Roll each piece into a 12"-long rope. Coil each rope into a snail shape. Place, 2" apart, on greased baking sheets.

CLOTHESPIN ROLLS: Cut each dough half into 12 pieces. Roll each piece into a 12"-long rope. Wrap each rope around a greased wooden peg clothespin (or a 4"-long piece of dowel, cut from a ½"-thick wooden dowel rod). Place, 2" apart, on greased baking sheets.
   Immediately after the rolls are baked, remove clothespins. If you wish, fill the holes with peanut butter or jelly.

CRESCENT ROLLS: With lightly floured rolling pin, roll out each dough half into a 16" circle. Spread each circle with 3 tblsp. butter or regular margarine, softened.

Cut each circle into 12 wedges. Roll up each wedge, starting at the wide end. Place rolled wedges, points down, 2" apart, on greased baking sheets. Curve the ends to form crescents.

PARKER HOUSE ROLLS: Melt 3 tblsp. butter or regular margarine. With lightly floured rolling pin, roll out each dough half to ¼" thickness. With floured 2½" round biscuit cutter, cut 18 circles from each dough half.

Brush tops of circles with melted butter. Then, fold circles, with top half overlapping bottom half, and place in rows, ½" apart, on greased large baking sheet. Makes 36 rolls.

FAN-TAN ROLLS: With lightly floured rolling pin, roll out one dough half into a 13x9" rectangle. Brush with 2 tblsp. butter or regular margarine, softened. Cut rectangle lengthwise into 6 strips. Stack strips evenly, buttered-side up. Cut stack into 12 pieces. Place each piece, cut-side up, in a greased 2½" muffin-pan cup. Repeat with remaining dough half.

BROWN-AND-SERVE ROLLS: Prepare and shape dough as directed for the dinner rolls of your choice (see preceding recipes). Let rise until doubled, about 30 minutes.

Bake in 275° oven 20 minutes until rolls are set but not browned.

Immediately remove from pans or baking sheets. Cool on racks. Place rolls in plastic bags. Refrigerate up to 3 days, or freeze up to 2 months.

To serve: Thaw rolls, if frozen. Place rolls on greased baking sheet. Bake in 400° oven 10 to 14 minutes or until golden brown.

No-knead Dinner Rolls

The brown-and-serve variation lets you store these rolls in your refrigerator or freezer for fresh-baked convenience in minutes!

1 pkg. active dry yeast
¼ c. warm water (105 to 115°)
1¼ c. warm milk (105 to 115°)
¼ c. sugar
¾ tsp. salt
1 egg
¼ c. vegetable oil
5 c. sifted flour
Vegetable oil

In large bowl, sprinkle yeast over warm water; stir until dissolved. Add warm milk, sugar, salt, egg, ¼ c. oil and 3 c. flour.

Using mixer at low speed, beat until well blended. Increase speed to medium; beat 2 minutes. Stir in remaining flour to make a soft dough.

Lightly brush top of dough with oil. Cover with towel and let rise in warm place until doubled, about 50 minutes.

Punch down dough. Turn out dough onto lightly floured surface. Knead just until dough is smooth, about 15 times. Divide dough in half. Cover and let rest 10 minutes.

Cut each half into 12 pieces. Shape each piece into a ball. Place balls in rows in 2 greased 8x8x2" baking pans.

Cover and let rise until doubled, about 45 minutes.

Bake in 375° oven 20 minutes, or until rolls are golden brown and sound hollow when tapped. Immediately remove from pans. Serve warm. Makes 24 rolls.

BROWN-AND-SERVE DINNER ROLLS: Prepare, shape and let dough rise as directed. Bake in 275° oven 25 minutes until rolls are set but not browned.

Immediately remove from pans. Cool on racks. Place rolls in plastic bags. Refrigerate up to 3 days, or freeze up to 2 months.

To serve: Thaw rolls, if frozen. Place rolls on greased baking sheet. Bake in 400° oven 7 minutes or until browned.

Bread Sticks

Bake them in a hot oven, and you'll have soft, chewy sticks; bake them longer, at a lower temperature, and you'll have crisp sticks, like the ones served in restaurants.

> 1 pkg. active dry yeast
> 1 tblsp. sugar
> 1 tsp. salt
> 2¾ to 3¼ c. sifted flour
> ¾ c. milk
> 1 tblsp. shortening
> ¼ c. water
> 1 egg white
> 1 tblsp. water
> Poppy seed, sesame seed or coarse salt

In large bowl, stir together yeast, sugar, salt and ¾ c. flour; set aside.

In 1-qt. saucepan over low heat, heat milk, shortening and ¼ c. water until very warm (120 to 130°).

Using mixer at low speed, gradually beat milk mixture into yeast mixture until well blended. Increase speed to medium; beat 2 minutes. Add ¾ c. flour. Increase speed to high; beat 2 minutes more.

Stir in enough additional flour to make a soft dough. Turn out dough onto lightly floured surface. Knead until smooth and elastic, about 5 to 8 minutes.

Place in greased large bowl, turning over dough so that top is greased. Cover with towel and let rise in warm place until doubled, about 45 minutes.

Punch down dough. Cover and let rest 10 minutes.

With lightly floured rolling pin, roll out dough into a 16x6" rectangle. Cut dough into 32 (½"-wide) strips.

Roll each strip into an 8"-long rope. Place ropes, 1" apart, on greased large baking sheets.

Cover and let rise 15 minutes.

In small bowl, mix together egg white and 1 tblsp. water. Brush each rope with egg white mixture; sprinkle with poppy seed, sesame seed or coarse salt.

Bake in 400° oven 15 minutes or until golden brown. Immediately remove from baking sheets. Cool on racks. Makes 32 bread sticks.

CRISP BREAD STICKS: Bake in 250° oven, turning occasionally, 45 to 60 minutes or until crisp and evenly browned.

TWISTED BREAD STICKS: After rolling each strip into a rope, twist rope twice before placing on greased baking sheets.

One-Hour Rolls

A Missouri woman shared her grandmother's recipe for these quick rolls. Pat the dough into the pan, then cut it into squares.

> 2 pkg. active dry yeast
> ¼ c. sugar
> 1 tsp. salt
> ½ tsp. baking soda
> 4½ c. sifted flour
> 1½ c. buttermilk
> ½ c. shortening
> ¼ c. butter or regular margarine, melted

In large bowl, stir together yeast, sugar, salt, baking soda and 2 c. flour; set aside.

In 2-qt. saucepan over low heat, heat buttermilk and shortening until very warm (120 to 130°). (Mixture will look curdled.)

Using mixer at low speed, gradually beat buttermilk mixture into yeast mixture until well blended. Increase speed to medium; beat 2 minutes.

Stir in remaining 2½ c. flour until well blended and mixture forms a soft dough that leaves side of bowl. Turn out dough onto lightly floured surface. Knead until smooth, about 1 minute. Cover with towel and let rest 10 minutes.

Brush 13x9x2" baking pan with 3 tblsp. melted butter. Pat dough evenly into pan. With sharp knife, cut dough into 24 pieces, cutting almost through to bottom of dough.

Cover and let rise in warm place until doubled, about 30 minutes. Brush rolls with remaining 1 tblsp. melted butter.

Bake in 425° oven 15 minutes, or until rolls are golden brown and sound hollow when tapped. Immediately remove from pan. Serve warm. Makes 24 rolls.

Cottage Cheese Rolls

The cheese bakes up in attractive specks on top of these rolls.

> 2 pkg. active dry yeast
> ¼ c. sugar
> ½ c. warm water (105 to 115°)
> 2 c. cream-style, small-curd cottage cheese
> 2 tsp. salt
> ½ tsp. baking soda
> 2 eggs
> 4¼ to 4¾ c. sifted flour
> 1 tblsp. butter or regular margarine, melted

In large bowl, sprinkle yeast and sugar over warm water; stir until dissolved. Add cottage cheese, salt, baking soda, eggs and 2 c. flour.

Using mixer at low speed, beat until well blended. Increase speed to medium; beat 3 minutes. Stir in enough additional flour to make a soft dough.

Cover with towel and let rise in warm place until doubled, about 1 hour.

Punch down dough. Turn out dough onto lightly floured surface and knead until no longer sticky, about 1 minute. Divide dough in half. Cover and let rest 10 minutes.

Cut each half into 12 pieces. Shape each piece into a ball. Place balls in rows in 2 greased 8x8x2" baking pans.

Cover and let rise until doubled, about 45 minutes.

Bake in 350° oven 25 to 30 minutes, or until rolls are dark golden brown and sound hollow when tapped. Immediately remove from pans. Brush tops of hot rolls with melted butter. Serve warm. Makes 24 rolls.

Corn Meal Rolls

"The kids really like 'em!" That's what a Kansas school lunchroom cook told us about these light and tender yeast rolls.

> 1 c. yellow corn meal
> 2 c. water
> ½ c. shortening
> 1½ tsp. salt
> ⅓ c. sugar
> 2 pkg. active dry yeast
> ¼ tsp. sugar
> ½ c. warm water (105 to 115°)
> 5 to 5½ c. sifted flour
> 2 eggs

In 2-qt. saucepan over high heat, bring corn meal and 2 c. water to a boil, stirring constantly. Reduce heat to medium. Cook, stirring constantly, until mixture is thick, about 3 minutes. Stir in shortening, salt and ⅓ c. sugar until well blended. Remove from heat. Let stand to cool until warm (105 to 115°).

In large bowl, sprinkle yeast and ¼ tsp. sugar over ½ c. warm water; stir until dissolved. Add 2 c. flour and corn meal mixture.

Using mixer at low speed, beat until well blended. Increase speed to medium; beat 2 minutes. Add eggs and 1 c. flour. Increase speed to high; beat 2 minutes more.

Stir in enough additional flour to make a soft dough. Turn out dough onto lightly floured surface. Knead until smooth and elastic, about 5 minutes.

Place in greased large bowl, turning over dough so that top is greased. Cover with towel and let rise in warm place until doubled, about 1 hour.

Punch down dough. Divide dough in half. Cover and let rest 10 minutes.

Divide each half into 16 pieces. With lightly floured hands, shape each piece into a ball. Place balls in rows in 2 greased 9x9x2" baking pans.

Cover and let rise until doubled, about 40 minutes.

Bake in 375° oven 15 to 20 minutes, or until rolls are golden brown and sound hollow when tapped. Immediately remove from pans. Serve warm. Makes 32 rolls.

Marbled Rolls

Two doughs—whole-wheat and white—are twisted together for each roll. These rolls are baked in muffin pans.

        1 pkg. active dry yeast
        ¼ c. packed brown sugar
        ¾ tsp. salt
        3¾ c. sifted all-purpose flour
        1⅓ c. milk
        ¼ c. shortening
        1 egg
        1 tsp. unsweetened cocoa
        1 c. plus 1 tblsp. stirred whole-wheat flour
        Vegetable oil
        1 egg
        1 tblsp. water

In large bowl, stir together yeast, brown sugar, salt and 1¼ c. all-purpose flour; set aside.

In 2-qt. saucepan over low heat, heat milk and shortening until very warm (120 to 130°).

Using mixer at low speed, gradually beat milk mixture into yeast mixture until well blended. Increase speed to medium; beat 2 minutes. Add 1 egg and 1¼ c. all-purpose flour. Increase speed to high; beat 2 minutes more.

Remove half of the batter (about 1⅓ c.) and place in another bowl. To one half of batter, stir in remaining 1¼ c. all-purpose flour to make a moderately stiff dough. Into remaining half of batter stir in cocoa and then whole-wheat flour to make a moderately stiff dough. Brush top of each dough lightly with oil. Cover and let rise in warm place until doubled, about 45 minutes.

Punch down each dough. Turn out doughs onto lightly floured surface. Knead each just until smooth, about 30 seconds. Cover and let rest 10 minutes.

Cut each dough into fourths. Roll each fourth into a 30"- long rope. Twist together one whole-wheat rope and one white rope, forming a twisted rope, about 24" long. Repeat with remaining ropes.

Cut each twisted rope into 6 pieces. Fold pieces in half and place, cut-ends down, in 24 greased 2½" muffin-pan cups. Gently press each piece into the muffin-pan cups to flatten slightly.

Cover and let rise until doubled, about 30 to 45 minutes.

In small bowl, mix together egg and 1 tblsp. water. Brush each roll with egg mixture.

Bake in 375° oven 15 to 20 minutes, or until rolls are browned and sound hollow when tapped. Immediately remove from pans. Serve warm. Makes 24 rolls.

Potato Rolls

Instant potato flakes makes these rolls light.

> 1 pkg. active dry yeast
> 2 tblsp. sugar
> 1 c. warm water (105 to 115°)
> ½ c. instant potato flakes
> ⅓ c. nonfat dry milk
> ¼ c. vegetable oil
> 1½ tsp. salt
> 1 egg
> 3 to 3½ c. sifted flour

In large bowl, sprinkle yeast and sugar over warm water; stir until dissolved. Add potato flakes, dry milk, oil, salt, egg and 1 c. flour.

Using mixer at low speed, beat until well blended. Increase speed to medium; beat 2 minutes.

Stir in enough additional flour to make a soft dough. Turn out dough onto lightly floured surface. Knead until smooth and elastic, about 5 minutes.

Place in greased large bowl, turning over dough so that top is greased. Cover with towel and let rise in warm place until doubled, about 1 hour.

Punch down dough. Divide dough in half. Cover and let rest 10 minutes.

Cut each half into 12 pieces. With greased hands, shape each piece into a ball. Place balls in rows in 2 greased 8x8x2" baking pans.

Cover and let rise until doubled, about 1 hour.

Bake in 400° oven 15 minutes, or until rolls are golden brown and sound hollow when tapped. Immediately remove from pans. Serve warm. Makes 24 rolls.

Honey-Wheat Buns

The creation of an Ohio woman—buns that capture the classic tastes of wheat and honey.

3 c. stirred whole-wheat flour
¾ c. unprocessed bran
¾ c. wheat germ
2 pkg. active dry yeast
½ c. nonfat dry milk
1 tsp. salt
3½ to 4½ c. sifted all-purpose flour
2 c. water
½ c. shortening
½ c. honey
2 eggs

In medium bowl, stir together whole-wheat flour, bran and wheat germ; set aside.

In large bowl, stir together yeast, dry milk, salt, 1 c. all-purpose flour and 2 c. whole-wheat flour mixture; set aside.

In 2-qt. saucepan over low heat, heat water, shortening and honey until very warm (120 to 130°).

Using mixer at low speed, gradually beat water mixture into yeast mixture until well blended. Increase speed to medium; beat 2 minutes. Add eggs and remaining whole-wheat flour mixture; beat 3 minutes more.

Stir in enough additional all-purpose flour to make a moderately stiff dough. Turn out dough onto lightly floured surface. Knead until smooth and elastic, about 15 minutes.

Place in greased large bowl, turning over dough so that top is greased. Cover with towel and let rise in warm place until doubled, about 1 hour.

Punch down dough. Divide dough into 16 pieces. Cover and let rest 5 minutes.

Shape each piece into a ball. Place balls, 2" apart, on greased large baking sheets. Flatten each ball slightly to make a 3" round.

Cover and let rise until doubled, about 45 minutes.

Bake in 350° oven 15 to 20 minutes, or until buns are golden brown and sound hollow when tapped. Immediately remove from baking sheets. Serve warm. Makes 16 buns.

Potato-Wheat Dinner Rolls

A Kansas cook tells us that she grinds wheat from her own farm to give these rolls an extra-fresh, nutlike flavor.

2 pkg. active dry yeast
1 tsp. granulated sugar
½ c. warm water (105 to 115°)
2 c. stirred whole-wheat flour
1 c. instant potato flakes
1 c. warm milk (105 to 115°)
½ c. packed brown sugar
½ c. butter or regular margarine, softened
1 tsp. salt
2 eggs
2 c. sifted all-purpose flour
1 egg yolk
1 tblsp. water

In large bowl, sprinkle yeast and granulated sugar over warm water; stir until dissolved. Add whole-wheat flour, potato flakes, warm milk, brown sugar, butter, salt and eggs.

Using mixer at low speed, beat until well blended. Increase speed to medium; beat 2 minutes.

Stir in enough all-purpose flour to make a soft dough. Turn out dough onto lightly floured surface. Knead until smooth and elastic, about 10 minutes.

Place in greased large bowl, turning over dough so that top is greased. Cover with towel and let rise in warm place until doubled, about 1 hour.

Punch down dough. Divide dough into 32 pieces. Cover and let rest 10 minutes.

On lightly floured surface, roll each piece into a 12"-long rope. Wrap each rope around a greased wooden peg clothespin (or a 4"-long piece of dowel, cut from a ½"-thick wooden dowel rod). Place, 2" apart, on greased large baking sheets.

Cover and let rise until doubled, about 30 minutes.

In small bowl, mix together egg yolk and water. Brush each roll with egg yolk mixture.

Bake in 375° oven 15 minutes, or until rolls are golden brown and sound hollow when tapped. Immediately remove clothespins. Serve warm. Makes 32 rolls.

Caraway Vienna Rolls

Crusty rolls crowned with a sprinkling of caraway seed. You could leave the tops plain, or substitute coarse salt for caraway seed.

>2 pkg. active dry yeast
>1 tblsp. sugar
>1 tsp. salt
>4½ to 5 c. sifted flour
>¾ c. milk
>¾ c. water
>2 tsp. caraway seed
>1 egg white
>1 tblsp. water
>Caraway seed

In large bowl, stir together yeast, sugar, salt and 1½ c. flour; set aside.

In 1-qt. saucepan, over low heat, heat milk and ¾ c. water until very warm (120 to 130°).

Using mixer at low speed, gradually beat milk mixture into yeast mixture until well blended. Increase speed to medium; beat 2 minutes. Add 1 c. flour and 2 tsp. caraway seed, beat 2 minutes more.

Stir in enough additional flour to make a moderately stiff dough. Turn out dough onto lightly floured surface. Knead until smooth and elastic, about 10 minutes.

Place in greased large bowl, turning over dough so that top is greased. Cover with towel and let rise in warm place until doubled, about 35 minutes.

Punch down dough. Turn out dough onto lightly floured surface. Cover and let rest 10 minutes.

Cut dough into 16 pieces. Shape each piece into an oval. Place, 2" apart, on greased large baking sheets.

Cover and let rise until doubled, about 20 to 30 minutes.

In small bowl, mix together egg white and 1 tblsp. water. Brush each roll with egg white mixture. Cut 2 diagonal slashes on top of each roll; sprinkle with additional caraway seed.

Bake in 400° oven 20 to 25 minutes, or until rolls are browned and sound hollow when tapped. Immediately remove from baking sheets. Serve warm. Makes 16 rolls.

Sesame-Onion Bow Ties

Make any meal special with these golden sesame-coated rolls. Just arrange them in a basket for a simple centerpiece.

3 tblsp. butter or regular margarine
1½ c. chopped onions
1 pkg. active dry yeast
1 tblsp. sugar
¾ tsp. salt
3¼ to 3½ c. sifted flour
1 c. very warm milk (120 to 130°)
1 egg yolk
1 tblsp. water
2 tblsp. sesame seed

In 10″ skillet over medium heat, melt butter. Add onions; cook until tender. Remove from heat; set aside.

In large bowl, stir together yeast, sugar, salt and 1 c. flour. Using mixer at low speed, gradually beat very warm milk into yeast mixture until well blended. Increase speed to medium; beat 2 minutes. Add cooked onions and ½ c. flour. Increase speed to high; beat 2 minutes more.

Stir in enough additional flour to make a soft dough. Turn out dough onto lightly floured surface. Knead until smooth and elastic, about 5 minutes.

Place in greased large bowl, turning over dough so that top is greased. Cover with towel and let rise in warm place until doubled, about 50 minutes.

Punch down dough. Cover and let rest 10 minutes.

Roll out dough into a 16x14″ rectangle. Cut in 28 (4x2″) rectangles. Tightly twist each rectangle in center to form bow ties. Place bow ties, 2″ apart, on greased baking sheets.

Cover and let rise until doubled, about 20 to 30 minutes.

In small bowl, mix together egg yolk and water. Brush each bow tie with egg yolk mixture; sprinkle with sesame seed.

Bake in 375° oven 15 to 20 minutes or until golden brown. Immediately remove from baking sheets. Serve warm. Makes 28 bow ties.

8
Sweet Yeast Breads

It doesn't matter whether you've been baking for years or are a first-time baker. There's a certain pride that comes from making attractive, mouth-watering coffeecakes and sweet yeast breads, even when you serve them at informal get-togethers.

This chapter begins with two recipes for basic sweet yeast dough—Shortcut Sweet Dough, which has only one rising, and Sweet Dough, which includes a coolrise variation. Both doughs can be used to make more than a dozen different breads.

For example, from just one batch of Sweet Dough, you'll be able to create four whimsical Animal Breads—a bear, a bunny, a turtle and an alligator. Use your imagination to make other animal shapes. Serve fresh hot Cinnamon Raisin Buns for Sunday breakfast without a fuss by putting a batch of Coolrise Sweet Dough in the refrigerator to rise overnight. Date Nut Coffeecake, Swedish Tea Rings and Orange Twists will be sought-after items at bake sales—all made from the same Sweet Dough recipe.

Because sweet yeast doughs usually contain more fat and sugar than many white bread doughs, they take a little longer to rise. It also takes a few minutes to shape these doughs, so don't rush them—the results are well worth the extra time involved.

This chapter ends with familiar favorites, including recipes for Hot Cross Buns, Baked Doughnuts and Sticky Cinnamon Rolls—all are individual sweet breads, good any time of the day, and we're sure there will never be a crumb left over!

Shortcut Sweet Dough

So named because this light and tender dough rises only once. It's made with oil instead of butter.

> 2 pkg. active dry yeast
> ¼ c. sugar
> 1 c. warm water (105 to 115°)
> ⅓ c. nonfat dry milk
> ¼ c. vegetable oil
> 1 tsp. salt
> 1 egg
> 3¾ to 4¼ c. sifted flour

In large bowl, sprinkle yeast and sugar over warm water; stir until dissolved. Add dry milk, oil, salt, egg and 2 c. flour.

Using mixer at low speed, beat until well blended. Increase speed to medium; beat 3 minutes.

Stir in enough additional flour to make a soft dough. Turn out dough onto lightly floured surface. Toss dough with flour until no longer sticky and knead 1 minute.

Cover and let rest 15 minutes.

Use as directed to make Cinnamon Bread, Houska, Date Nut Coffeecake, Coconut-Almond Ring Twist, Easter Egg Bread, Grecian Feast Loaf, Daisy Coffee Breads, Coconut Macaroon Coffeecake and many more (recipes follow).

Sweet Dough

Use this versatile dough to make all sorts of goodies, including Cinnamon Bread and Houska. To save time, make the Coolrise Sweet Dough and let the first rising be done in the refrigerator.

> 3 pkg. active dry yeast
> ¾ c. sugar
> 1½ tsp. salt
> 8 to 9 c. sifted flour
> 2½ c. milk
> ¾ c. butter or regular margarine
> 2 eggs

In large bowl, stir together yeast, sugar, salt and 2 c. flour; set aside.

In 2-qt. saucepan over low heat, heat milk and butter until very warm (120 to 130°).

Using mixer at low speed, gradually beat milk mixture into yeast mixture until well blended. Increase speed to medium; beat 2 minutes. Add eggs and 2½ c. flour. Increase speed to high; beat 2 minutes more.

Stir in enough additional flour to make a soft dough. Turn out dough onto lightly floured surface. Knead until smooth and elastic, about 5 minutes.

Place in greased large bowl, turning over dough so that top is greased. Cover with towel and let rise in warm place until doubled, about 1 hour.

Punch down dough. Cover and let rest 10 minutes.

Use as directed to make Animal Breads, Cinnamon Bread, Grecian Feast Loaf, Potica, Swedish Tea Rings, Apricot Coffee Braids and many more (recipes follow).

COOLRISE SWEET DOUGH: Prepare and knead Sweet Dough as directed. Place dough in greased large bowl, turning over dough so that top is greased. Cover tightly with plastic wrap. Refrigerate 2 to 24 hours.

Punch down dough. On lightly floured surface, knead 1 minute, or until dough is no longer sticky, adding additional flour if necessary. Cover and let rest 30 minutes.

Use as directed to make Houska, Daisy Coffee Breads, Potica, Cherry Swirl, Kolaches, Orange Twists and many more (recipes follow).

Animal Breads

Children's eyes will open wide when you offer them bread shaped like a bear, a bunny, a turtle or an alligator.

        1 recipe Sweet Dough
        Raisins
        1 egg white
        1 tblsp. water

Prepare Sweet Dough. Let rise as directed.

For each animal bread use one fourth of the dough. Shape it following the directions below.

For best results, assemble 2 animal shapes directly on the same greased large baking sheet, placing breads 4" apart. Be sure to pinch the dough firmly when attaching the body pieces. To make a better bond, moisten surfaces to be joined with some egg white.

After shaping the animal breads, cover and let rise until doubled, about 45 minutes.

In small bowl, mix together remaining egg white and water. Brush each bread with egg white mixture.

Bake in 350° oven 30 minutes, or until each bread is golden brown and sounds hollow when tapped. Immediately remove from baking sheets. Cool on racks. Makes 4 animal breads.

BEAR BREAD: Divide dough in half.

For body: Shape one half into a ball and place on greased baking sheet. Flatten slightly with hand.

For head: Divide remaining dough in half. Shape one half into a ball and place next to body for head; pinch together to seal well. Flatten head slightly with hand.

For paws, ears and nose: Divide the remaining dough into 6 pieces plus 1 tiny piece for nose. Shape the 6 pieces into balls; attach, by pinching, 4 to the body for paws and 2 to the head for ears. With finger, make an indentation in each ear. Pinch the tiny piece of dough in center of face for nose.

With tip of knife, cut a hole in center of body for belly button and 2 holes in head for eyes. Moisten 3 raisins with some egg white. Press raisins into holes. Continue as directed.

BUNNY BREAD: Divide dough in half.

For body: Shape one half into a ball and place on greased baking sheet. Flatten slightly with hand.

For head: Divide remaining dough in half. Shape one half into a ball and place next to body for head; pinch together to seal well. Flatten head slightly with hand.

For feet and ears: Divide remaining dough into 6 pieces. Shape 4 pieces into 2"-long ropes; attach, by pinching, 2 ropes to the bottom of body for feet and 2 ropes to the head for ears. Pinch tips of ears to make points and turn one ear tip slightly down towards head.

For paws: Shape remaining pieces into 2 balls and attach, by pinching, to top of body. With tip of knife, cut a hole in center of body for belly button and 2 holes in head for eyes. Moisten 3 raisins with some egg white. Press raisins into holes. Continue as directed.

TURTLE BREAD: Cut off one third of the dough.

For body: Shape larger piece into a ball and place on greased baking sheet. Flatten slightly with hand.

For head: Divide remaining dough in half. Shape one half into a ball and place next to body for head; pinch together to seal well. Flatten head slightly with hand.

For feet and tail: Divide the remaining dough into 5 pieces. Shape 4 pieces into balls; attach, by pinching, to body for feet. Roll remaining piece into 1"-long rope; attach, by pinching, to body. Pinch tip of tail to make a point.

With tip of knife, make 2 holes in head for eyes. Moisten 2 raisins with some egg white. Press raisins into holes.

With scissors, snip body about ½" deep, at ½" intervals, to resemble turtle shell; snip each foot twice for toes. Continue as directed.

ALLIGATOR BREAD: Cut off one fifth of the dough.

For body: Shape larger piece of dough into 12"-long rope; pinch both ends to make points. Place on greased baking sheet, curving one end of rope. Cut a slit in other end of rope for mouth. To hold mouth open during baking, place a greased small ball of aluminum foil in mouth. (Remove foil after baking.)

For feet: Divide remaining dough into 4 pieces. Roll each piece into a 2"-long rope. Attach to body by pinching; curve each foot slightly.

With tip of knife, cut 2 holes in head for eyes. Moisten 2 raisins with some egg white. Press raisins into holes.

With scissors, snip body about ½" deep, at ½" intervals, to form scales; snip each foot twice for toes. Continue as directed.

Cinnamon Bread

You can choose from two sweet doughs to make a delectable cinnamon-swirled loaf with a crusty, sugary top.

> ½ recipe Sweet Dough, or
>   1 recipe Shortcut Sweet Dough
> ¼ c. sugar
> 1 tblsp. ground cinnamon
> 1 tblsp. butter or regular margarine, melted
> 1 egg white
> 1 tblsp. water

Prepare desired Sweet Dough. Let rise or rest as directed.

In small bowl, stir together sugar and cinnamon. Reserve 2 tsp. cinnamon mixture.

On lightly floured surface with floured rolling pin, roll out dough into a 16x9" rectangle. Brush rectangle with melted butter. Sprinkle with remaining cinnamon mixture. Starting with one short side, roll up rectangle, jelly-roll fashion. Pinch seam and ends to seal.

Place seam-side down in greased 9x5x3" loaf pan. Cover and let rise until doubled, about 1 hour and 10 minutes.

In small bowl, mix together egg white and water. Brush loaf with egg white mixture; sprinkle with reserved 2 tsp. cinnamon mixture.

Bake in 375° oven 30 to 40 minutes, or until loaf is golden brown and sounds hollow when tapped. Immediately remove from pan. Cool on rack. Makes 1 loaf.

Houska

*An Iowa woman of Czechoslovakian descent makes this braided loaf
at Christmastime just as her mother did.*

> ½ recipe Sweet Dough, or
>   ½ recipe Coolrise Sweet Dough, or
>   1 recipe Shortcut Sweet Dough
> ½ c. golden raisins
> ½ c. chopped almonds
> ¼ c. chopped, candied cherries
> ¼ c. chopped, candied pineapple
> 1 egg
> 1 tblsp. water

Prepare desired Sweet Dough, stirring raisins, almonds, cherries
and pineapple into dough before kneading. Let rise or rest as
directed.

Divide dough into fourths. On lightly floured surface, roll each
fourth into a 12"-long rope. Braid 3 ropes; pinch ends to seal.
Place braid on greased large baking sheet.

Divide remaining rope into thirds. Roll each third into a
14"-long rope. Braid ropes; pinch ends together. Carefully place
small braid on top of the large braid; tuck ends of top braid under
bottom braid, stretching top braid if necessary.

Cover and let rise until doubled, about 1 hour.

In small bowl, mix together egg and water. Brush loaf with egg
mixture.

Bake in 350° oven 30 to 35 minutes, or until loaf is golden
brown and sounds hollow when tapped. Immediately remove from
baking sheet. Cool on rack. Makes 1 large loaf.

Date Nut Coffeecake

Looks very tempting—you make cuts in this S-shaped bread before baking so that the filling peeks through the finished crust.

> ½ recipe Sweet Dough, or
> > ½ recipe Coolrise Sweet Dough, or
> > 1 recipe Shortcut Sweet Dough
>
> Date Nut Filling (recipe follows)
> Quick Vanilla Glaze (see Index)

Prepare desired Sweet Dough. Let rise or rest as directed. Prepare Date Nut Filling.

On lightly floured surface with floured rolling pin, roll out dough into a 20x18″ rectangle.

Reserve ⅓ c. filling; set aside. Spread remaining filling, lengthwise in a 3″-wide strip, down center of rectangle. With scissors or sharp knife, cut dough on both sides of filling from edge of dough to filling at 2″ intervals.

Alternately bring up strips from opposite sides, crossing them over filling and tucking the ends underneath dough.

Arrange filled dough in an S shape. Place on greased large baking sheet. Spoon reserved ⅓ c. filling into open spaces between the crossed dough strips.

Cover and let rise until doubled, about 45 minutes.

Bake in 350° oven 30 to 35 minutes, or until coffeecake is golden brown and sounds hollow when tapped. Immediately remove from baking sheet. Cool on rack 10 minutes.

Meanwhile, prepare Quick Vanilla Glaze; drizzle over warm coffeecake. Serve warm. Makes 1 large coffeecake.

DATE NUT FILLING: In 2-qt. saucepan over medium-high heat, stir together 1 (8-oz.) pkg. pitted dates, chopped, 1 c. chopped pecans, ⅔ c. water, ¼ c. packed brown sugar and 1 tblsp. lemon juice. Cook, stirring constantly, until mixture boils and thickens. Remove from heat; cool. Makes about 2 c.

Apricot Coffee Braids

Attractively braided and dusted with sugar, these loaves hold a surprise: When sliced, they reveal a golden apricot filling.

¾ c. dried apricot halves
1½ c. water
⅓ c. sugar
¾ tsp. ground ginger
½ recipe Sweet Dough, or
   ½ recipe Coolrise Sweet Dough, or
   1 recipe Shortcut Sweet Dough
1 tblsp. butter or regular margarine, melted
Confectioners' sugar

In 2-qt. saucepan over high heat, bring apricots and water to a boil. Reduce heat to medium. Simmer, uncovered, until apricots are very tender, about 15 minutes. Drain apricots and mash well. Stir in sugar and ginger. Cool; set aside.

Prepare desired Sweet Dough. Let rise or rest as directed.

Divide dough in half. On lightly floured surface, roll out one half into a 14x9" rectangle. Cut lengthwise into 3 (14x3") strips. Spread 2 tblsp. of the apricot mixture lengthwise, down the center of 1 strip. Bring the lengthwise edges of the strip up over the filling and pinch together to form a rope. Repeat with remaining 2 strips of dough.

Place ropes, seam-side down, on greased baking sheet; braid together. Pinch together ends and tuck under braid. Repeat with remaining dough and apricot filling, placing second braid on another greased baking sheet.

Cover and let rise in warm place until doubled, 45 minutes to 1 hour.

Bake in 375° oven 25 to 30 minutes, or until braids are golden brown and sound hollow when tapped. Immediately remove from baking sheets. Cool on racks 10 minutes.

Brush warm braids with melted butter and generously sift confectioners' sugar over tops. Serve warm. Makes 2 braids.

Coconut-Almond Ring Twist

This beautiful yeast coffeecake is delicately flavored with a filling of toasted coconut and almonds, plus a hint of lemon.

1 recipe Shortcut Sweet Dough
⅓ c. coconut, toasted
⅓ c. finely chopped, toasted almonds
⅓ c. sugar
1 tblsp. lemon juice
1 tblsp. butter or regular margarine, melted
1 egg white
1 tblsp. water

Prepare Shortcut Sweet Dough. Let rest as directed.

In small bowl, mix together toasted coconut, toasted almonds, sugar and lemon juice until well blended; set aside.

Divide dough in half. On lightly floured surface with floured rolling pin, roll out each half into a 20x8" rectangle. Brush each rectangle with melted butter.

Sprinkle almond mixture over each rectangle to within ½" from edges. Starting with one long side, roll up each rectangle, jelly-roll fashion. Moisten seams with some water; pinch to seal.

Place ropes, seam-side down, on greased large baking sheet. Twist ropes together and shape into a tight ring; pinch together ends and tuck under.

Cover and let rise until doubled, about 45 minutes.

In small bowl, mix together egg white and water. Brush ring with egg white mixture.

Bake in 350° oven 25 to 30 minutes, or until ring is golden brown and sounds hollow when tapped. Immediately remove from baking sheet. Cool on rack. Makes 1 coffeecake.

Mincemeat Coffee Breads

Spread with citrus-flavored frosting, these long, narrow loaves with their savory filling are a natural for holiday breakfasts.

½ recipe Sweet Dough, or
   ½ recipe Coolrise Sweet Dough, or
   1 recipe Shortcut Sweet Dough
3 c. prepared mincemeat
Lemon-Orange Butter Frosting
   (recipe follows)
⅓ c. chopped walnuts
¼ c. sliced maraschino cherries, drained

Prepare desired Sweet Dough. Let rise or rest as directed.

Divide dough into fourths. On lightly floured surface with floured rolling pin, roll out each fourth into a 12x7" rectangle. Spread ¾ c. mincemeat, lengthwise in a 3½"-wide strip, down center of each rectangle. Bring long sides of each rectangle up over mincemeat; pinch seams and ends to seal.

Place loaves, seam-side down, 3" apart, on greased large baking sheets. Cut crosswise slashes on top of each loaf, 2" long and 1½" apart.

Cover and let rise until doubled, about 45 minutes to 1 hour.

Bake in 350° oven 25 minutes, or until loaves are golden brown and sound hollow when tapped. Immediately remove from baking sheets. Cool on racks 10 minutes.

Meanwhile, prepare Lemon-Orange Butter Frosting; frost tops of warm loaves. Sprinkle with walnuts and cherries. Serve warm. Makes 4 loaves.

LEMON-ORANGE BUTTER FROSTING: In bowl stir together 3 c. sifted confectioners' sugar, ¼ c. butter or regular margarine, softened, 2 tsp. lemon juice, 2 tsp. orange juice, ½ tsp. grated lemon rind and ½ tsp. grated orange rind until smooth and creamy. If frosting is too stiff, stir in additional orange juice, 1 tsp. at a time, until thin enough to spread.

Easter Egg Bread

Show off your children's colorfully painted Easter eggs in a sweet coffee ring. The eggs cook as the dough bakes.

> 6 uncooked eggs in shell
> Easter egg color
> ½ recipe Sweet Dough, or
>   ½ recipe Coolrise Sweet Dough, or
>   1 recipe Shortcut Sweet Dough
> 1 egg yolk
> 1 tblsp. milk

Carefully wash uncooked eggs. Tint shells with egg color and set aside to dry.

Prepare desired Sweet Dough. Let rise or rest as directed.

Divide dough in half. On lightly floured surface, roll each half into a 36"-long rope.

Place ropes, side by side, on greased large baking sheet. Loosely twist together ropes, leaving 6 spaces for eggs; pinch together ends to form a ring. Place 1 egg in each space.

Cover and let rise until doubled, about 1 hour.

In small bowl, mix together egg yolk and milk. Brush ring with egg yolk mixture.

Bake in 375° oven 20 minutes, or until ring is golden brown and sounds hollow when tapped. Immediately remove from baking sheet. Cool on rack. Makes 1 large coffee ring.

Grecian Feast Loaf

This handsome currant bread, scented with lemon and mace, is traditionally served at Easter and Christmas in Greek homes both here and abroad. Three small rounds of dough are baked together to form a single three-petaled loaf that symbolizes the Trinity.

> ½ recipe Sweet Dough, or
>   ½ recipe Coolrise Sweet Dough, or
>   1 recipe Shortcut Sweet Dough
> ⅔ c. currants
> 2 tsp. grated lemon rind
> ¼ tsp. ground mace
> 1 egg yolk
> 1 tblsp. water

Prepare desired Sweet Dough, stirring currants, lemon rind and mace into dough before kneading. Let rise or rest as directed.

Divide dough into thirds. Shape each third into a smooth ball. Arrange on greased baking sheet to form a three-leaf clover, leaving ¾" space between balls of dough.

Cover and let rise until doubled, about 1 hour.

In small bowl, mix together egg yolk and water. Brush loaf with egg yolk mixture.

Bake in 350° oven 25 to 30 minutes, or until loaf is browned and sounds hollow when tapped. Immediately remove from baking sheet. Cool on rack. Makes 1 loaf.

Daisy Coffee Breads

Pull apart these flower-shaped coffeecakes into individual rolls; each has its own apricot-filled center.

½ recipe Sweet Dough, or
  ½ recipe Coolrise Sweet Dough, or
  1 recipe Shortcut Sweet Dough
Golden Apricot Filling (recipe follows)
Quick Vanilla Glaze (recipe follows)

Prepare desired Sweet Dough. Let rise or rest as directed. Prepare Golden Apricot Filling.

Divide dough in half. On lightly floured surface with floured rolling pin, roll out one half into a 14x7" rectangle. Cut into 14 (7x1") strips. Twist 2 strips together and wind into a coil. Repeat with remaining strips.

Place 1 coil in center of greased baking sheet. Arrange the remaining coils around the center coil to form a flower shape. Repeat with remaining dough half, placing coils on another greased baking sheet.

Cover and let rise until doubled, about 40 to 50 minutes.

Make a depression in center of each coil. Fill each depression with Golden Apricot Filling.

Bake in 350° oven 25 minutes, until breads are golden brown and sound hollow when tapped. Immediately remove from baking sheets. Cool on racks 10 minutes.

Meanwhile, prepare Quick Vanilla Glaze; drizzle over warm breads. Serve warm. Makes 2 coffee breads.

GOLDEN APRICOT FILLING: In 2-qt. saucepan over high heat, bring 1 c. chopped dried apricots and ½ c. water to a boil. Reduce heat to medium. Cover and cook until apricots are tender, about 5 minutes. Remove from heat. Add 2 tblsp. butter or regular margarine and mash well. Stir in ¾ c. sugar; cool. Makes about 1 c.

QUICK VANILLA GLAZE: In small bowl stir 1¼ c. sifted confectioners' sugar, 4½ tsp. milk and ¼ tsp. vanilla until smooth.

Potica

A spiral-shaped coffee ring that's filled with a mix of poppy seed, honey and a squeeze of fresh lemon juice. Serve this native Yugoslavian bread lightly dusted with confectioners' sugar.

> ½ recipe Sweet Dough, or
>   ½ recipe Coolrise Sweet Dough
> 1 c. water
> ½ c. poppy seed
> ⅓ c. ground walnuts
> ¼ tsp. ground cinnamon
> 2 tblsp. honey
> 1 tsp. lemon juice
> 1 egg
> 1 egg yolk
> 1 tblsp. milk

Prepare desired Sweet Dough. Let rise or rest as directed.

Meanwhile, in 1-qt. saucepan over high heat, bring water and poppy seed to a boil. Remove from heat. Cover and let stand 30 minutes. Place poppy seed mixture in cheesecloth-lined strainer; press out as much liquid as possible.

In medium bowl, stir together drained poppy seed, walnuts and cinnamon.

In small bowl, mix together honey, lemon juice and egg. Stir honey mixture into poppy seed mixture; set aside.

On lightly floured surface with floured rolling pin, roll out dough into a 20x12" rectangle. Spread poppy seed mixture to within ½" from edges. Starting with one long side, tightly roll up, jelly-roll fashion; pinch seam to seal.

Place roll, seam-side down, on greased large baking sheet. Shape roll into a flat coil.

Cover and let rise until doubled, about 1 hour.

In small bowl, mix together egg yolk and milk. Brush coil with egg yolk mixture.

Bake in 350° oven 25 to 30 minutes, or until coffee ring is golden brown and sounds hollow when tapped. Immediately remove from baking sheet. Cool on rack. Makes 1 large coffee ring.

Swedish Tea Rings

Filled with colorful bits of candied fruit, these festive wreaths make inviting centerpieces for any breakfast table.

½ recipe Sweet Dough, or
   ½ recipe Coolrise Sweet Dough, or
   1 recipe Shortcut Sweet Dough
½ c. butter or regular margarine
2 tsp. grated lemon rind
½ c. sugar
1 c. ground almonds
1½ c. chopped, mixed candied fruit
2 tblsp. water
2 tblsp. sugar

Prepare desired Sweet Dough. Let rise or rest as directed.

In small bowl using mixer at medium speed, beat together butter, lemon rind and ½ c. sugar. Add almonds and beat until well blended; set aside.

Divide dough in half. On lightly floured surface with floured rolling pin, roll out one half into a 14x10" rectangle. Spread rectangle with half of the almond mixture to within ½" from edges. Sprinkle with half of the candied fruit. Starting with one long side, roll up rectangle, jelly-roll fashion. Pinch seam to seal.

Place roll, seam-side down, on a greased baking sheet. Shape into a ring; pinch together ends to seal. With scissors, cut from outside edge of ring three quarters of the way through towards the center at 1" intervals. Turn each cut piece on its side.

Repeat with remaining dough half, almond mixture and candied fruit. Cover and let rise in warm place until doubled, about 45 minutes to 1 hour.

Bake in 350° oven 30 minutes, or until tea rings are golden brown and sound hollow when tapped. Immediately remove from baking sheets. Place on racks.

In small bowl, mix together water and 2 tblsp. sugar. Immediately brush sugar mixture over hot tea rings; cool slightly. Serve warm. Makes 2 tea rings.

Coconut Macaroon Coffeecake

So rich, you could even make this for dessert. It serves up nicely, too, because it's baked in a springform pan.

1 recipe Shortcut Sweet Dough
1 (8-oz.) pkg. cream cheese
¼ c. sugar
½ tsp. almond extract
1 egg
1⅓ c. coconut, toasted
1 egg white, slightly beaten
½ c. sliced almonds

Prepare Shortcut Sweet Dough. Let rest as directed.

Meanwhile, in small bowl, using mixer at medium speed, beat cream cheese, sugar, almond extract and egg until well blended. Stir in toasted coconut. Cover and set aside.

With floured hands, pat three fourths of the dough into bottom and halfway up side of greased 10″ springform pan. Spread cream cheese mixture to within ½″ from edge.

On lightly floured surface with floured rolling pin, roll remaining one-fourth dough into a 9½″ circle. Roll dough loosely around rolling pin; unroll over filling. Pinch together edges to seal.

Cover and let rise until doubled, about 1 hour.

Brush dough with beaten egg white; sprinkle with almonds.

Bake in 350° oven 45 minutes, or until coffeecake is golden brown and sounds hollow when tapped. Cool in pan on rack 10 minutes. With metal spatula, loosen coffeecake from pan. Remove side of pan. Cool on rack. Makes 1 coffeecake.

Cherry Swirl

A ring-shaped coffeecake that's good any time of year. We've included a heart-shaped variation for your special Valentine; use cherry, red raspberry or strawberry preserves for the filling.

> ½ recipe Sweet Dough, or
> ½ recipe Coolrise Sweet Dough
> 1 (10-oz.) jar cherry preserves
> ½ c. chopped pecans
> Thin Confectioners' Glaze (recipe follows)

Prepare desired Sweet Dough. Let rise or rest as directed.

In small bowl, stir together preserves and pecans; set aside.

Divide dough in half. On lightly floured surface with floured rolling pin, roll out each half into a 18x10" rectangle. Spread preserve mixture on each rectangle to within 2" from edges.

Starting with one long side, roll up each rectangle, jelly-roll fashion; pinch seams and ends to seal. Place rolls on greased large baking sheet. Twist together rolls and shape into a ring; pinch ends together and tuck under.

Cover and let rise until doubled, about 1 hour.

Bake in 375° oven 25 to 30 minutes, or until ring is golden brown and sounds hollow when tapped. Immediately remove from baking sheet. Cool on rack.

Meanwhile, prepare Thin Confectioners' Glaze; drizzle over cooled ring. Makes 1 large coffeecake.

THIN CONFECTIONERS' GLAZE: In small bowl, mix 1 c. sifted confectioners' sugar, 1 tblsp. butter or regular margarine, melted, and 1 to 2 tblsp. milk until smooth and thin enough to drizzle. If you wish, add red food color to tint glaze.

CHERRY HEARTS: Prepare and shape rolls as directed. Place each roll in center of a greased large baking sheet. Lightly mark center of 1 roll with finger then, bring each end up and around to make a heart shape. Pinch together ends to seal. Repeat with remaining roll. Continue as directed. Makes 2 heart-shaped loaves.

Cinnamon Raisin Buns

Even the strong-willed won't be able to resist these extra-special sweet rolls. They're baked with a topping of brown sugar and heavy cream, then drizzled with creamy icing.

½ recipe Sweet Dough, or
  ½ recipe Coolrise Sweet Dough, or
  1 recipe Shortcut Sweet Dough
1 c. raisins
1 c. packed brown sugar
3 tsp. ground cinnamon
1 tblsp. butter or regular margarine, melted
½ c. heavy cream
¼ tsp. vanilla
Creamy Confectioners' Sugar Icing (recipe follows)

Prepare desired Sweet Dough kneading in raisins. Let dough rise or rest as directed.

Divide dough in half. Cover and let rest 10 minutes.

In small bowl, mix together ¾ c. brown sugar and 2½ tsp. cinnamon.

On lightly floured surface with floured rolling pin, roll out each half into a 12x8″ rectangle. Brush each rectangle with melted butter, sprinkle with brown sugar mixture and gently pat down. Starting with one long side, roll up each rectangle, jelly-roll fashion. Pinch seams to seal. Cut each roll into 12 slices.

Place slices, cut-side down, in 2 greased 9x9x2″ baking pans. Cover and let rise until doubled, about 45 minutes.

Meanwhile, in small bowl, stir together cream, vanilla, ¼ c. brown sugar and ½ tsp. cinnamon. Pour cream mixture evenly over raised slices.

Bake in 375° oven 25 minutes, or until buns are browned and sound hollow when tapped. Immediately remove from pans. Cool, top-side up, on racks 10 minutes.

Meanwhile, prepare Creamy Confectioners' Sugar Icing; drizzle over warm buns. Serve warm. Makes 24 buns.

CREAMY CONFECTIONERS' SUGAR ICING: In small bowl, stir 1½ c. sifted confectioners' sugar, 2 tblsp. butter or regular margarine, melted, 5 tsp. milk and ½ tsp. vanilla until smooth.

Kolaches

These Czechoslovakian sweet buns can have many different fillings. We've included apricot and prune, but you could use ready-made fruit, poppy seed or nut fillings.

½ recipe Sweet Dough, or
   ½ recipe Coolrise Sweet Dough, or
   1 recipe Shortcut Sweet Dough
Prune Filling (recipe follows), or
   Apricot Filling (recipe follows)
Confectioners' sugar

Prepare desired Sweet Dough. Let rise or rest as directed. Prepare desired Filling.

Divide dough in half. On lightly floured surface with floured rolling pin, roll out each half into a 12" square. Cut dough into 9 (4") squares. Place squares, 2" apart, on greased large baking sheets. Place 1 rounded tblsp. filling in center of each square. Fold 2 opposite corners of each square over the filling, overlapping 1"; pinch to seal.

Cover with towel and let rise until doubled, about 45 minutes.

Bake in 350° oven 15 to 20 minutes, or until kolaches are golden brown and sound hollow when tapped. Immediately remove from baking sheets. Cool on racks. Sift confectioners' sugar over tops of kolaches. Makes 18 kolaches.

PRUNE FILLING: In 2-qt. saucepan over high heat, bring 2 c. water and 2 c. chopped, dried, pitted prunes to a boil. Reduce heat to medium. Cover and cook 8 minutes, or until prunes are tender. Drain.

In food processor bowl with metal blade, place drained, cooked prunes. Add ½ c. sugar. Cover and process until smooth. Makes 1¾ c.

APRICOT FILLING: Substitute 2 c. chopped, dried apricots for prunes. Cook, drain and process as directed. Makes 1¾ c.

ROUND KOLACHES: Prepare desired Sweet Dough and Filling. Divide dough into 18 pieces. With greased hands, shape into balls. Place balls, 3" apart, on greased large baking sheets. Cover and let rise as directed. Make a depression in center of each ball. Spoon 1 rounded tblsp. filling into each depression. Continue as directed.

Apricot-Prune Pinwheels

Make these attractive pinwheel-shaped buns for breakfast.

½ recipe Sweet Dough, or
   ½ recipe Coolrise Sweet Dough, or
   1 recipe Shortcut Sweet Dough
3 c. water
¾ c. chopped, dried pitted prunes
¾ c. chopped, dried apricots
¼ c. finely chopped walnuts
⅓ c. sugar
1 egg white, slightly beaten
Sugar

Prepare desired Sweet Dough. Let rise or rest as directed.

Meanwhile, in 2-qt. saucepan over high heat, bring water to a boil. Add prunes and apricots. Reduce heat to low. Cover and cook about 10 minutes, or until fruit is tender; drain.

In medium bowl, stir together drained fruit, walnuts and ⅓ c. sugar; set aside.

Divide dough in half. On lightly floured surface with floured rolling pin, roll out each half into a 15x10" rectangle. Cut each into 6 (5") squares. Place 6 squares on each of 2 greased large baking sheets.

Spoon 1 rounded tblsp. filling into center of each square. With scissors, diagonally cut dough from each corner to within ½" from filling.

Fold every other point towards the center, overlapping points and pinching to seal.

Cover and let rise until doubled, about 1 hour.

Brush each pinwheel with beaten egg white. Sprinkle with sugar.

Bake in 350° oven 15 to 18 minutes, or until pinwheels are golden brown and sound hollow when tapped. Immediately remove from baking sheets. Cool on racks. Makes 12 pinwheels.

Orange Twists

To vary the flavor of these individual sweet treats, use grated lemon rind instead of orange rind, or try a mix of both.

> ½ recipe Sweet Dough, or
> ½ recipe Coolrise Sweet Dough, or
> 1 recipe Shortcut Sweet Dough
> 1 c. sugar
> 2 tblsp. grated orange rind
> ¼ c. butter or regular margarine, softened

Prepare desired Sweet Dough. Let rise or rest as directed.

In small bowl, stir together sugar and orange rind; set aside.

Divide dough in half. On lightly floured surface with floured rolling pin, roll out one half into a 16x12" rectangle. Spread 1 tblsp. softened butter, lengthwise, in a 4"-wide strip, down center of rectangle. Sprinkle with one fourth of the sugar mixture.

Fold one third of the rectangle lengthwise over the buttered and sugared portion of the rectangle. Spread the top of this portion with 1 tblsp. softened butter and sprinkle with one fourth of the sugar mixture.

Fold the remaining third of the rectangle over the buttered and sugared portion. Pinch to seal lengthwise edge. Repeat with remaining dough half, softened butter and sugar mixture.

Cut each folded rectangle crosswise into 16 strips. Twist each strip twice. Place, 2" apart, on greased baking sheets. Cover and let rise until doubled, about 45 minutes.

Bake in 375° oven 15 minutes, or until twists are golden brown and sound hollow when tapped. Immediately remove from baking sheets. Serve warm. Makes 32 twists.

ORANGE TWIST COFFEE BREADS: Prepare and shape twists as directed. Place 16 twisted strips in each of 2 greased 9x9x2" baking pans.

Cover and let rise until doubled, about 1 hour.

Bake in 375° oven 25 to 30 minutes, or until breads are golden brown and sound hollow when tapped. Immediately remove from pans. Serve warm. Makes 2 coffee breads.

Rhubarb Coffeecake

Fresh rhubarb spiced with cinnamon is the rosy filling in this lattice-topped yeast cake. It's best when served warm.

> 1 pkg. active dry yeast
> ¼ tsp. sugar
> ¼ c. warm water (105 to 115°)
> ½ c. milk
> 2 tblsp. butter or regular margarine, melted
> 1 tsp. salt
> 1 egg
> 3 c. sifted flour
> ½ c. sugar
> 4 tsp. flour
> 2½ c. diced rhubarb (¾ lb.)
> 3 tblsp. water
> 1 tsp. ground cinnamon
> ⅓ c. sugar
> 1 tblsp. butter or regular margarine, melted

In large bowl, sprinkle yeast, and ¼ tsp. sugar over warm water; stir until dissolved. Add milk, melted butter, salt, egg, 1 c. flour and ¼ c. sugar.

Using mixer at low speed, beat until well blended. Increase speed to medium; beat 2 minutes. Add ½ c. flour. Increase speed to high; beat 2 minutes more.

Stir in remaining 1½ c. flour to make a soft dough. Turn out dough onto lightly floured surface. Knead until smooth and elastic, about 5 minutes. Cover with towel and let rest 15 minutes.

Meanwhile, in 2-qt. saucepan, stir together ¼ c. sugar and 4 tsp. flour. Stir in rhubarb and 3 tblsp. water. Over high heat, bring to a boil, stirring occasionally. Reduce heat to low. Cover and simmer 5 to 8 minutes, or until rhubarb is tender. Remove from heat; set aside.

In small bowl, mix together cinnamon and ⅓ c. sugar; set aside.

Press three fourths of the dough into bottom and halfway up sides of greased 13x9x2" baking pan. Brush with 1 tblsp. melted butter. Sprinkle with half of the cinnamon mixture. Spread rhubarb mixture evenly over dough.

With lightly floured rolling pin, roll out remaining dough into a 9" square. With fluted pastry wheel, cut dough into 12 (9x¾") strips.

Place half of the strips, about 1" apart, over rhubarb. Repeat with remaining strips, placing them in the opposite direction, forming a diamond or square pattern. Sprinkle remaining cinnamon mixture over top.

Cover and let rise in warm place until doubled, about 25 minutes.

Bake in 350° oven 35 minutes, or until coffeecake is golden brown. Cool in pan on rack 10 minutes. Serve warm. Makes 1 coffeecake.

Relay Farm Coffeecakes

The dairy farmer's wife who shared this recipe likes to double the ingredients and shape the dough into six ring-shaped cakes.

>2 pkg. active dry yeast
>1 tsp. sugar
>½ c. warm water (105 to 115°)
>1½ c. milk
>½ c. shortening
>½ c. honey
>2 tsp. salt
>7 to 7½ c. sifted flour
>2 eggs
>Walnut Filling (recipe follows)
>2 recipes Confectioners' Sugar Icing (see Index)

In large bowl, sprinkle yeast and sugar over warm water; stir until dissolved. Set aside.

In 2-qt. saucepan over low heat, heat milk, shortening, honey and salt until warm (105 to 115°).

Using mixer at low speed, beat milk mixture and 3 c. flour into yeast mixture until well blended. Add eggs. Increase speed to medium; beat 2 minutes.

Stir in enough additional flour to make a soft dough. Turn out dough onto lightly floured surface. Knead until smooth and elastic, about 10 minutes.

Place in greased large bowl, turning over dough so that top is greased. Cover with towel and let rise in warm place until doubled, about 1 hour 30 minutes.

Punch down dough. Divide into 6 pieces. Cover and let rest 10 minutes. Meanwhile, prepare Walnut Filling.

On lightly floured surface with floured rolling pin, roll out one piece into a 26x4″ rectangle. Sprinkle with one sixth of the filling. Starting with one long side, roll up each rectangle. Pinch seam to seal. Repeat with remaining pieces and filling.

Coil 1 rope in center of greased large baking sheet. Continue coiling 2 more ropes around first coil. Repeat with remaining 3 ropes on another baking sheet. With scissors, cut slits, 1″ apart, in top of coils.

Cover and let rise until doubled, about 1 hour.

Bake in 375° oven 20 minutes, or until coffeecakes are golden brown and sound hollow when tapped. Immediately remove from baking sheets. Cool on racks.

Prepare Confectioners' Sugar Icing; drizzle over cooled coffeecakes. Makes 2 coffeecakes.

WALNUT FILLING: In small bowl, mix together 1 c. packed brown sugar, ½ c. chopped walnuts and 2 tsp. ground cinnamon.

Sunburst Coffeecakes

Elegant-looking—orange and coconut crescent rolls bake in round cake pans to form two sunburst shapes. The dough rises just once.

1 pkg. active dry yeast
1 tsp. salt
¼ c. sugar
3½ c. sifted flour
1 c. milk
¼ c. butter or regular margarine
1 egg
½ c. coconut, toasted
2 tsp. grated orange rind
½ c. sugar
2 tblsp. butter or regular margarine, melted
Orange Glaze (recipe follows)

In large bowl, stir together yeast, salt, ¼ c. sugar and 1½ c. flour; set aside.

In 1-qt. saucepan over low heat, heat milk and ¼ c. butter until very warm (120 to 130°).

Using mixer at low speed, gradually beat milk mixture into yeast mixture until well blended. Increase speed to medium; beat

2 minutes. Add egg and ½ c. flour; beat 2 minutes more.

Stir in remaining flour until well blended and a firm dough forms. Cover with towel and let rest 15 minutes.

In small bowl, stir together toasted coconut, orange rind and ½ c. sugar; set aside.

Turn out dough onto lightly floured surface. Knead 1 minute, or until dough is no longer sticky, adding additional flour if necessary. Divide dough in half.

With floured rolling pin, roll out each half into a 12″ circle. Brush both circles with melted butter. Sprinkle coconut mixture evenly over each circle.

Cut each circle into 12 wedges. Roll up each wedge, starting at the wide end. Place rolled wedges, points down, in 2 greased 9″ round baking pans. Curve the ends gently to form crescents.

Cover and let rise in warm place until doubled, about 45 minutes.

Bake in 375° oven 20 minutes, or until coffeecakes are golden brown and sound hollow when tapped. Carefully remove from pans. Cool on racks 10 minutes.

Meanwhile, prepare Orange Glaze; drizzle over warm coffeecakes. Serve warm. Makes 2 coffeecakes.

ORANGE GLAZE: In medium bowl, mix 2 c. sifted confectioners' sugar, 1 tsp. grated orange rind and 2 to 3 tblsp. orange juice until smooth and thin enough to drizzle.

Orange-Nut Glazed Raisin Bread

Makes two flavorful, raisin-studded loaves—drizzled with a sweet orange-and-walnut glaze.

> 2 pkg. active dry yeast
> ½ c. sugar
> 1 tsp. salt
> 1 tsp. ground ginger
> 5 to 6 c. sifted flour
> 1¼ c. milk
> ½ c. butter or regular margarine
> 2 eggs
> 1 tsp. grated orange rind
> 1½ c. raisins
> Orange-Nut Glaze (recipe follows)

In large bowl, stir together yeast, sugar, salt, ginger and 1½ c. flour; set aside.

In 2-qt. saucepan over low heat, heat milk and butter until very warm (120 to 130°).

Using mixer at low speed, gradually beat milk mixture into yeast mixture until well blended. Increase speed to medium; beat 2 minutes. Add eggs, orange rind and 1½ c. flour. Increase speed to high; beat 2 minutes more.

Stir in raisins and enough additional flour to make a moderately soft dough. Turn out dough onto lightly floured surface. Knead just until smooth, about 3 minutes.

Place in greased large bowl, turning over dough so that top is greased. Cover with towel and let rise in warm place until doubled, about 1 hour.

Punch down dough. Divide dough in half. Cover and let rest 15 minutes.

On lightly floured surface with floured rolling pin, roll out each half into a 16x8" rectangle.

Starting with one short side, roll up each rectangle, jelly-roll fashion. Pinch seam and ends to seal.

Place each roll, seam-side down, in greased 9x5x3" loaf pan. Cover and let rise until doubled, about 1 hour.

Diagonally slash each loaf, crosswise, 3 times.

Bake in 375° oven 25 minutes. Cover loosely with foil; bake 15 to 20 minutes more, or until loaves are browned and and sound hollow when tapped. Immediately remove from pans. Place on racks.

Immediately prepare Orange-Nut Glaze; spread over tops of warm loaves. Cool on racks. Makes 2 loaves.

ORANGE-NUT GLAZE: In small bowl, stir together 1 c. sifted confectioners' sugar, ½ c. finely chopped walnuts and 2 tsp. butter or regular margarine, softened. Stir in 2 to 4 tblsp. orange juice until glaze is thin enough to spread.

Butter Crescents

Plain or filled with a mix of peanut butter and honey, these sweet rolls can easily be reheated and served for breakfast.

1 pkg. active dry yeast
1 tsp. sugar
½ c. warm water (105 to 115°)
½ c. milk
½ tsp. salt
1 egg
½ c. butter or regular margarine, melted
¼ c. sugar
4¼ to 4¾ c. sifted flour
3 tblsp. butter or regular margarine, melted

In large bowl, sprinkle yeast and 1 tsp. sugar over warm water; stir until dissolved. Add milk, salt, egg, ½ c. melted butter, ¼ c. sugar and 2 c. flour.

Using mixer at low speed, beat until well blended. Increase speed to medium; beat 2 minutes.

Stir in enough additional flour to make a soft dough. Turn out dough onto lightly floured surface. Knead until smooth and elastic, about 5 minutes.

Place in greased large bowl, turning over dough so that top is greased. Cover with towel and let rise in warm place until doubled, about 1 hour.

Punch down dough. Divide dough in half. Cover and let rest 10 minutes.

On lightly floured surface with floured rolling pin, roll out each half into a 12" circle. Brush both circles with 3 tblsp. melted butter. Cut each circle into 12 wedges.

Roll up each wedge, starting at the wide end. Place rolled wedges, points down, 2" apart, on greased large baking sheets. Curve the ends gently to form crescents.

Cover and let rise until doubled, about 30 minutes.

Bake in 400° oven 12 to 15 minutes, or until crescents are golden brown and sound hollow when tapped. Immediately remove from baking sheets. Serve warm. Makes 24 crescents.

PEANUT BUTTER CRESCENTS: Use only ½ c. melted butter. In small bowl, mix ⅓ c. peanut butter, ⅓ c. honey and ½ tsp. ground cinnamon until well blended. Spread each circle with peanut butter mixture before cutting into wedges.

Hot Cross Buns

These sweet cinnamon and currant buns are associated with the Lenten season and usually served on Good Friday. Each bun is topped with a cross of white icing.

> 2 pkg. active dry yeast
> ½ c. sugar
> 2 tsp. ground cinnamon
> ¾ tsp. salt
> 5¾ to 6¼ c. sifted flour
> 6 tblsp. butter or regular margarine
> 1½ c. milk
> 3 eggs
> 1¼ c. currants
> 1 egg yolk
> 2 tsp. water
> 1 c. sifted confectioners' sugar
> ½ tsp. vanilla
> 1 tblsp. milk

In large bowl, stir together yeast, sugar, cinnamon, salt and 2 c. flour; set aside.

In 2-qt. saucepan over low heat, heat butter and 1½ c. milk until very warm (120 to 130°).

Using mixer at low speed, gradually beat milk mixture into yeast mixture until well blended. Increase speed to medium; beat 2 minutes. Add 3 eggs and 1½ c. flour. Increase speed to high; beat 2 minutes more.

Stir in currants and enough additional flour to make a soft dough. Turn out dough onto lightly floured surface. Knead until smooth and elastic, about 8 to 10 minutes.

Place in greased large bowl, turning over dough so that top is greased. Cover with towel and let rise in warm place until doubled, about 50 minutes.

Punch down dough. Cover and let rest 10 minutes.

Divide dough into 24 pieces. Shape each piece into a ball. Place balls in greased 13x9x2" baking pan or 2 greased 8x8x2" baking pans.

Cover and let rise until doubled, about 35 minutes.

In small bowl, mix together egg yolk and water. Brush balls with egg yolk mixture.

Bake in 375° oven 20 to 25 minutes, or until buns are golden brown and sound hollow when tapped. Immediately remove buns from baking pan. Cool buns completely on rack.

In small bowl, stir confectioners' sugar, vanilla and 1 tblsp. milk until smooth. Drip icing from tip of spoon over center of each cooled bun to form a cross. Makes 24 buns.

Baked Doughnuts

Since these are baked, not deep-fried, don't worry about using a doughnut cutter to cut the dough; a biscuit cutter will do, because as these spiced sweet cakes rise and bake, the "holes" disappear.

2 pkg. active dry yeast
½ c. sugar
1 tsp. salt
1 tsp. ground nutmeg
½ tsp. ground cinnamon
4½ c. sifted flour
1¾ c. milk
½ c. shortening
2 eggs
¼ c. butter or regular margarine, melted
Confectioners' sugar

In large bowl, stir together yeast, sugar, salt, nutmeg, cinnamon and 2 c. flour; set aside.

In 2-qt. saucepan over low heat, heat milk and shortening until very warm (120 to 130°).

Using mixer at low speed, gradually beat milk mixture into yeast mixture until well blended. Increase speed to medium; beat 2 minutes. Add eggs and 1 c. flour. Increase speed to high; beat 2 minutes more.

Stir in remaining flour to make a soft dough. Cover tightly with plastic wrap. Refrigerate 2 to 24 hours.

On heavily floured surface with floured rolling pin, roll out dough to ½" thickness. Cut dough with floured 2¾" biscuit cutter and place, 2" apart, on greased large baking sheets.

Cover with towel and let rise in warm place until doubled, about 30 minutes.

Bake in 425° oven 10 minutes, or until doughnuts are golden brown. Immediately remove from baking sheets and brush doughnuts with melted butter. Sift confectioners' sugar over doughnuts. Serve warm. Makes 24 to 30 doughnuts.

Sweet Whirls

Spoon your favorite jam into the centers of these coiled rolls. They're flavored with orange rind and cardamom.

> 2 pkg. active dry yeast
> ½ c. sugar
> 1 tsp. salt
> ¼ tsp. ground cardamom
> 4½ to 5½ c. sifted flour
> 1¼ c. milk
> ½ c. butter or regular margarine
> 2 eggs
> 1 tsp. grated orange rind
> Quick Orange Glaze (recipe follows)
> Strawberry, cherry, raspberry or apricot jam

In large bowl, stir together yeast, sugar, salt, cardamom and 1½ c. flour; set aside.

In 2-qt. saucepan over low heat, heat milk and butter until very warm (120 to 130°).

Using mixer at low speed, gradually beat milk mixture into yeast mixture until well blended. Increase speed to medium; beat 2 minutes. Add eggs, orange rind and 1 c. flour. Increase speed to high; beat 2 minutes more.

Stir in enough additional flour to make a soft dough. Turn out dough onto lightly floured surface. Knead until smooth and elastic, about 8 minutes. Cover with towel; let rest 20 minutes.

With lightly floured rolling pin, roll out dough into a 16x8" rectangle. Cut into 16 (8x1") strips. Roll each strip into 12"-long rope. Holding one end of a rope down on greased baking sheet, wind rope into a coil; tuck end under. Repeat with remaining ropes, placing 2" apart, on greased baking sheets.

Cover and let rise in warm place until doubled, about 50 minutes.

Prepare Quick Orange Glaze; set aside. Make an indentation in center of each coil. Spoon about 1 tsp. jam into each indentation.

Bake in 375° oven 12 minutes. Brush each roll with glaze. Bake 5 minutes more, or until rolls are golden brown and sound hollow when tapped. Immediately remove from baking sheets. Cool on racks. Makes 16 rolls.

QUICK ORANGE GLAZE: In small bowl, stir together ¼ c. orange juice and 2 tblsp. sugar.

Sugar-crusted Rolls

You might guess that these flaky, rich rolls are made with a Danish pastry—but they're not!

3½ c. sifted flour
1 tsp. salt
1 c. butter or regular margarine
1 pkg. active dry yeast
¼ c. sugar
¼ c. warm water (105 to 115°)
¾ c. dairy sour cream
2 tsp. vanilla
2 eggs
½ c. sugar

Into large bowl, sift together flour and salt. With pastry blender; cut in butter until coarse crumbs form. Set aside.

In medium bowl, sprinkle yeast and ¼ c. sugar over warm water; stir until dissolved. Add sour cream, vanilla and eggs. With wire whisk, beat until well blended.

Add sour cream mixture to flour-butter mixture; stir until mixture forms a soft dough that leaves side of bowl. Cover tightly with plastic wrap. Refrigerate 12 to 24 hours.

Divide dough in half. On heavily floured surface with floured rolling pin, roll out one half into 18x12" rectangle. (Keep remaining dough refrigerated.)

Fold dough, crosswise, into thirds, making a 12x6" rectangle. Repeat rolling and folding twice more, adding flour to surface as necessary to keep dough from sticking.

Cut dough in half to make 2 (6") squares. Turn in all corners of one dough square to make a circle. Sprinkle with 2 tblsp. sugar. Roll out dough into a 12" circle. Cut circle into 8 wedges.

Roll up each wedge, starting at the wide end. Place rolled wedges, points down, 2" apart, on greased large baking sheets. Curve ends to form crescents. Repeat with remaining 6" square.

Repeat with remaining half of dough. Cover with towel and let rise in warm place until doubled, about 45 minutes.

Bake in 375° oven 12 to 15 minutes, or until rolls are golden brown and sound hollow when tapped. Immediately remove from baking sheets. Cool on racks. Makes 32 rolls.

Cinnamon-Sugar Hearts

A New York farm wife makes these crisp individual hearts especially for Valentine's Day.

1 pkg. active dry yeast
½ c. warm water (105 to 115°)
¾ c. sifted all-purpose flour
¾ c. stirred whole-wheat flour
⅛ tsp. salt
⅔ c. butter or regular margarine
1 egg yolk
1 tblsp. butter or regular margarine, melted
⅔ c. sugar
2 tsp. ground cinnamon

In small bowl, sprinkle yeast over warm water; stir until dissolved. Set aside.

In large bowl, stir together all-purpose flour, whole-wheat flour and salt. With pastry blender, cut in ⅔ c. butter until coarse crumbs form.

Stir in yeast mixture and egg yolk until well blended. Cover tightly with plastic wrap and refrigerate 2 hours or overnight.

Turn out dough onto lightly floured surface. Knead just until smooth, about 10 times. With floured rolling pin, roll out dough into a 12x10" rectangle. Brush with 1 tblsp. melted butter.

In small bowl, stir together sugar and cinnamon. Sprinkle half of the sugar mixture over buttered dough. Starting with one long side, roll up rectangle, jelly-roll fashion to center of rectangle. Then roll up opposite long side to center of rectangle. Cut into 12 slices.

Sprinkle some of the remaining sugar mixture on sheet of waxed paper. Place one slice, cut-side down, on the sugared waxed paper. Flatten slightly with palm of hand.

Roll out dough until very thin (less than ⅛" thick), turning over slice once so that both sides are sugared. As you roll slices they will resemble crude hearts. Repeat with remaining sugar mixture and slices.

Carefully place hearts, 1" apart, on ungreased baking sheets.

Bake in 400° oven 10 to 12 minutes or until golden brown. Immediately remove from baking sheets. Cool slightly on racks. Serve warm or cold. Makes 12 hearts.

Sticky Cinnamon Rolls

Heavenly—swirled with cinnamon and lightly glazed with caramel.

> 1 pkg. active dry yeast
> ¼ c. granulated sugar
> ¼ c. warm water (105 to 115°)
> ¾ c. warm milk (105 to 115°)
> ¼ c. shortening
> 1 tsp. salt
> 1 egg
> 3¼ to 3¾ c. sifted flour
> ½ c. packed brown sugar
> ½ c. light corn syrup
> 6 tblsp. butter or regular margarine, melted
> 1 tsp. ground cinnamon
> ¼ c. granulated sugar
> 2 tblsp. butter or regular margarine, melted

In large bowl, sprinkle yeast and ¼ c. granulated sugar over warm water; stir until dissolved. Add warm milk, shortening, salt, egg and 1 c. flour.

Using mixer at low speed, beat until well blended. Increase speed to high; beat 2 minutes.

Stir in enough additional flour to make a soft dough. Turn out dough onto lightly floured surface. Knead until smooth and elastic, about 5 minutes.

Place in greased large bowl, turning over dough so that top is greased. Cover with towel and let rise in warm place until doubled, about 1 hour.

Punch down dough. Cover and let rest 10 minutes. Meanwhile, in 13x9x2" baking pan, stir brown sugar, corn syrup and 6 tblsp. melted butter until well blended. In small bowl, stir together cinnamon and ¼ c. granulated sugar.

On lightly floured surface with lightly floured rolling pin, roll out dough into a 15x10" rectangle. Brush with 2 tblsp. melted butter; sprinkle with cinnamon mixture.

Starting with one long side, roll up jelly-roll fashion. Pinch seam to seal. Cut roll into 15 slices. Arrange slices, cut-side down, on top of brown sugar mixture in pan.

Cover and let rise until doubled, about 45 minutes.

Bake in 375° oven 20 to 25 minutes or until golden brown. Immediately invert rolls onto platter. Serve warm. Makes 15 rolls.

Golden Pecan Cinnamon Buns

Makes 30 light-as-a-feather, whole-wheat buns, each filled with plump golden raisins and topped with Brown Butter Icing.

> 2 pkg. active dry yeast
> 1¼ tsp. salt
> 3 c. stirred whole-wheat flour
> 2 c. boiling water
> 1½ c. golden raisins
> ⅓ c. shortening
> ⅓ c. honey
> 1 egg
> 2 c. sifted all-purpose flour
> Cinnamon Filling (recipe follows)
> ¼ c. butter or regular margarine, melted
> Brown Butter Icing (recipe follows)

In bowl, stir together yeast, salt and 2 c. whole-wheat flour.

In medium bowl, pour boiling water over raisins; let stand 5 minutes. Drain, reserving liquid. Add enough water to reserved liquid to make 1⅔ c.; cool to very warm (120 to 130°).

Using mixer at low speed, gradually beat reserved liquid into yeast mixture until well blended. Add shortening, honey and egg. Increase speed to medium; beat 2 minutes.

Stir in raisins, remaining whole-wheat flour and enough all-purpose flour to make a soft dough. Turn out dough onto lightly floured surface. Knead until smooth and elastic, 10 minutes.

Place in greased large bowl, turning over dough so that top is greased. Cover with towel and let rise in warm place until doubled, about 1 hour.

Punch down dough. Divide in half. Cover and let rest 10 minutes. Meanwhile, prepare Cinnamon Filling.

On lightly floured surface with lightly floured rolling pin, roll out each half into a 15x10" rectangle. Brush each rectangle with melted butter, then sprinkle with filling.

Starting with one long side, roll up, jelly-roll fashion. Pinch seams to seal. Cut each roll into 15 slices. Arrange slices, cut-side down, in 2 greased 13x9x2" baking pans.

Cover and let rise until doubled, about 45 minutes.

Bake in 375° oven 25 minutes, or until buns are golden brown and sound hollow when tapped. Immediately remove from pans. Cool on racks 10 minutes. Meanwhile, prepare Brown Butter Icing; drizzle over warm buns. Serve warm. Makes 30 buns.

CINNAMON FILLING: In small bowl, mix together 1¼ c. packed brown sugar, 1 c. pecan halves, ⅓ c. wheat germ and 4 tsp. ground cinnamon.

BROWN BUTTER ICING: In 1-qt. saucepan over low heat, heat 3 tblsp. butter or regular margarine until lightly browned. Remove from heat. Stir in 2 c. sifted confectioners' sugar and 3 tblsp. milk until smooth. If icing is too thick, stir in additional milk, 1 tsp. at a time, until thin enough to drizzle.

Quick Caramel Rolls

A Canadian farm wife used to make these sweet, sticky rolls as an after-school treat for her seven hungry boys.

> 2 tsp. light corn syrup
> ⅓ c. packed brown sugar
> ¼ c. butter or regular margarine
> ⅓ c. pecan halves
> 1 pkg. active dry yeast
> 1 tsp. granulated sugar
> ¾ c. warm water (105 to 115°)
> 2½ c. All-purpose Baking Mix (see Index)
> ¼ c. packed brown sugar
> 2 tblsp. butter or regular margarine, softened

In 1-qt. saucepan over medium heat, bring corn syrup, ⅓ c. brown sugar and ¼ c. butter to a boil, stirring constantly. Pour into 9" round baking pan. Sprinkle with pecan halves; set aside.

In large bowl, sprinkle yeast and granulated sugar over warm water; stir until dissolved. Stir in All-purpose Baking Mix. (Dough will be soft.) Turn out dough onto well-floured surface. Knead just until smooth, about 10 times. With well-floured rolling pin, roll out dough into a 16x9" rectangle.

In small bowl, mix together ¼ c. brown sugar and 2 tblsp. softened butter; spread over rectangle. Starting with one long side, roll up rectangle, jelly-roll fashion. Pinch together seam to seal. Cut roll into 10 slices.

Place slices, cut-side down, on top of pecan halves in pan. Cover and let rise in warm place until doubled, about 45 minutes.

Bake in 400° oven 20 to 25 minutes or until golden brown. Immediately invert rolls onto plate. Serve warm. Makes 10 rolls.

9
Extra-Special
Yeast Breads

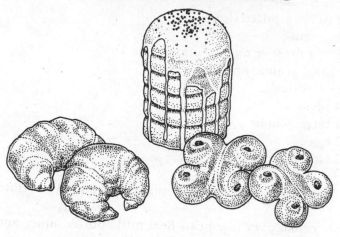

Many of the recipes in this chapter are graced with long heritages, and are made to celebrate festive occasions: sugar-topped German Stollen, fruit-studded Italian Panettone and Swedish St. Lucia Buns are all yuletide breads.

Some have traditional shapes like Kulich, Easter loaves that resemble the snow-capped domes of Russian churches; the almond-filled crescents called Bear Claws; or Giant Cinnamon Swirl, a coffeecake that one Ohio family treasures year 'round.

These showcase breads are more challenging to prepare than basic yeast breads. But, if you take your time making them, we're certain that you won't have any difficulties.

When you have the opportunity to bake, plan ahead for busy occasions. Choose a recipe, make it, and after it's baked and cooled, freeze the bread. If the bread is topped with a frosting or glaze, like braided Viennese Striezel, freeze the bread without the frosting. After the bread thaws, frost it and your guests will never know that you made it a few weeks before.

The recipe for Croissants includes ''Freeze and Bake Later'' directions. So do the recipes for Danish Twists and Danish Wreaths, making it a cinch to present fresh-baked pastries, hot from the oven, in less than 30 minutes.

So tour the world right from your own kitchen by making and sampling many of the ethnic breads on the following pages.

Holiday Bread

Each anise-flavored loaf is adorned with a twisted rope of dough.

> 2 pkg. active dry yeast
> 6 tblsp. sugar
> 1½ tsp. salt
> 7 to 7½ c. sifted flour
> ¾ c. milk
> ¾ c. butter or regular margarine
> ½ tsp. ground anise
> ½ c. water
> 4 eggs
> 1 tblsp. water
> 1 egg
> 2 tsp. sesame seed

In large bowl, stir together yeast, sugar, salt and 2½ c. flour; set aside.

In 2-qt. saucepan over low heat, heat milk, butter, anise and ½ c. water until very warm (120 to 130°).

Using mixer at low speed, gradually beat milk mixture into yeast mixture until well blended. Increase speed to medium, beat 2 minutes. Add 4 eggs and ½ c. flour; beat 2 minutes more.

Stir in enough additional flour to make a soft dough. Turn out dough onto lightly floured surface. Knead until smooth and elastic, about 8 to 10 minutes.

Place in greased large bowl, turning over dough so that top is greased. Cover with towel and let rise in warm place until doubled, about 1 hour 30 minutes.

Punch down dough. Divide dough in half. Cover and let rest 10 minutes.

Pinch off a 2"-piece of dough from each half; set aside. Shape remaining two halves into loaves. Place each loaf in greased 9x5x3" loaf pan.

Divide each 2"-piece in half. Roll each half into 9"-long rope. Twist 2 ropes together and place lengthwise across one loaf, tucking ends under. Repeat with remaining ropes.

Cover and let rise until doubled, about 1 hour.

In small bowl, mix together 1 tblsp. water and 1 egg. Brush loaves with egg mixture. Sprinkle with sesame seed.

Bake in 350° oven 50 to 55 minutes, or until loaves are golden brown and sound hollow when tapped. Remove from pans. Cool on racks. Makes 2 loaves.

Giant Cinnamon Swirl

A large, sweet, cinnamon-and-pecan coffeecake is a year 'round favorite of one Ohio family.

        1 pkg. active dry yeast
        2 tblsp. granulated sugar
        1 tsp. salt
        2¾ to 3¼ c. sifted flour
        1 c. milk
        3 tblsp. shortening
        ½ c. chopped pecans
        ¼ c. packed brown sugar
        2 tsp. ground cinnamon
        ¼ c. granulated sugar
        ¼ c. butter or regular margarine, melted

In large bowl, stir together yeast, 2 tblsp. granulated sugar, salt and 1½ c. flour; set aside.

In 1-qt. saucepan over low heat, heat milk and shortening until very warm (120 to 130°).

Using mixer at low speed, gradually beat milk mixture into yeast mixture until well blended. Increase speed to medium; beat 2 minutes.

Stir in enough additional flour to make a soft dough. Turn out dough onto lightly floured surface. Knead until smooth and elastic, about 5 minutes.

Place in greased large bowl, turning over dough so that top is greased. Cover with towel and let rise in warm place until doubled, about 1 hour.

On sheet of waxed paper, mix together pecans, brown sugar, cinnamon and ¼ c. granulated sugar; set aside.

Punch down dough. Divide dough into fourths. Cover and let rest 10 minutes.

On lightly floured surface, roll each dough piece into a 12"-long rope. Dip each rope into melted butter, then roll in pecan mixture until well coated.

Coil one rope in center of greased large baking sheet. Continue coiling remaining ropes, one at a time, around first coiled rope to make 1 giant coil.

Cover and let rise until doubled, about 1 hour.

Bake in 350° oven 30 to 35 minutes, or until coffeecake is golden brown and sounds hollow when tapped. Immediately remove from baking sheet. Serve warm. Makes 1 large coffeecake.

Kulich

The colorful iced tops of these Russian Easter breads are said to resemble the snow-capped domes of a church.

1 pkg. active dry yeast
¼ c. sugar
1 tsp. salt
1 tsp. grated lemon rind
2¾ to 3¼ c. sifted flour
½ c. milk
¼ c. water
2 tblsp. butter or regular margarine
1 egg
¼ c. chopped almonds
¼ c. raisins
Confectioners' Sugar Icing (recipe follows)
Multi-colored sprinkles

In large bowl, stir together yeast, sugar, salt, lemon rind and ¾ c. flour; set aside.

In 1-qt. saucepan over low heat, heat milk, water and butter until very warm (120 to 130°).

Using mixer at low speed, gradually beat milk mixture into yeast mixture until well blended. Increase speed to medium; beat 2 minutes. Add egg and ¾ c. flour. Increase speed to high; beat 2 minutes more.

Stir in almonds, raisins and enough additional flour to make a soft dough. Turn out dough onto lightly floured surface. Knead until smooth and elastic, about 8 to 10 minutes.

Place in greased large bowl, turning over dough so that top is greased. Cover with towel and let rise in warm place until doubled, about 1 hour.

Punch down dough. Divide dough in half. Cover and let rest 10 minutes.

Shape each half into a ball and place each in greased 1-lb. coffee can.

Cover and let rise until doubled, about 1 hour.

Bake in 350° oven 30 to 35 minutes, or until loaves are golden brown and sound hollow when tapped. Immediately remove from cans. Cool on racks.

Prepare Confectioners' Sugar Icing. Frost tops with icing, allowing icing to run down the sides. Sprinkle multi-colored sprinkles over iced loaves. Makes 2 loaves.

CONFECTIONERS' SUGAR ICING: In small bowl, stir together 1¼ c. sifted confectioners' sugar, 4 tsp. milk and ¼ tsp. almond extract until smooth and thin enough to drizzle. If icing is too thick, stir in additional milk, 1 tsp. at a time, until thin enough to drizzle.

Stollen

On Christmas morning in Germany, you'll be likely to find thin slices of this fruitcake-like bread at your breakfast table.

1 c. halved candied cherries
1 c. golden raisins
¼ c. orange juice
2 pkg. active dry yeast
½ c. granulated sugar
1 tsp. salt
¼ tsp. ground mace
5½ to 6¼ c. sifted flour
½ c. milk
½ c. water
½ c. butter or regular margarine
1 tsp. grated lemon rind
2 eggs
1 c. toasted, blanched whole almonds
2 tblsp. butter or regular margarine, melted
Confectioners' sugar

In small bowl, stir together cherries, raisins and orange juice; set aside.

In large bowl, stir together yeast, granulated sugar, salt, mace and 1½ c. flour.

In 2-qt. saucepan over low heat, heat milk, water and ½ c. butter until very warm (120 to 130°).

Using mixer at low speed, gradually beat milk mixture into yeast mixture until well blended. Increase speed to medium; beat 2 minutes. Add lemon rind, eggs and 1½ c. flour; beat 2 minutes more.

Stir in fruit mixture, almonds and enough additional flour to make a soft dough. Turn out dough onto lightly floured surface. Knead until smooth and elastic, about 5 minutes.

Place in greased large bowl, turning over dough so that top is greased. Cover with towel and let rise in warm place until doubled, about 1 hour 30 minutes.

Punch down dough. Divide dough in half. Cover and let rest 10 minutes.

On lightly floured surface with floured rolling pin, roll out each half into a 12x9″ oval. Fold each oval in half lengthwise. Place loaves, 4″ apart, on greased large baking sheet.

Cover and let rise until doubled, about 1 hour. Brush loaves with 1 tblsp. melted butter.

Bake in 350° oven 35 minutes, or until loaves are browned and sound hollow when tapped. Immediately remove from baking sheet. Cool on racks 10 minutes.

Brush warm loaves with remaining 1 tblsp. melted butter and sift confectioners' sugar over loaves. Makes 2 loaves.

Panettone

Studded with candied fruits and raisins, these Italian-inspired breads are most popular during the Christmas holidays.

> 2 pkg. active dry yeast
> ½ c. sugar
> 1 tsp. salt
> 4½ to 5½ c. sifted flour
> ½ c. milk
> ½ c. water
> ½ c. butter or regular margarine
> 3 eggs
> ½ c. mixed candied fruit
> ½ c. raisins
> 1 egg
> 1 tblsp. water

In large bowl, stir together yeast, sugar, salt and 1½ c. flour; set aside.

In 2-qt. saucepan over low heat, heat milk, ½ c. water and butter until very warm (120 to 130°).

Using mixer at low speed, gradually beat milk mixture into yeast mixture until well blended. Increase speed to medium; beat 2 minutes. Add 3 eggs and 1 c. flour. Increase speed to high; beat 2 minutes more.

Stir in candied fruit, raisins and enough additional flour to make a soft dough. Turn out dough onto lightly floured surface. Knead until smooth and elastic, about 10 minutes.

Place in greased large bowl, turning over dough so that top is greased. Cover with towel and let rise in warm place until doubled, about 1 hour.

Punch down dough. Divide dough in half. Cover and let rest 10 minutes.

Shape each half into a round loaf. Place loaves, 4" apart, on greased large baking sheet.

Cover and let rise until doubled, about 1 hour.

In small bowl, mix together 1 egg and 1 tblsp. water. Brush loaves with egg mixture.

Bake in 350° oven 30 to 35 minutes, or until loaves are golden brown and sound hollow when tapped. Immediately remove from baking sheet; cool on racks. Makes 2 loaves.

Viennese Striezel

Every country in Europe boasts of a beautiful braided loaf of yeast bread. The Viennese add raisins and candied cherries to the rich, sweet dough and then arrange it in a loaf, three braids high.

> 1 pkg. active dry yeast
> ¼ c. sugar
> ½ tsp. salt
> ¼ tsp. ground nutmeg
> 2¾ to 3 c. sifted flour
> ½ c. milk
> ¼ c. water
> 2 tblsp. shortening
> 1 egg
> ¼ c. raisins
> ¼ c. chopped candied cherries
> 2 tblsp. chopped candied orange peel
> Viennese Striezel Frosting (recipe follows)
> 2 tblsp. chopped walnuts

In large bowl, stir together yeast, sugar, salt, nutmeg and 1 c. flour; set aside.

In 1-qt. saucepan over low heat, heat milk, water and shortening until very warm (120 to 130°).

Using mixer at low speed, gradually beat milk mixture into yeast mixture until well blended. Increase speed to medium; beat 2 minutes. Add egg and ¾ c. flour. Increase speed to high, beat 2 minutes more.

Stir in raisins, cherries, orange peel and enough additional flour to make a soft dough. Turn out dough onto lightly floured surface. Knead until smooth and elastic, about 5 minutes.

Place in greased large bowl, turning over dough so that top is greased. Cover with towel and let rise in warm place until doubled, about 1 hour.

Punch down dough. Divide into 9 pieces. Cover and let rest 10 minutes.

On lightly floured surface, roll each piece into a 15"-long rope. Braid 4 ropes; pinch ends together. Place on greased large baking sheet. Make a depression lengthwise down center of braid to help keep second braid in place.

Braid 3 ropes and place in depression on top of first braid; tuck ends of top braid under bottom braid. Make another depression down center of second braid.

Braid remaining 2 ropes and place in depression on top of second braid; tuck ends of top braid under bottom braid.

Cover and let rise until doubled, about 1 hour.

Bake in 350° oven 35 to 40 minutes, or until loaf is golden brown and sounds hollow when tapped. Immediately remove from baking sheet. Cool on rack 10 minutes.

Meanwhile, prepare Viennese Striezel Frosting and frost warm loaf. Sprinkle with walnuts. Makes 1 loaf.

VIENNESE STRIEZEL FROSTING: In small bowl, stir 1 c. sifted confectioners' sugar, 4½ tsp. milk and ½ tsp. vanilla until smooth.

Azorian Sweet Bread

These lemon-flavored Portuguese egg breads are appropriate at Easter, Christmas, weddings and on other special occasions.

>3 pkg. active dry yeast
>1 c. sugar
>1½ tsp. salt
>8 to 9 c. sifted flour
>1½ c. water
>½ c. butter or regular margarine
>4 eggs
>2 tsp. grated lemon rind
>1 egg, beaten

In large bowl, stir together yeast, sugar, salt and 2½ c. flour; set aside.

In 2-qt. saucepan over low heat, heat water and butter until very warm (120 to 130°).

Using mixer at low speed, gradually beat water mixture into yeast mixture until well blended. Increase speed to medium; beat 2 minutes. Add 4 eggs, lemon rind and 2 c. flour; beat 2 minutes more.

Stir in enough additional flour to make a soft dough. Turn out dough onto lightly floured surface. Knead until smooth and elastic, about 10 minutes.

Place in greased large bowl, turning over dough so that top is greased. Cover with towel and let rise in warm place until doubled, about 1 hour 15 minutes.

Punch down dough. Divide dough in half. Cover and let rest 10 minutes.

Shape each half into a ball. Place each ball in greased 9" round baking pan. Flatten each ball slightly with hand.

Cover and let rise until doubled, about 30 minutes.

Brush each loaf with beaten egg.

Bake in 350° oven 25 to 35 minutes, or until loaves are a dark, golden brown and sound hollow when tapped. Immediately remove from pans. Cool on racks. Makes 2 loaves.

Krendel

A sweet, pretzel-shaped Russian bread that has a hint of saffron. At Christmastime, it's served with lemon tea or hot chocolate.

2 pkg. active dry yeast
½ tsp. salt
1 c. sugar
6 to 6½ c. sifted flour
1⅓ c. milk
⅓ c. butter or regular margarine
⅛ tsp. ground saffron
½ tsp. vanilla
3 eggs
1 c. golden raisins
½ c. sliced almonds
1 egg white
1 tblsp. water
2 tblsp. sugar

In large bowl, stir together, yeast, salt, 1 c. sugar and 2 c. flour.

In 2-qt. saucepan over low heat, heat milk, butter and saffron until very warm (120 to 130°).

Using mixer at low speed, gradually beat milk mixture into yeast mixture until well blended. Increase speed to medium; beat 2 minutes. Add vanilla, 3 eggs and 1 c. flour; beat 2 minutes more.

Stir in raisins, almonds and enough additional flour to make a soft dough. Turn out dough onto lightly floured surface. Knead until smooth and elastic, about 8 minutes.

Place in greased large bowl, turning over dough so that top is greased. Cover with towel and let rise in warm place until doubled, about 1 hour 30 minutes.

Punch down dough. Cover and let rest 10 minutes.

Roll dough into 48"-long rope. On greased large baking sheet holding both ends of rope, form a large loop. Twist ends of rope once, 6" from ends. Bring down ends of rope and pinch to opposite side of loop to make a pretzel shape.

Cover and let rise until doubled, about 1 hour.

In small bowl, mix together egg white and 1 tblsp. water. Brush loaf with egg white mixture. Sprinkle with 2 tblsp. sugar.

Bake in 350° oven 30 minutes. Cover loosely with foil; bake 20 to 25 minutes more, or until loaf is golden brown and sounds hollow when tapped. Immediately remove from baking sheet. Cool on rack. Makes 1 loaf.

Challah

These braided egg breads are traditionally served in Jewish homes on Friday night—the beginning of the Sabbath—and at feast times.

2 pkg. active dry yeast
⅓ c. sugar
2 tsp. salt
7 to 8 c. sifted flour
1½ c. very warm water (120 to 130°)
½ c. vegetable oil
6 eggs
1 egg yolk
1 tblsp. water
Poppy seed (optional)

In large bowl, stir together yeast, sugar, salt and 2 c. flour.

Using mixer at low speed, gradually beat in very warm water and oil until well blended. Increase speed to medium; beat 2 minutes. Add 6 eggs and 2 c. flour; beat 2 minutes more.

Stir in enough additional flour to make a soft dough. Turn out dough onto lightly floured surface. Knead until smooth and elastic, about 5 minutes.

Place in greased large bowl, turning over dough so that top is greased. Cover with towel and let rise in warm place until doubled, about 1 hour 30 minutes.

Punch down dough. Divide dough into 3 pieces. Cover and let rest 10 minutes.

Divide one piece into thirds. Roll each third into a 12"-long rope. Braid ropes; pinch ends together. Place on greased baking sheet. Repeat with another piece of dough.

Divide remaining dough into 6 pieces. Roll each piece into a 14"-long rope. Braid 3 ropes; pinch ends together. Carefully place small braid on top of one large braid; tuck ends of top braid under bottom braid, stretching top braid if necessary. Braid remaining 3 ropes and place on remaining large braid.

Cover and let rise until doubled, about 1 hour.

In small bowl, mix together egg yolk and water. Brush each loaf with egg yolk mixture. If you wish, sprinkle loaves with poppy seed.

Bake in 350° oven 30 minutes, or until loaves are golden brown and sound hollow when tapped. Immediately remove from baking sheets. Cool on racks. Makes 2 loaves.

RAISIN CHALLAH: Stir 1½ c. raisins into soft dough before kneading.

Gouda Loaves

Instead of cheese 'n' crackers for appetizers, present wedges of these cheese rounds encased in a crusty, mustard-flavored dough.

> 1 pkg. active dry yeast
> 1 tsp. sugar
> ¼ c. warm water (105 to 115°)
> ¾ c. milk
> 2 tblsp. butter or regular margarine
> 1 tblsp. Dijon mustard
> ½ tsp. salt
> 3 to 3½ c. sifted flour
> 2 (8-oz.) pkg. Gouda cheese, wax removed
> 1 egg
> 1 tblsp. water

In large bowl, sprinkle yeast and sugar over warm water; stir until dissolved. Add milk, butter, mustard, salt and 1½ c. flour.

Using mixer at low speed, beat until well blended. Increase speed to medium; beat 2 minutes.

Stir in enough additional flour to make a soft dough. Turn out dough onto lightly floured surface. Knead until smooth and elastic, about 5 minutes.

Place in greased large bowl, turning over dough so that top is greased. Cover tightly with plastic wrap. Refrigerate 2 to 24 hours.

Punch down dough. Turn out onto lightly floured surface. Knead until dough is no longer sticky, adding additional flour if necessary. Cover with towel and let rest 15 minutes.

Cut off one-sixth dough; set aside. Divide remaining dough in half. With lightly floured rolling pin, roll out each half into an 8″ circle.

Place a cheese round in center of each circle. Gather dough around cheese, pinching gathers together to seal. Place loaves, gathered-side down, 4″ apart, on greased large baking sheet.

Use remaining dough to make decorative designs, like leaves, balls or ropes, and attach to tops of loaves.

Cover and let rest in warm place 20 minutes.

In small bowl, mix together egg and water. Brush loaves with egg mixture.

Bake in 400° oven 20 to 25 minutes, or until loaves are golden brown and sound hollow when tapped. Immediately remove from baking sheet. Cool on rack at least 1 hour before slicing. Makes 2 loaves.

Swiss Bread Ring

Its filling of cheese, bacon and chopped onion makes this bread suitable for an appetizer or a main dish. Bake it in a tube pan.

> 2 pkg. active dry yeast
> 1 tblsp. sugar
> 2 tsp. salt
> 3¼ to 4¼ c. sifted flour
> 1 c. milk
> ½ c. butter or regular margarine
> 2 tblsp. Dijon mustard
> 6 slices bacon, diced
> 1 medium onion, chopped
> 1 egg
> 1 egg, separated
> 1 (8-oz.) pkg. cream cheese
> ½ lb. Swiss or Gruyère cheese, shredded (2 c.)
> Sesame seed (optional)

In large bowl, stir together yeast, sugar, salt and 1 c. flour; set aside.

In 2-qt. saucepan over low heat, heat milk, butter and mustard until very warm (120 to 130°).

Using mixer at low speed, gradually beat milk mixture into yeast mixture until well blended. Increase speed to medium; beat 2 minutes. Add 1 c. flour; beat 2 minutes more.

Stir in enough additional flour to make a soft dough. Turn out dough onto lightly floured surface. Knead until smooth and elastic, about 10 minutes. Cover with towel and let rest 15 minutes.

Meanwhile, in 10" skillet over medium-high heat, cook bacon and onion until browned. Drain bacon and onion on paper towels.

In small bowl, using mixer at medium speed, beat cream cheese, 1 egg and 1 egg yolk until smooth. Stir in bacon-onion mixture and shredded cheese until well blended.

On lightly floured surface with floured rolling pin, roll out dough into a 24x8" rectangle. Shape cheese mixture into a cylinder, lengthwise down center of dough. Fold each side of dough over cheese mixture, overlapping about 2"; pinch seam to seal.

Place roll in well-greased 10" tube pan, seam-side down and overlapping ends slightly; pinch ends to seal.

Cover and let rest in warm place 10 minutes.

In small bowl, with fork, slightly beat reserved egg white. Brush roll with egg white. Sprinkle with sesame seed.

Bake in 375° oven 1 hour, or until ring is golden brown and sounds hollow when tapped. Remove from pan. Cool on rack at least 15 minutes for easier slicing. Serve warm. Makes 8 main-dish or 16 appetizer servings.

To Reheat: Wrap ring in foil. Heat wrapped ring in 350° oven 30 minutes or until heated through.

Three-Braid Bread

You'll find a strand of white, one of whole-wheat and one of rye bread in each of these multicolored loaves.

>
> 2 pkg. active dry yeast
> 2 tblsp. granulated sugar
> 1½ tsp. salt
> 4¼ to 4¾ c. sifted all-purpose flour
> ¼ c. vegetable oil
> 2 c. milk
> 1 egg
> 2 tblsp. packed brown sugar
> 1 c. stirred whole-wheat flour
> 2 tblsp. unsweetened cocoa
> 2 tblsp. molasses
> 1 c. stirred rye flour
> Milk

In large bowl, stir together yeast, granulated sugar, salt and 2 c. all-purpose flour; set aside.

In 2-qt. saucepan over low heat, heat oil and 2 c. milk until very warm (120 to 130°).

Using mixer at low speed, gradually beat milk mixture into yeast mixture until well blended. Increase speed to medium; beat 2 minutes. Add egg and 1¼ c. all-purpose flour. Increase speed to high; beat 2 minutes more.

Measure batter and divide equally into 3 bowls.

Into first bowl, stir in 1 c. all-purpose flour to make a soft dough.

Into second bowl, stir in brown sugar and then whole-wheat flour to make a moderately stiff dough.

Into third bowl, stir in cocoa, molasses and then rye flour to make a soft dough. If necessary, stir in a small amount of all-purpose flour, 1 tblsp. at a time, until dough is stiff enough to knead.

On lightly floured surface, knead each dough until smooth and elastic, about 5 minutes.

Place each dough into separate greased medium bowls, turning over dough so that each top is greased. Cover with towels and let rise in warm place until doubled, about 50 minutes.

Punch down each dough. Divide each dough in half. Cover and let rest 5 minutes.

On lightly floured surface, roll each piece into a 14"-long rope. Using 1 rope from the 3 different doughs, braid 3 ropes, pinch ends together. Place braid in greased 8½x4½x2½" loaf pan, tucking ends of braid under. Repeat with remaining ropes.

Cover and let rise until doubled, about 30 minutes. Brush loaves with milk.

Bake in 375° oven 25 minutes, or until loaves are browned and sound hollow when tapped. Immediately remove from pans; cool on racks. Makes 2 loaves.

Whole-Wheat Pita

Each round of pita has a pocket that forms during baking—just right for stuffing with your favorite sandwich filling.

> 2 pkg. active dry yeast
> 2 tblsp. packed brown sugar
> 2 tsp. salt
> 4 c. stirred whole-wheat flour
> 2½ c. very warm water (120 to 130°)
> ¼ c. shortening
> 1 to 1½ c. sifted all-purpose flour
> Yellow corn meal

In large bowl, stir together yeast, brown sugar, salt and 3 c. whole-wheat flour.

Using mixer at low speed, beat very warm water and shortening into yeast mixture until well blended. Increase speed to medium; beat 2 minutes.

Stir in remaining 1 c. whole-wheat flour and enough additional all-purpose flour to make a soft dough. Turn out dough onto lightly floured surface. Knead until smooth and elastic, about 10 minutes.

Place in greased large bowl, turning over dough so that top is greased. Cover with towel and let rise in warm place until doubled, about 1 hour.

Punch down dough. Divide dough into 12 pieces. Cover and let rest 10 minutes. Meanwhile, sprinkle 4 greased baking sheets with corn meal.

On lightly floured surface with floured rolling pin, roll out each piece of dough into 6" circle. Place 3 circles, 2" apart, on each baking sheet.

Cover and let rise until doubled, about 30 minutes.

Bake in 475° oven 8 to 10 minutes or until pitas are lightly browned. Immediately remove from baking sheets. Cool on racks. When pitas are cool, place in plastic bags to keep them soft.

To serve, cut pita in half crosswise. If pockets have not formed, slit with knife. Makes 12 pitas.

Poppy Seed Crescents

A Missouri woman whose father came from Poland in 1912 still keeps in touch with relatives there, and these sweet rolls are just one of her many favorite Polish recipes. To save time, you can use ready-made poppy seed filling.

      1 pkg. active dry yeast
      3 tblsp. sugar
      ½ tsp. salt
      3½ to 4 c. sifted flour
      ¾ c. evaporated milk
      ¼ c. butter or regular margarine
      ¼ c. water
      1 egg
      3 egg yolks
      Poppy Seed Filling (recipe follows)
      1 tblsp. water

In large bowl, stir together yeast, sugar, salt and 1 c. flour; set aside.

In 1-qt. saucepan over low heat, heat evaporated milk, butter and ¼ c. water until very warm (120 to 130°).

Using mixer at low speed, gradually beat milk mixture into yeast mixture until well blended. Increase speed to medium; beat 2 minutes. Add egg, 2 egg yolks and 1 c. flour; beat 2 minutes more.

Stir in enough additional flour to make a soft dough. Turn out dough onto lightly floured surface. Knead until smooth and elastic, about 5 to 8 minutes.

Place in greased large bowl, turning over dough so that top is greased. Cover with towel and let rise in warm place until doubled, about 1 hour.

Punch down dough. Cover and let rise again until doubled, about 40 minutes.

During rising time: Prepare Poppy Seed Filling.

Punch down dough. Divide dough in half. Cover and let rest 10 minutes.

On lightly floured surface with floured rolling pin, roll out each half into a 12" circle.

Brush each circle with filling. Cut each circle into 12 wedges. Roll up each wedge, starting at the wide end. Place rolled wedges, points down, 2" apart, on greased large baking sheets. Curve the ends gently to form crescents.

Cover and let rise until doubled, about 45 minutes.

In small bowl, mix together 1 egg yolk and 1 tblsp. water. Brush crescents with egg yolk mixture.

Bake in 425° oven 10 minutes, or until crescents are golden brown and sound hollow when tapped. Immediately remove from baking sheets. Cool on racks. Makes 24 crescents.

POPPY SEED FILLING: In 1-qt. saucepan over high heat, bring 5 tblsp. poppy seed, ¼ c. sugar, ¼ c. water and ½ tsp. grated lemon rind to a boil, stirring constantly. Boil 1 minute. Remove from heat and cool to room temperature, about 30 minutes. Makes ½ c.

Sauerkraut Buns

Shared by a farm wife from New Mexico, here's a recipe for soft rolls filled with beef and sauerkraut—also called bierrocks.

> 2 pkg. active dry yeast
> 3 tblsp. sugar
> 1½ tsp. salt
> 6½ to 7½ c. sifted flour
> 1⅔ c. milk
> ⅔ c. butter or regular margarine
> 2 eggs
> 1 lb. ground chuck
> 1 medium onion, chopped
> ¼ tsp. pepper
> 1 tsp. salt
> 2 c. sauerkraut, drained, or chopped cabbage

In large bowl, stir together yeast, sugar, 1½ tsp. salt and 2 c. flour; set aside.

In 2-qt. saucepan over low heat, heat milk and butter until very warm (120 to 130°).

Using mixer at low speed, gradually beat milk mixture into yeast mixture until well blended. Increase speed to medium; beat 2 minutes. Add eggs and 1 c. flour. Increase speed to high; beat 2 minutes more.

Stir in enough additional flour to make a soft dough. Turn out dough onto lightly floured surface. Knead until smooth and elastic, about 5 minutes.

Place in greased large bowl, turning over dough so that top is greased. Cover with towel and let rise in warm place until doubled, about 1 hour.

During last 20 minutes of rising time: In 10" skillet over medium-high heat, cook ground chuck, onion, pepper and 1 tsp. salt until meat is browned. Stir in sauerkraut; cook 1 to 2 minutes more. Remove from heat.

Punch down dough. Divide dough in half. Cover and let rest 10 minutes.

On lightly floured surface with floured rolling pin, roll out each half into a 16x12" rectangle. Cut each rectangle into 12 (4") squares.

Spoon 2 level tblsp. meat mixture in center of each square. Bring all corners to center; pinch ends and seams to seal. Place squares, seam-side down, 2" apart, on greased large baking sheets.

Cover and let rest in warm place 10 minutes.

Bake in 350° oven 15 to 20 minutes, or until rolls are golden brown and sound hollow when tapped. Immediately remove from baking sheets. Serve warm. Makes 24 buns.

St. Lucia Buns

To initiate the Christmas season, it is a Swedish custom that a young girl of the family is chosen to represent St. Lucia, the Queen of Light. Dressed in a white gown and wearing a wreath of lighted candles on her head, she presents these coiled sweet buns to her family on the morning of the saint's feast day, December 13.

2 pkg. active dry yeast
1 tsp. salt
1 tsp. ground cardamom
⅓ c. sugar
4 to 4⅔ c. sifted flour
1¼ c. milk
½ c. butter or regular margarine
1 egg
Raisins
1 egg white, slightly beaten
Sugar

In large bowl, stir together yeast, salt, cardamom, ⅓ c. sugar and 1½ c. flour; set aside.

In 2-qt. saucepan over low heat, heat milk and butter until very warm (120 to 130°).

Using mixer at low speed, gradually beat milk mixture into yeast mixture until well blended. Increase speed to medium; beat 2 minutes. Add egg and 1 c. flour; beat 2 minutes more.

Stir in enough additional flour to make a soft dough. Turn out dough onto lightly floured surface. Knead until smooth and elastic, about 5 minutes.

Place in greased large bowl, turning over dough so that top is greased. Cover with towel and let rise in warm place until doubled, about 45 minutes.

Punch down dough. Divide dough in half. Cover and let rest 10 minutes.

Divide each half into 16 pieces. On lightly floured surface, roll each piece into a 10"-long rope.

To make an S shape: Holding 2 ropes together, coil ends to form an S shape. Repeat with remaining ropes and place, 2" apart, on greased baking sheets.

To make a butterfly shape: Coil both ends of a rope into the center of that rope; then repeat with a second rope. Place the two coiled ropes back-to-back on greased baking sheet to make a butterfly shape. Repeat with remaining ropes and place, 2" apart, on greased baking sheets.

Press a raisin deep into center of each coil. Cover dough and let rise until doubled, about 40 minutes.

Brush each coil with egg white. Sprinkle with sugar.

Bake in 400° oven 10 to 12 minutes, or until buns are golden brown and sound hollow when tapped. Immediately remove from baking sheets. Cool on racks. Makes 16 buns.

Lenten Buns

Made only for Easter in Scandinavian countries, these cardamom-spiced buns are filled with almond paste and whipped cream.

1 pkg. active dry yeast
½ c. granulated sugar
1 tsp. ground cardamom
4½ c. sifted flour
1½ c. milk
½ c. butter or regular margarine
1 egg
1 egg, beaten
1 c. almond paste (8 oz.)
1 c. heavy cream
Confectioners' sugar

In bowl, stir together yeast, sugar, cardamom and 1½ c. flour.

In 2-qt. saucepan over low heat, heat milk and butter until very warm (120 to 130°).

Using mixer at low speed, gradually beat milk mixture into yeast mixture. Add 1 egg; beat until well blended. Increase speed to medium; beat 2 minutes.

Stir in remaining 3 c. flour until well blended and mixture forms a soft dough. Cover with towel and let rise in warm place until doubled, about 1 hour.

Punch down dough. (Dough will be sticky.) Turn out dough onto lightly floured surface and knead until dough is no longer sticky, about 1 minute, adding additional flour if necessary.

Divide dough into 16 pieces. Shape each piece into a ball. Place balls, 3" apart, on greased large baking sheets.

Cover and let rise until doubled, about 1 hour.

Brush each bun with beaten egg.

Bake in 350° oven 20 to 25 minutes, or until buns are golden brown and sound hollow when tapped. Immediately remove from baking sheets. Cool on racks.

Meanwhile, in bowl with fork, mix almond paste and 3 tblsp. heavy cream until well blended. Cover and set aside.

In chilled small bowl using mixer at medium speed, beat remaining heavy cream until soft peaks form.

Slice off the top third of each bun and set aside. Spread bottom portion of each bun with almond paste mixture. Pipe whipped cream over almond paste; replace tops. Sift confectioners' sugar over buns. Serve immediately. Makes 16 buns.

Brioche Dough

Legend has it that this buttery egg dough originated in the French district of Brie. You can make the dough either conventionally or with the coolrise method; use it to make individual brioches or one giant-size brioche.

> 1 pkg. active dry yeast
> ¼ c. sugar
> ¼ c. warm water (105 to 115°)
> ½ c. milk
> ¼ c. butter or regular margarine, melted
> ½ tsp. salt
> ½ tsp. grated lemon rind
> 3½ to 4 c. sifted flour
> 2 eggs

In large bowl, sprinkle yeast and sugar over warm water; stir until dissolved. Add milk, melted butter, salt, lemon rind and 1½ c. flour.

Using mixer at low speed, beat until well blended. Increase speed to medium; beat 2 minutes. Add eggs. Increase speed to high; beat 2 minutes more.

Stir in enough additional flour to make a soft dough. Turn out dough onto lightly floured surface. Knead until smooth and elastic, about 10 minutes.

Place in greased large bowl, turning over dough so that top is greased. Cover with towel and let rise in warm place until doubled, 1 hour.

Punch down dough. Cover and let rest 10 minutes.

Use as directed to make Individual Brioches, Giant Brioche or Brioche with Sausage (recipes follow).

COOLRISE BRIOCHE DOUGH: Prepare and knead dough as directed. Place dough in greased large bowl, turning over dough so that top is greased. Cover tightly with plastic wrap. Refrigerate 2 to 24 hours.

Punch down dough. On lightly floured surface, knead until dough is no longer sticky, about 30 seconds. Cover with towel and let rest 30 minutes.

Use as directed to make Individual Brioches or Giant Brioche (recipes follow).

Individual Brioches

Golden brown rolls with a delicate buttery flavor—each one shaped like a muffin with a small knob on top.

        1 recipe Brioche Dough or
            1 recipe Coolrise Brioche Dough
        1 egg yolk
        1 tblsp. milk

Prepare Brioche dough. Let rise and punch down dough as directed.

Divide three fourths of the dough into 18 equal pieces. Shape each piece into a ball and place in 18 greased 3" muffin-pan cups or individual fluted brioche pans.

Divide remaining dough into 18 equal pieces. Shape each piece into a teardrop shape. Make a deep indentation in center of each large ball. Insert a teardrop piece, pointed-end down, into each indentation.

Cover and let rise until doubled, about 1 hour.

In small bowl, mix together egg yolk and milk. Brush each brioche with egg yolk mixture.

Bake in 400° oven 10 minutes, or until brioches are golden brown and sound hollow when tapped. Immediately remove from pans. Serve warm. Makes 18 brioches.

Giant Brioche

Perfect for holding a dip! Just cut the knob from the top of the loaf and carefully scoop out the bread, leaving a shell. Fill the shell with your favorite dip, replace the knob and break up the scooped-out bread to serve as "dippers."

        1 recipe Brioche Dough or
            1 recipe Coolrise Brioche Dough
        1 egg yolk
        1 tblsp. milk

Prepare Brioche Dough. Let rise and punch down dough as directed.

Pinch off ½ c. dough; shape into a teardrop shape. Set aside.

Shape remaining dough into a ball. Place in greased 1½-qt.

casserole, soufflé dish or large brioche pan. Make a deep indentation in center of ball. Insert teardrop piece, pointed-end down, into indentation.

Cover and let rise until doubled, about 1 hour.

Bake in 375° oven 30 minutes. Cover loosely with foil; bake 10 to 15 minutes more, or until brioche is golden brown and sounds hollow when tapped. Immediately remove from dish. Makes 1 large brioche.

Brioche with Sausage

Serve slices of these sausage-filled breads, warm or cold, with an assortment of mustards.

> 1 recipe Brioche Dough
> 2 (1-lb.) pkg. bulk pork sausage
> 2 c. water
> 1 egg yolk
> 1 tblsp. milk

Prepare Brioche dough but use only 2 tblsp. sugar and omit lemon rind; let rise as directed.

Meanwhile, shape each pkg. of sausage into an 8"-long log. In 10" skillet over high heat bring sausage logs and water to a boil. Reduce heat to medium-low. Cover and simmer 20 minutes. Drain sausage on paper towels.

Punch down dough. Cut off a 2" piece of dough; set aside. Divide remaining dough in half; cover and let rest 10 minutes.

On lightly floured surface with floured rolling pin, roll out each half into a 10x8" rectangle. Place a sausage log in center of each rectangle.

Fold dough over sausage logs; pinch seams and ends to seal. Tuck under ends, and place each roll, seam-side down, 4" apart, on greased large baking sheet.

Use reserved dough to make decorative designs, like leaves, balls or ropes and attach to top of each roll. Cover and let rest in warm place 20 minutes.

In small bowl, mix together egg yolk and milk. Brush loaves with egg yolk mixture.

Bake in 375° oven 35 minutes, or until loaves are golden brown and sound hollow when tapped. Immediately remove from baking sheet. Serve warm or cold. Makes 2 loaves.

Swedish Sweet Dough

Made with heavy cream, this rich dough rises in the refrigerator. It will keep up to two days in the fridge, so you can make the dough well in advance.

3½ c. sifted flour
1 tsp. salt
⅓ c. sugar
½ c. butter
1 pkg. active dry yeast
1 tsp. sugar
¼ c. warm water (105 to 115°)
1 c. heavy cream
2 eggs
1 tblsp. vegetable oil

Into large bowl, sift together flour, salt and ⅓ c. sugar. With pastry blender, cut in butter until coarse crumbs form; set aside.

In medium bowl, sprinkle yeast and 1 tsp. sugar over warm water; stir until dissolved. Add heavy cream and eggs. With wire whisk, beat until well blended.

Add yeast mixture to flour-butter mixture; stir until soft dough forms that leaves side of bowl. Brush oil over dough. Cover tightly with plastic wrap. Refrigerate 24 to 48 hours.

Use as directed to make Bear Claws, Swedish Sweet Rolls and Pineapple-Cheese Ring (recipes follow).

Bear Claws

Not a bit hard to make—but you'll need to make the refrigerator Swedish Sweet Dough the day before.

1 recipe Swedish Sweet Dough
Sweet Almond Filling (recipe follows)
1 egg white, slightly beaten
⅓ c. sliced almonds
Sugar

At least 1 day before serving, prepare Swedish Sweet Dough and Sweet Almond Filling as directed.

On heavily floured surface with floured rolling pin, roll out dough into a 26x12" rectangle. Cut dough lengthwise into thirds to make 3 (26x4") strips.

Divide Sweet Almond Filling into thirds.

On heavily floured surface, roll each piece of Sweet Almond Filling into a 26"-long rope. Place 1 rope on each dough strip. Fold each long side of dough over filling, overlapping ½"; pinch seams to seal.

Cut each filled strip into 6 equal pieces. Place pieces, seam-side down, 3" apart, on greased baking sheets.

With knife, make crosswise cuts, 1" apart, halfway across width of each dough piece. Curve ends of each piece to form a fan shape that resembles claws.

Brush each claw with egg white. Sprinkle with almonds and sugar.

Let rise, uncovered, until dough is light and almost doubled, about 25 minutes.

Bake in 350° oven 18 to 20 minutes or until golden brown. Immediately remove from baking sheets. Cool on racks. Makes 18 bear claws.

SWEET ALMOND FILLING: In small bowl, using mixer at medium speed, beat ¼ c. butter and ⅓ c. granulated sugar until light and fluffy. Add 2 egg whites and ½ tsp. grated lemon rind; beat until well blended.

Add 1 c. almond paste (8 oz.), 1 tblsp. at a time, beating until well blended after each addition. Stir in ½ c. finely chopped almonds. Cover and refrigerate 1 to 3 days. Makes 2 c.

Swedish Sweet Rolls

Use a pastry wheel to make easy work of cutting the dough into thin strips. Then twist the strips together and tie into loose knots—they'll form lovely rosette-shaped rolls when baked.

> 1 recipe Swedish Sweet Dough
> 1 egg white, slightly beaten
> ¼ c. chopped almonds
> Confectioners' sugar

At least 1 day before serving, prepare Swedish Sweet Dough. Divide dough in half. (Refrigerate one half.)

On heavily floured surface with floured rolling pin, roll out one half into a 12x10" rectangle. With pastry wheel, cut dough into 24 (10x½") strips.

Place 3 strips side by side. Pinch strips together at both ends, making one large strip. Twist strip several times, then gently tie strip in a loose knot, tucking ends under. Repeat with remaining strips.

Roll out, cut and shape remaining dough half in the same way.

Place knots, 2" apart, on greased large baking sheets. Cover and let rise until doubled, about 45 minutes.

Brush rolls with egg white. Sprinkle with almonds.

Bake in 350° oven 15 to 20 minutes, or until rolls are golden brown and sound hollow when tapped. Immediately remove from baking sheets. Cool on racks. Sift confectioners' sugar over rolls. Makes 16 rolls.

Pineapple-Cheese Ring

A festive, two-tiered coffeecake generous enough to serve a crowd. You can use raspberry or apricot preserves instead of pineapple.

> 1 recipe Swedish Sweet Dough
> 2 (3-oz.) pkg. cream cheese
> ½ c. ricotta cheese
> ¼ c. granulated sugar
> 1 tblsp. flour
> 1 egg
> 1 (10-oz.) jar pineapple preserves
> 1 egg white
> 1 tblsp. water
> Confectioners' sugar

At least 1 day before serving, prepare Swedish Sweet Dough as directed.

In small bowl using mixer at medium speed, beat cream cheese, ricotta cheese, granulated sugar, flour and egg until well blended, about 1 minute.

On heavily floured surface with floured rolling pin, roll out two thirds of the dough into a 18x10" rectangle. Spread cheese filling to within ½" from edges. Starting with one long side, roll up, jelly-roll fashion; pinch seam to seal. Carefully place roll, seam-side down, in greased 10" tube pan. Pinch ends together to seal.

Roll out remaining dough into a 16x8" rectangle. Spread

preserves to within ½" from edges. Starting with one long side, roll up, jelly-roll fashion; pinch seam to seal. Carefully place roll, seam-side down, on top of dough in pan. Pinch ends together to seal.

Starting from outside edge of top roll and cutting to center, snip roll with scissors, ½" deep and 1" apart.

Cover and let rise until doubled, about 1 hour.

In small bowl, mix together egg white and water. Brush dough with egg white mixture.

Bake in 350° oven 45 minutes, or until coffeecake is golden brown and sounds hollow when tapped. Cool in pan on rack. Remove from pan. Sift confectioners' sugar over coffeecake. Makes 16 servings.

Danish Pastry Dough

No one can deny that it takes at least a few hours for even the most experienced baker to make this dough. But once you've sampled just one of the pastries, like Danish Twists, you'll know that your time has been well spent!

1½ c. butter, softened
4⅓ to 4⅔ c. sifted flour
2 pkg. active dry yeast
¼ c. sugar
½ tsp. salt
¾ c. milk
½ c. water
1 egg

In small bowl using mixer at medium speed, beat butter and ⅓ c. flour until well blended. On a sheet of plastic wrap, spread butter mixture into a 12x6" rectangle. Wrap and refrigerate until very cold.

In large bowl, stir together yeast, sugar, salt and 1¼ c. flour; set aside.

In 1-qt. saucepan over low heat, heat milk and water until very warm (120 to 130°).

Using mixer at low speed, gradually beat milk mixture into yeast mixture until well blended. Increase speed to medium; beat 2 minutes. Add egg and 1¼ c. flour; beat 2 minutes more.

Stir in enough additional flour to make a soft dough. Turn out dough onto lightly floured surface. Knead until smooth and elastic, about 5 minutes. Cover and let rest 10 minutes.

On lightly floured surface with floured rolling pin, roll out dough into a 14" square. Lay rectangle of cold butter on half of dough. Fold over other half of dough. Pinch together edges of dough to seal well.

Roll out dough into a 20x12" rectangle. Fold dough, crosswise, into thirds. Roll out again into a 20x12" rectangle. (If butter gets too soft and rolling becomes difficult, refrigerate dough about 15 minutes between rollings.) Repeat rolling and folding dough twice more.

Wrap dough in plastic wrap. Refrigerate 1 to 24 hours before shaping.

Use as directed to make Danish Coffee Rings, Cockscomb Coffeecakes, Danish Twists and Danish Wreaths (recipes follow).

Danish Coffee Rings

Yields two large rings, each filled with a custard-like cheese mixture—perfect for any informal get-together.

> 1 recipe Danish Pastry Dough
> Cream Cheese Filling (recipe follows)
> Sugar
> 1 egg
> 1 tblsp. water

Prepare Danish Pastry Dough and Cream Cheese Filling.

On surface sprinkled with sugar, roll out dough to a 20x12" rectangle; cut in half crosswise. Cover and refrigerate one half.

On surface sprinkled with sugar, roll out one half into a 20x10" rectangle. Cut in half lengthwise.

Spread a fourth of the filling lengthwise down center of one 20x5" rectangle. Starting with one long side, roll up jelly-roll fashion. Pinch seam and ends to seal. Repeat with second 20x5" rectangle and a fourth of the filling.

Twist the 2 rolls together and form into a ring, firmly pinching together ends to seal.

Place on greased baking sheet. Cover with plastic wrap; refrigerate 1 to 24 hours. Repeat with remaining dough half and filling.

Place another baking sheet under each baking sheet with coffeecake. (This will help prevent bottoms of coffeecakes from burning during baking.)

In small bowl mix together egg and water. Brush coffeecakes with egg mixture.

Bake in 400° oven 5 minutes. Reduce temperature to 350° and bake 20 to 25 minutes more or until golden brown. Immediately remove from baking sheets. Serve warm. Makes 2 coffeecakes.

CREAM CHEESE FILLING: In small bowl using mixer at medium speed, beat 1 (8-oz.) pkg. cream cheese, softened, and ¼ c. sugar until smooth. Add 1 egg yolk, 1 tblsp. flour and ½ tsp. vanilla; beat until smooth and creamy. Makes 1 c.

Cockscomb Coffeecakes

These look like giant Bear Claws. You can fill them with either apricot or almond filling.

> 1 recipe Danish Pastry Dough
> Golden Apricot Filling (see Index) or
>   Almond Filling (recipe follows)
> Sugar
> 1 egg
> 1 tblsp. water

Prepare Danish Pastry Dough and desired filling.

On surface sprinkled with sugar, roll out dough to a 20x12" rectangle; cut in half crosswise. Cover and refrigerate one half.

On surface sprinkled with sugar, roll out one half into an 18x10" rectangle. Spread a fourth of the filling lengthwise over the center third of the dough. Fold a third of the dough over the filling. Spread the top of the folded third of dough with a fourth of the filling. Fold remaining third of dough over the filling. Pinch together lengthwise edges to seal.

With scissors, make cuts, 1¼" apart, along folded side of dough, cutting two thirds of the way through the dough. Place on greased baking sheet, curving dough so that cut side fans out. Cover with plastic wrap; refrigerate 1 to 24 hours. Repeat with remaining dough half and filling.

Place another baking sheet under each baking sheet with coffeecake. (This will help prevent bottoms of coffeecakes from burning during baking.)

In small bowl mix together egg and water. Brush coffeecakes with egg mixture.

Bake in 400° oven 5 minutes. Reduce temperature to 350° and bake 20 minutes more or until golden brown. Immediately remove from baking sheets. Serve warm. Makes 2 coffeecakes.

ALMOND FILLING: In small bowl using mixer at medium speed, beat 1 egg white until foamy. Beat in ⅔ c. almond paste, a small amount at a time. Add ¼ c. butter, 1 tblsp. at a time, beating until smooth and creamy. Makes about 1 c.

Danish Twists

For breakfast you can have hot fresh pastry in about 15 minutes if you keep the unbaked twists in your freezer.

> 1 recipe Danish Pastry Dough
> ½ recipe Golden Apricot Filling (see Index), or
>   ½ recipe Almond Filling (see preceding recipe), or
>   ½ c. jam, preserves or marmalade
> Sugar
> ½ c. coconut (optional)
> Confectioners' Glaze (recipe follows)

Prepare Danish Pastry Dough and desired filling.

On surface sprinkled with sugar, roll out dough into a 20x12" rectangle; cut in half crosswise. Cover and refrigerate one half.

On surface sprinkled with sugar, roll out one half into a 16x12" rectangle. Spread half of the filling or jam, lengthwise, over half of the rectangle; sprinkle with ¼ c. coconut.

Fold other half of rectangle over filling; gently pat down. Cut crosswise into 16 (6x1") strips.

Carefully twist each strip 3 or 4 times. Place, 2" apart, on greased baking sheets. Cover with plastic wrap; refrigerate 1 to 24 hours. Repeat with remaining dough half and filling.

Place another baking sheet under each baking sheet with pastries. (This will help prevent bottoms of pastries from burning during baking.)

Bake in 400° oven 10 to 15 minutes or until golden brown. Immediately remove from baking sheets. Cool on racks 10 minutes.

Meanwhile, prepare Confectioners' Glaze and drizzle over warm pastries. Serve warm. Makes 32 pastries.

CONFECTIONERS' GLAZE: In small bowl, stir 1½ c. sifted confectioners' sugar, 2 tblsp. milk and ½ tsp. vanilla until smooth.

To Freeze and Bake Later: After shaping pastries, place on baking sheets and freeze until firm. Remove from baking sheets; wrap tightly in foil. Store in freezer up to 3 weeks.

Unwrap and place frozen pastries, 2″ apart, on greased baking sheets. Place another baking sheet under each baking sheet with pastries.

Bake frozen pastries in 425° oven 10 to 12 minutes or until golden brown. Drizzle with glaze and serve as directed.

Danish Wreaths

Made from strips of Danish Pastry Dough, braided together and shaped into rings. Once baked, they're topped with vanilla glaze.

> 1 recipe Danish Pastry Dough
> Sugar
> Confectioners' Glaze (see preceding recipe)

Prepare Danish Pastry Dough.

On surface sprinkled with sugar, roll out dough into a 20x12″ rectangle; cut in half crosswise. Cover and refrigerate one half.

On surface sprinkled with sugar, roll out one half into an 18x12″ rectangle. Cut crosswise into 18 (12x1″) strips.

Cut each strip in half to form 36 (6x1″) strips. Braid 2 strips together and form into a ring, firmly pinching together ends to seal. Repeat with remaining strips.

Place rings, 2″ apart, on greased baking sheets. Cover with plastic wrap; refrigerate 1 to 24 hours. Repeat with remaining dough half.

Place another baking sheet under each baking sheet with pastries. (This will help prevent bottoms of pastries from burning during baking.)

Bake in 400° oven 10 to 15 minutes or until golden brown. Immediately remove from baking sheets. Cool on racks 10 minutes.

Meanwhile, prepare Confectioners' Glaze and drizzle over warm pastries. Serve warm. Makes 3 doz. pastries.

To Freeze and Bake Later: See Danish Twists (preceding recipe) for directions.

Croissants

Like puff pastry, croissant dough is rolled, then folded and rerolled many times, making multiple layers of dough separated by layers of butter. Fresh from the oven, these flaky, crescent-shaped rolls are hard to resist.

> 1 pkg. active dry yeast
> 2 tsp. sugar
> ¼ c. warm water (105 to 115°)
> ¾ c. room temperature milk
> 2 tblsp. vegetable oil
> ½ tsp. salt
> 2½ to 2¾ c. sifted flour
> 1 c. cold butter
> 2 tblsp. flour
> 1 egg
> 1 tblsp. water

In large bowl sprinkle yeast and sugar over ¼ c. warm water; stir until dissolved. Stir in room temperature milk, oil, salt and enough of the 2½ to 2¾ c. flour to make a very soft dough that pulls away from side of bowl.

Turn out dough onto lightly floured surface. Cover with towel and let rest 5 minutes. Dough will be sticky.

Using rubber or metal spatula, knead dough just until smooth but *not* elastic, about 30 seconds.

Pour 7 c. water into medium bowl. Mark water line with a piece of tape. Empty bowl, dry and grease. Place dough in bowl, turning over dough so that top is greased.

Cover tightly with plastic wrap; let rise in warm place until dough comes up to the tape mark, about 1 hour to 1 hour 30 minutes. Dough will rise 3½ times in bulk.

Using rubber spatula, stir down dough. Cover with plastic wrap; let rise in warm place just until doubled, about 45 minutes, or refrigerate overnight.

Using rubber spatula, stir down dough. Cover tightly with plastic wrap. Refrigerate until dough is chilled, 30 minutes to 1 hour *or* place in freezer just until dough is chilled, about 15 minutes. (Do not freeze.)

Meanwhile, in small bowl using mixer at low speed, beat cold butter until pliable but still cold. Add 2 tblsp. flour; beat until well blended. Butter should be soft enough to spread but still cold. If butter becomes too soft, refrigerate briefly.

On lightly floured surface, roll out dough into an 18x10" rectangle. Starting at one narrow side, evenly spread butter over two thirds of dough to ½" of edges. Fold unbuttered third of dough over the buttered center third of dough. Fold remaining buttered third over top, making a 10x6" rectangle. (You now have 3 layers of dough separated by 2 layers of butter.)

Roll out dough into an 18x10" rectangle, starting 1" from 6" side and rolling to 1" of opposite 6" side to prevent butter from pushing out. Fold, crosswise, into thirds making a 10x6" rectangle. Dust lightly with flour; wrap in plastic wrap. Refrigerate 1 hour.

Unwrap dough and place on lightly floured surface. Gently tap dough with rolling pin to break up flecks of butter in dough. Roll out dough into a 16x10" rectangle; fold, crosswise, into thirds. Repeat rolling and folding once more. Dust dough lightly with flour; wrap in plastic wrap.

Refrigerate 1 hour 30 minutes, or overnight. (If refrigerating overnight, place a baking sheet and then a 5 lb. weight, such as a bag of flour, on top of the dough to prevent it from rising.)

On lightly floured surface, roll out dough into a 24x12" rectangle. Cut in half crosswise. Cover and refrigerate one half.

Cut other half into 4 (6") squares. Cut each square in half diagonally. Gently stretch the sides of each triangle so that each side is about 7" long. Starting at one side of each triangle, roll up toward opposite point.

Place, 2" apart, on greased baking sheet with the center point of each roll touching the baking sheet. Do not tuck center points under roll. Curve ends of each roll to form crescent shape. Repeat with remaining dough half.

Cover loosely with plastic wrap. Let rise at room temperature (72 to 75°) until almost doubled and dough feels light and springy, about 1 hour 30 minutes.

In small bowl, mix together egg and 1 tblsp. water. Brush crescents with egg mixture. Place another baking sheet under each baking sheet with crescents. (This will help prevent bottoms of crescents from burning during baking.)

Bake in 425° oven 15 to 20 minutes or until golden brown. Immediately remove from baking sheets. Cool on racks 10 minutes before serving. Serve warm. Makes 16 croissants.

ALMOND CROISSANTS: Prepare Almond Filling (see Index).
Prepare croissants as directed but before shaping, spread each triangle with 1 tblsp. Almond Filling. Roll up triangles and brush with egg mixture as directed. Croissants may then be sprinkled with sliced almonds, if desired. Let rise and bake as directed.

SWISS CHEESE CROISSANTS: Prepare croissants as directed but before shaping, sprinkle each triangle with 2 tblsp. shredded Swiss cheese. Roll up triangles and continue as directed.

To Freeze and Bake Later: Prepare croissant dough and shape as directed. Place crescents on baking sheets. Cover crescents loosely with plastic wrap; freeze until firm. Wrap tightly in foil. Store in freezer up to 2 weeks.
Unwrap and place frozen crescents, 2" apart, on greased baking sheets. Cover loosely with plastic wrap. Let thaw and rise at room temperature until almost doubled, about 2 hours to 2 hours 30 minutes. Brush with egg mixture and bake as directed.
Or, prepare croissant dough, shape dough and let crescents rise as directed. Freeze risen crescents and wrap as directed above. Unwrap frozen crescents and brush frozen crescents with egg mixture. Bake frozen crescents 20 minutes, as directed.

10
Batter Breads

Look in the recipe box of an experienced country cook, and you'll find at least a couple of recipes for batter breads. Smart bakers know that these shortcut yeast recipes can be timesavers, especially when it comes to making homemade bread; the batters don't have to be kneaded or shaped, and you can use them for coffeecakes, breads and rolls.

The method is simple. The ingredients are mixed together until a stiff batter forms—stiff enough to allow a wooden spoon to stand up by itself. After the last addition of flour, the batter is stirred for about a minute, just long enough to develop the gluten.

Since the batter rises in the same bowl in which it's made, you need only set the bowl aside in a warm place to rise. Batter yeast breads will rise faster than kneaded yeast breads, so it's wise to keep an eye on them during the last minutes of rising. You can tell when the batter has risen—it will be double in bulk.

Stir down the risen batter with a wooden spoon and keep stirring it for about 30 seconds more, making sure that all the bubbles are broken. No shaping is necessary; batter breads take the shape of the container in which they bake.

It's not hard to see why batter breads are in so many cooks' recipe files—especially once you've sampled batter breads such as Sally Lunn, Anadama Bread, Peanut Batter Bread, Cracked Wheat Casserole Bread, Raised Breakfast Rolls and One-Hour Spoon Rolls.

Whole-Wheat Batter Bread

Wheat germ and molasses are flavorful additions to this casserole bread that rises in less than a hour.

2 pkg. active dry yeast
½ c. wheat germ
⅓ c. nonfat dry milk
2 tsp. salt
2½ c. stirred whole-wheat flour
2 c. water
⅓ c. molasses
2 tblsp. shortening
2¼ c. sifted all-purpose flour

In large bowl, stir together yeast, wheat germ, dry milk, salt and 1½ c. whole-wheat flour; set aside.

In 2-qt. saucepan over low heat, heat water, molasses and shortening until very warm (120 to 130°).

Using mixer at low speed, gradually beat water mixture into yeast mixture until well blended. Increase speed to medium; beat 2 minutes.

Using wooden spoon, gradually stir in remaining 1 c. whole-wheat flour and 2¼ c. all-purpose flour until mixture is well blended and forms a stiff batter. Cover with towel and let rise in warm place until doubled, about 40 minutes.

Using wooden spoon, stir down batter and continue stirring for 30 seconds. Turn batter into greased 2-qt. soufflé dish. Let rise, uncovered, until batter is level with top of dish, about 15 minutes.

Bake in 400° oven 20 minutes. Cover loosely with foil; bake 20 minutes more, or until loaf is browned and sounds hollow when tapped. Immediately remove from dish. Cool on rack. Makes 1 loaf.

Cinnamon-Wheat Muffin Bread

This bread has the texture of English muffins, but it's baked in a loaf. Slice, toast and serve it with honey or butter at breakfast.

2 pkg. active dry yeast
2 tblsp. sugar
2 tsp. salt
2 tsp. ground cinnamon
3 c. sifted all-purpose flour
2 c. stirred whole-wheat flour
2 c. milk
½ c. water
1 c. raisins
2 tblsp. warm water
½ tsp. baking soda
Corn meal

In large bowl, stir together yeast, sugar, salt, cinnamon, 1½ c. all-purpose flour and 1 c. whole-wheat flour; set aside.

In 2-qt. saucepan over low heat, heat milk and ½ c. water until very warm (120 to 130°).

Using mixer at low speed, gradually beat milk mixture into yeast mixture until well blended. Increase speed to medium; beat 2 minutes.

Using wooden spoon, gradually stir in raisins, remaining 1½ c. all-purpose flour and 1 c. whole-wheat flour until mixture is well blended and forms a stiff batter. Cover with towel and let rise in warm place until doubled, about 45 minutes.

Using wooden spoon, stir down batter. In small bowl, mix together 2 tblsp. warm water and baking soda; add to batter. Using spoon, beat 1 minute. (Batter will be streaked if baking soda is not thoroughly stirred into batter.)

Dust 3 well-greased 1-lb. coffee cans with corn meal. Turn batter into cans. Let rise, uncovered, until doubled, about 30 minutes.

Bake in 400° oven 25 to 30 minutes or until loaves sound hollow when tapped. Immediately remove from cans. Cool on racks. To serve, cut each loaf into ½"-thick slices; toast. Makes 3 loaves.

Cracked Wheat Casserole Bread

Cracked wheat adds a chewy texture and nutlike flavor to these whole-wheat casserole loaves.

    1½ c. water
    1¼ c. cracked wheat
    1 c. milk
    ¼ c. butter or regular margarine
    2 pkg. active dry yeast
    3 tblsp. sugar
    2 tsp. salt
    2¾ c. sifted all-purpose flour
    2 c. stirred whole-wheat flour
    2 eggs

In 2-qt. saucepan over high heat, bring water and cracked wheat to a boil. Reduce heat to medium-low; simmer, uncovered, 2 minutes. Remove from heat. Stir in milk and butter; let cool until mixture is very warm (120 to 130°).

In large bowl, stir together yeast, sugar, salt, 1 c. all-purpose flour and 1 c. whole-wheat flour.

Using mixer at low speed, gradually beat cracked wheat mixture into yeast mixture until well blended. Increase speed to medium; beat 2 minutes. Add eggs and 1 c. all-purpose flour. Increase speed to high; beat 2 minutes more.

Using wooden spoon, gradually stir in remaining ¾ c. all-purpose flour and 1 c. whole-wheat flour until mixture is well blended and forms a stiff batter. Cover with towel and let rise in warm place until doubled, about 45 minutes.

Using wooden spoon, stir down batter. Turn batter into 2 well-greased 1½-qt. casserole or soufflé dishes. Let rise, uncovered, until doubled, about 30 minutes.

Bake in 375° oven 45 minutes or until loaves sound hollow when tapped. Immediately remove from dishes. Cool on racks. Makes 2 loaves.

Dilly Casserole Bread

To allow the delicate dill and green onion flavors to fully develop, wrap this cottage cheese bread in foil and let it stand a day.

>1 pkg. active dry yeast
>2 tblsp. sugar
>2 tsp. dill seed
>1 tsp. salt
>¼ tsp. baking soda
>2½ c. sifted flour
>1 c. large-curd, cream-style cottage cheese
>¼ c. water
>1 tblsp. butter or regular margarine
>1 egg
>¼ c. chopped green onions

In large bowl, stir together first 5 ingredients and 1¼ c. flour; set aside.

In 2-qt. saucepan over low heat, heat cottage cheese, water and butter until very warm (120 to 130°).

Using mixer at low speed, gradually beat cottage cheese mixture into yeast mixture until well blended. Add egg. Increase speed to medium; beat 2 minutes more.

Using wooden spoon, gradually stir in green onions and remaining 1¼ c. flour until mixture is well blended and forms a stiff batter. Cover and let rise in warm place until doubled, about 50 minutes.

Using wooden spoon, stir down batter. Turn batter into well-greased 1½-qt. casserole or soufflé dish. Let rise, uncovered, until doubled, about 30 minutes.

Bake in 350° oven 25 minutes. Cover loosely with foil; bake 15 minutes more or until loaf sounds hollow when tapped. Immediately remove from casserole. Cool on rack about 20 minutes. Serve warm. Makes 1 loaf.

Anadama Bread

It's said that a New England fisherman had a lazy wife who wouldn't cook. Since the husband did all of the cooking, he created this bread and called it—"Anna, damn her."

1 pkg. active dry yeast
1 tsp. salt
2¾ c. sifted flour
1 c. water
½ c. yellow corn meal
¼ c. molasses
3 tblsp. shortening
1 egg

In large bowl, stir together yeast, salt and 1¼ c. flour; set aside.

In 2-qt. saucepan over low heat, heat water, corn meal, molasses and shortening until very warm (120 to 130°).

Using mixer at low speed, gradually add corn meal mixture to yeast mixture until well blended. Increase speed to medium; beat 2 minutes. Add egg and ½ c. flour; beat 2 minutes more.

Gradually stir in remaining 1 c. flour until mixture is well blended and forms a stiff batter. Turn batter into well-greased 8½x4½x2½" loaf pan. Spread batter evenly into corners of pan. Let rise, uncovered, in warm place until doubled, about 1 hour.

Bake in 375° oven 50 minutes or until loaf sounds hollow when tapped. Immediately remove from pan. Cool on rack. Makes 1 loaf.

Cheddar Batter Bread

You wouldn't guess that this tender-crumbed, crusty loaf is a simple batter bread. It's a Missouri farm family's favorite.

2 pkg. active dry yeast
3 tblsp. sugar
2 tsp. salt
4 c. sifted flour
1½ c. milk
1 tblsp. butter or regular margarine
1½ c. shredded sharp Cheddar cheese

In large bowl, stir together yeast, sugar, salt and 2 c. flour; set aside.

In 2-qt. saucepan over low heat, heat milk and butter until very warm (120 to 130°).

Using mixer at low speed, gradually beat milk mixture into yeast mixture until well blended. Increase speed to medium; beat 2 minutes.

Using wooden spoon, gradually stir in cheese and remaining 2 c. flour until mixture is well blended and forms a stiff batter. Cover with towel and let rise in warm place until doubled, about 50 minutes.

Using wooden spoon stir down batter. Turn batter into well-greased 9x5x3" loaf pan. Spread batter evenly into corners of pan. Do not let rise.

Bake in 350° oven 40 minutes. Cover loosely with foil; bake 15 to 20 minutes more or until loaf sounds hollow when tapped. Immediately remove from pan. Cool on rack. Makes 1 loaf.

Beer Batter Loaf

The beer in this crisp-crusted rye bread adds a malt flavor. For a stronger flavor, you could use ale or dark beer.

     2 pkg. active dry yeast
     3 tblsp. sugar
     2 tsp. salt
     2½ c. sifted all-purpose flour
     2 c. stirred rye flour
     1 c. beer
     1 c. water
     2 tblsp. butter or regular margarine
     1 egg
     Milk

In large bowl, stir together yeast, sugar, salt, 1 c. all-purpose flour and 1 c. rye flour; set aside.

In 2-qt. saucepan over low heat, heat beer, water and butter until very warm (120 to 130°).

Using mixer at low speed, gradually beat beer mixture into yeast mixture until well blended. Increase speed to medium; beat 2 minutes. Add egg and ½ c. all-purpose flour; beat 2 minutes more.

Using wooden spoon, gradually stir in remaining 1 c. all-purpose flour and 1 c. rye flour until mixture is well blended and forms a stiff batter. Cover with towel and let rise in warm place until doubled, about 50 minutes.

Using wooden spoon, stir down batter and continue stirring 30 seconds. Turn batter into well-greased 2-qt. casserole or soufflé dish. Brush with milk. Do not let rise.

Bake in 400° oven 45 to 50 minutes or until loaf sounds hollow when tapped. Immediately remove from dish. Cool on rack. Makes 1 loaf.

Cheese-Caraway Bread

Slices of this loaf flavored with caraway and sharp Cheddar make a good sandwich partner with either ham or corned beef.

> 1 pkg. active dry yeast
> 1 tblsp. sugar
> 1 tsp. salt
> 1 tsp. caraway seed
> 1 c. shredded sharp Cheddar cheese
> 3 c. sifted flour
> 1 c. water
> 2 tblsp. butter or regular margarine

In large bowl, stir together first 5 ingredients and 1½ c. flour; set aside.

In 1-qt. saucepan over low heat, heat water and butter until very warm (120 to 130°).

Using mixer at low speed, gradually beat water mixture into yeast mixture until well blended. Increase speed to medium; beat 2 minutes.

Using wooden spoon, gradually stir in remaining 1½ c. flour until mixture is well blended and forms a stiff batter. Cover with towel and let rise in warm place until doubled, about 45 minutes.

Using wooden spoon, stir down batter. Turn batter into well-greased 9x5x3" loaf pan. Spread batter evenly into corners of pan. Let rise, uncovered, until doubled, about 40 minutes.

Bake in 350° oven 45 minutes, or until loaf is browned and sounds hollow when tapped. Immediately remove from pan. Cool on rack. Makes 1 loaf.

Pizza Batter Bread

"Try using this pepperoni-studded bread to spice up your grilled cheese sandwiches," suggests an Illinois farm wife.

    1 pkg. active dry yeast
    1 tblsp. sugar
    1 tsp. salt
    ½ tsp. dried oregano leaves
    2 cloves garlic, minced
    3 c. sifted flour
    1¼ c. water
    2 tblsp. butter or regular margarine
    1 egg
    ¼ c. finely diced pepperoni

In large bowl, stir together first 5 ingredients and 1 c. flour; set aside.

In 1-qt. saucepan over low heat, heat water and butter until very warm (120 to 130°).

Using mixer at low speed, gradually beat water mixture into yeast mixture until well blended. Increase speed to medium; beat 2 minutes. Add egg and ¾ c. flour; beat 2 minutes more.

Using wooden spoon, gradually stir in pepperoni and remaining 1¼ c. flour until mixture is well blended and forms a stiff batter. Cover with towel and let rise in warm place until doubled, about 45 minutes.

Using wooden spoon, stir down batter. Turn batter into well-greased 8½x4½x2½" loaf pan. Spread batter evenly into corners of pan. Let rise, uncovered, until doubled, about 30 minutes.

Bake in 375° oven 40 to 45 minutes, or until loaf is browned and sounds hollow when tapped. Immediately remove from pan. Cool on rack. Makes 1 loaf.

Peanut Batter Bread

Children love this bread; it turns a peanut butter-and-jelly sandwich into a triple treat. Makes delicious toast, too!

        1 pkg. active dry yeast
        ¼ c. packed brown sugar
        ¼ c. finely chopped peanuts
        1 tsp. salt
        3 c. sifted flour
        1¼ c. water
        ¼ c. peanut butter

In large bowl, stir together yeast, brown sugar, peanuts, salt and 1½ c. flour; set aside.

In 1-qt. saucepan over low heat, heat water and peanut butter until very warm (120 to 130°).

Using mixer at low speed, gradually beat water mixture into yeast mixture until well blended. Increase speed to medium; beat 2 minutes.

Using wooden spoon, gradually stir in remaining 1½ c. flour until mixture is well blended and forms a stiff batter. Cover with towel and let rise in warm place until doubled, about 40 minutes.

Using wooden spoon, stir down batter and continue stirring 30 seconds. Turn batter into greased 9x5x3″ loaf pan. Spread batter evenly into corners of pan. Let rise, uncovered, until doubled, about 40 minutes.

Bake in 350° oven 45 to 50 minutes, or until loaf is browned and sounds hollow when tapped. Immediately remove from pan. Cool on rack. Makes 1 loaf.

Babka

The Polish word for "grandmother" gave this Easter bread its name. The fluted tube pan that is used is thought to have reminded someone of a woman's long, full skirt.

1 pkg. active dry yeast
½ c. sugar
1 tsp. salt
½ tsp. ground cinnamon
4 c. sifted flour
1¼ c. milk
½ c. butter or regular margarine
4 egg yolks
1 tsp. vanilla
1 tsp. rum flavor
½ c. golden raisins
¼ c. ground almonds
Confectioners' sugar

In large bowl, stir together yeast, sugar, salt, cinnamon and 1½ c. flour; set aside.

In 2-qt. saucepan over low heat, heat milk and butter until very warm (120 to 130°).

Using mixer at low speed, gradually beat milk mixture into yeast mixture until well blended. Beat in egg yolks, vanilla and rum flavor until well blended. Increase speed to medium; beat 2 minutes. Add 1½ c. flour. Increase speed to high; beat 2 minutes more.

Stir in raisins and remaining 1 c. flour until mixture is well blended and forms a moderately stiff batter.

Generously butter a 10″ fluted tube pan. Coat pan with ground almonds.

Turn dough into prepared pan. Cover with towel and let rise in warm place until doubled, about 1 hour 30 minutes.

Bake in 350° oven 45 minutes or until golden brown. Cool in pan on rack 10 minutes. Remove from pan. Cool completely. Sift confectioners' sugar over top of cake. Makes 1 babka.

Refrigerator Babka

A variation of traditional Babka, made with a dough that rises overnight in the refrigerator. Slice thickly and serve warm.

2 pkg. active dry yeast
1 tsp. salt
½ c. sugar
4½ c. sifted flour
¾ c. milk
½ c. water
½ c. butter or regular margarine
2 eggs
¼ c. ground almonds
4 tsp. ground cinnamon
1 c. sugar
⅓ c. butter or regular margarine, melted

In large bowl, stir together yeast, salt, ½ c. sugar and 1½ c. flour; set aside.

In 2-qt. saucepan over low heat, heat milk, water and ½ c. butter until very warm (120 to 130°).

Using mixer at low speed, gradually beat milk mixture into yeast mixture until well blended. Increase speed to medium; beat 2 minutes. Add eggs and 1½ c. flour; beat 2 minutes more.

Stir in remaining 1½ c. flour until well blended. Cover tightly with plastic wrap. Refrigerate 12 to 24 hours.

In small bowl, stir together almonds, cinnamon and 1 c. sugar.

Pinch off a 2" piece dough; shape into a ball. Dip ball into ⅓ c. melted butter, then roll in almond mixture until well coated. Place ball in greased and floured 10" fluted tube pan.

Repeat with remaining dough, melted butter and almond mixture, layering balls in pan. Cover with towel and let rise in warm place until doubled, about 2 hours.

Bake in 350° oven 50 to 55 minutes, or until babka is golden brown and sounds hollow when tapped. Cool in pan on rack 10 minutes. Remove from pan. Serve warm. Makes 1 babka.

Gugelhupf

To celebrate their victory over Turkish invaders in 1683, Viennese bakers created this rich yeast cake and modeled it after the shape of a sultan's turban—high and round, with fluted edges.

1 pkg. active dry yeast
¼ tsp. sugar
¼ c. warm water (105 to 115°)
½ c. sugar
¼ c. butter or regular margarine
2 eggs
2½ c. sifted flour
¼ tsp. salt
½ c. milk
½ c. golden raisins
1 tsp. grated lemon rind
1 tblsp. butter or regular margarine, melted
¼ c. finely ground almonds
18 blanched whole almonds
Confectioners' sugar

In small bowl, sprinkle yeast and ¼ tsp. sugar over warm water; stir until dissolved. Set aside.

In large bowl using mixer at medium speed, beat ½ c. sugar and ¼ c. butter until light and fluffy. Add eggs, one at a time, beating well after each addition. Add flour, salt, milk and yeast mixture; beat until smooth and well blended.

Stir in raisins and lemon rind. Cover and let rise in warm place until doubled, about 2 hours.

During last 10 minutes of rising time: Generously grease 10" fluted tube pan with 1 tblsp. melted butter. Coat pan with ground almonds. Arrange whole almonds in bottom of pan.

Using wooden spoon, stir down batter. Turn into prepared pan. Cover and let rise until doubled, about 1 hour.

Bake in 350° oven 15 minutes. Cover loosely with foil; bake 15 minutes more, or until bread is golden brown and toothpick inserted in center comes out clean. Cool in pan on rack 10 minutes. Remove from pan. Cool on rack. Sift confectioners' sugar over loaf. Makes 1 loaf.

Sally Lunn

An American tradition with British origins: two centuries ago, a girl named Sally Lunn sold warm slices of bread, rich in eggs, as a teatime treat near her home in Bath, England.

> 1 pkg. active dry yeast
> ⅓ c. sugar
> 1 tsp. salt
> 4 c. sifted flour
> ½ c. milk
> ½ c. water
> ½ c. butter or regular margarine
> 3 eggs

In large bowl, stir together yeast, sugar, salt and 1¼ c. flour; set aside.

In 2-qt. saucepan over low heat, heat milk, water and butter until very warm (120 to 130°).

Using mixer at low speed, gradually beat milk mixture into yeast mixture until well blended. Increase speed to medium; beat 2 minutes. Add eggs and 1 c. flour. Increase speed to high; beat 2 minutes more.

Using wooden spoon, gradually stir in remaining 1¾ c. flour until mixture is well blended and forms a stiff batter. Cover with towel and let rise in warm place until doubled, about 50 minutes.

Using wooden spoon, stir down batter and continue stirring 30 seconds. Turn batter into greased and floured 9″ tube pan. Let rise, uncovered, until doubled, about 50 minutes.

Bake in 350° oven 45 to 50 minutes or until bread is golden brown. Immediately remove from pan. Cool on rack about 20 minutes. Makes 1 coffee bread.

Citrus Crumb Coffeecake

Doubly good, because it's made with both orange juice and rind.

> Citrus Crumb Topping (recipe follows)
> 1 pkg. active dry yeast
> ½ c. sugar
> ½ tsp. salt
> 2¼ c. sifted flour
> ⅓ c. butter or regular margarine
> ¼ c. milk
> ¼ c. water
> 2 eggs
> 2 tblsp. frozen orange juice concentrate
> Vanilla Icing (recipe follows)

Prepare Citrus Crumb Topping; set aside.

In large bowl, stir together yeast, sugar, salt and 1 c. flour; set aside.

In 1-qt. saucepan over low heat, heat butter, milk and water until very warm (120 to 130°).

Using mixer at low speed, gradually beat butter mixture into yeast mixture until well blended. Increase speed to medium; beat 2 minutes. Add eggs, orange juice concentrate and ½ c. flour; beat 2 minutes more.

Using wooden spoon, gradually stir in remaining ¾ c. flour until mixture is well blended and forms a thick batter. Turn batter into well-greased 9x9x2″ baking pan. Spread batter evenly into corners of pan. Crumble topping over batter. Let rise, uncovered, in warm place until doubled, about 50 minutes.

Bake in 375° oven 45 minutes or until cake is browned. Cool in pan on rack 10 minutes.

Meanwhile, prepare Vanilla Icing. Remove cake from pan; set on rack over sheet of waxed paper. Drizzle icing over cake and cool about 20 minutes. Makes 1 coffeecake.

CITRUS CRUMB TOPPING: In small bowl using mixer at medium speed, beat ⅓ c. butter or regular margarine, softened, until creamy. Add ⅓ c. sugar and 1 egg yolk; beat until well blended.

Reduce speed to low. Add ½ c. flour and 2 tsp. grated orange rind; beat just until combined. Stir in ½ c. chopped pecans.

VANILLA ICING: In small bowl, stir 1 c. sifted confectioners' sugar, 1 tblsp. milk and 1 tsp. vanilla until smooth.

Kaffee Kuchen Ring

Almost like a pound cake, this fluted, lemon-flavored ring is ideal for dessert. Makes a handsome hostess gift, too.

> 1 pkg. active dry yeast
> 1 tsp. sugar
> ¼ c. warm water (105 to 115°)
> ¾ c. warm milk (105 to 115°)
> 3½ c. sifted flour
> Blanched whole almonds
> ½ c. butter or regular margarine
> 1 c. sugar
> 4 eggs
> 1 tsp. grated lemon rind
> ¾ tsp. salt
> ¼ tsp. ground nutmeg

In small bowl, sprinkle yeast and 1 tsp. sugar over warm water; stir until dissolved. Stir in warm milk and 1 c. flour until smooth. Cover with waxed paper and let rise in warm place until bubbly, about 15 minutes.

Meanwhile, butter a 10″ fluted tube pan. Arrange whole almonds in bottom of pan.

In large bowl using mixer at medium speed, beat butter and 1 c. sugar until light and fluffy. Add eggs, one at a time, beating well after each addition. Add lemon rind, salt, nutmeg, remaining 2½ c. flour and yeast mixture; beat until mixture is well blended and forms a thick batter.

Pour batter into prepared pan. Cover with towel and let rise in warm place until doubled, about 1 hour 15 minutes.

Bake in 350° oven 40 to 45 minutes or until golden brown. Cool in pan on rack 10 minutes. Immediately remove from pan. Cool on rack. Makes 1 coffeecake.

Baba au Rhum

A French specialty that is supposedly named after Ali Baba of The Arabian Nights. *Babas are very light, sweet, individual dessert breads dipped in a rum sauce. Use the delicate batter to make a ring-shaped, orange-glazed cake called Savarin.*

> 1 pkg. active dry yeast
> ⅓ c. warm water (105 to 115°)
> ½ c. butter or regular margarine, melted
> ¼ c. sugar
> ½ tsp. salt
> 1¾ c. sifted flour
> 3 eggs
> 1 tsp. vanilla
> Rum Sauce (recipe follows)

In large bowl, sprinkle yeast over warm water; stir until dissolved. Add melted butter, sugar, salt and ½ c. flour. Using mixer at medium speed, beat 2 minutes.

Add eggs, one at a time, beating well after each addition. Add vanilla and ½ c. flour; beat 2 minutes more.

Using wooden spoon, gradually stir in remaining ¾ c. flour until mixture is well blended and forms a thick batter. Cover with towel and let rise in warm place until doubled, about 50 minutes.

Using wooden spoon, stir down batter. Spoon batter evenly into 12 well-greased 3″ muffin-pan cups, filling two-thirds full. Let rise, uncovered, until batter is level with tops of cups, about 25 minutes.

Bake in 350° oven 20 to 30 minutes or until golden brown. Immediately remove from pans. Cool on racks 5 minutes. Meanwhile, prepare Rum Sauce.

Dip each baba in sauce until all the sauce is absorbed. Serve warm. Makes 12 babas.

Rum Sauce: In 2-qt. saucepan over high heat, bring 1 c. water and ½ c. sugar to a boil, stirring constantly; boil 1 minute. Remove from heat. Stir in ½ c. rum.

SAVARIN: Substitute 2 tsp. grated orange rind for vanilla, and Fresh Orange Sauce for Rum Sauce.

Spoon batter into well-greased 6 c. ring mold. Let rise, uncovered, until doubled, about 45 minutes.

Bake in 350° oven 35 minutes or until golden brown.

Meanwhile, prepare Fresh Orange Sauce. Immediately remove Savarin from mold; place on rack. Brush sauce over Savarin until all sauce is absorbed. Brush ¾ c. orange marmalade, melted, over Savarin. Serve immediately, or let cool completely and wrap in foil. Store up to 2 days. Makes 1 ring.

Fresh Orange Sauce: In 2-qt. saucepan over high heat, bring ¾ c. fresh orange juice, ⅔ c. sugar and ½ c. water to a boil, stirring constantly; boil 1 minute. Remove from heat.

One-Hour Spoon Rolls

A Colorado woman's recipe for no-rise yeast rolls—they're ready in less than an hour from start to finish! Leftover batter can be kept in the refrigerator up to two days; before baking, let the refrigerated batter stand at room temperature 15 minutes.

> 1 pkg. active dry yeast
> ¼ c. sugar
> 4 c. sifted self-rising flour
> 2 c. water
> ¾ c. butter or regular margarine
> 1 egg

In large bowl, stir together yeast, sugar and 1½ c. flour.

In 2-qt. saucepan over low heat, heat water and butter until very warm (120 to 130°).

Using mixer at low speed, gradually beat water mixture into yeast mixture until well blended. Increase speed to medium; beat 2 minutes. Add egg and 1 c. flour; beat 2 minutes more.

Gradually stir in remaining 1½ c. flour until mixture is well blended and forms a thick batter. Spoon batter evenly into 18 well-greased 3" muffin-pan cups, filling two-thirds full. Do not let rise.

Bake in 400° oven 15 to 20 minutes or until golden brown. Immediately remove from pans. Serve warm. Makes 18 rolls.

Seeded Wheat Rolls

For more than 20 years, an Ohio farm woman has been making these sesame seed-topped rolls. She especially likes this recipe because it makes only a dozen—just the right number of rolls for her family of six without any left over.

> 1 pkg. active dry yeast
> ¼ c. stirred whole-wheat flour
> 2 tblsp. sugar
> 1 tsp. salt
> 2 c. sifted all-purpose flour
> ½ c. milk
> ½ c. water
> 3 tblsp. vegetable oil
> 1 egg
> Sesame or poppy seed

In large bowl, stir together yeast, whole-wheat flour, sugar, salt and 1 c. all-purpose flour; set aside.

In 2-qt. saucepan over low heat, heat milk and water until very warm (120 to 130°).

Using mixer at low speed, gradually beat milk mixture into yeast mixture until well blended. Increase speed to medium; beat 2 minutes. Add oil and egg; beat 2 minutes more.

Using wooden spoon, gradually stir in remaining 1 c. all-purpose flour until mixture is well blended and forms a thick batter. Spoon batter evenly into 12 well-greased 3″ muffin-pan cups, filling about one-half full. Sprinkle batter with sesame or poppy seed. Cover with towel and let rise in warm place until doubled, about 1 hour.

Bake in 425° oven 25 minutes, or until rolls are dark golden brown and sound hollow when tapped. Immediately remove from pans. Serve warm. Makes 12 rolls.

Quick Pan Rolls

Used in a Texas school cafeteria, these egg-rich rolls are baked in a pan and cut into squares—no shaping required!

1 pkg. active dry yeast
½ c. nonfat dry milk
¼ c. sugar
1 tsp. salt
4 c. sifted flour
1½ c. water
⅓ c. butter or regular margarine
2 eggs

In large bowl, stir together yeast, dry milk, sugar, salt and 1½ c. flour; set aside.

In 2-qt. saucepan over low heat, heat water and butter until very warm (120 to 130°).

Using mixer at low speed, gradually beat water mixture into yeast mixture until well blended. Increase speed to medium; beat 2 minutes. Add eggs and 1 c. flour; beat 2 minutes more.

Using wooden spoon, gradually stir in remaining 1½ c. flour until mixture is well blended and forms a thick batter. Cover with towel and let rise in warm place until doubled, about 50 minutes.

Turn batter into well-greased 13x9x2" baking pan. Spread batter evenly into corners of pan. Do not let rise.

Bake in 350° oven 30 to 35 minutes or until browned. Cut into squares. Serve warm. Makes 24 rolls.

Swiss-Bacon Batter Rolls

Bake a batch of these muffin-shaped rolls and keep half a dozen in your freezer. So flavorful, with mellow Swiss cheese and smoky bacon, they're good anytime.

8 slices bacon, diced
2 pkg. active dry yeast
1 tblsp. sugar
1 tsp. salt
3 c. sifted flour
1 c. milk
½ c. water
1 egg
1 c. shredded Swiss cheese

In 10" skillet over medium heat, cook bacon until browned. Drain on paper towels. Reserve 2 tblsp. drippings.

In large bowl, stir together yeast, sugar, salt and 1½ c. flour; set aside.

In 1-qt. saucepan over low heat, heat milk, water and reserved drippings until very warm (120 to 130°).

Using mixer at low speed, beat milk mixture into yeast mixture until well blended. Increase speed to medium; beat 2 minutes. Add egg and ½ c. flour; beat 2 minutes more.

Using wooden spoon, gradually stir in cheese and remaining 1 c. flour until mixture is well blended and forms a stiff batter. Cover with towel and let rise in warm place until doubled, about 30 minutes.

Using wooden spoon, stir down batter. Spoon batter evenly into 18 well-greased 3" muffin-pan cups, filling two-thirds full. Let rise, uncovered, until doubled, about 30 minutes.

Bake in 400° oven 18 to 20 minutes or until golden brown. Immediately remove from pans. Serve warm. Makes 18 rolls.

To Freeze and Serve Later: Let rolls cool completely. Place on baking sheet and freeze until firm, about 2 hours. Wrap each roll in heavy-duty foil; freeze up to 1 month. Heat foil-wrapped, frozen rolls in 400° oven 25 minutes or until heated through.

Individual Onion-Herb Loaves

Baked in large custard cups, these little herbed loaves would complement a main course of roast turkey or grilled fish.

    ¼ c. butter or regular margarine
    2 medium onions, chopped
    2 pkg. active dry yeast
    2 tblsp. sugar
    1 tsp. salt
    ½ tsp. dried marjoram leaves
    ½ tsp. dried oregano leaves
    ½ tsp. dried thyme leaves
    3¼ c. sifted flour
    1¼ c. very warm water (120 to 130°)
    1 egg

In 7" skillet over medium heat, melt butter. Add onions; cook until onions are golden. Remove from heat; set aside.

In large bowl, stir together yeast, sugar, salt, marjoram, oregano, thyme and 1½ c. flour; set aside.

Using mixer at low speed, beat very warm water into yeast mixture until well blended. Increase speed to medium; beat 2 minutes. Add egg and ½ c. flour; beat 2 minutes more.

Using wooden spoon, gradually stir in onion mixture and remaining 1¼ c. flour until mixture is well blended and forms a stiff batter. Spoon batter evenly into 6 well-greased 10-oz. custard cups, filling one-half full. Let rise, uncovered, in warm place until doubled, about 1 hour.

Bake in 375° oven 35 to 40 minutes or until browned. Immediately remove from cups. Serve warm. Makes 6 loaves.

To Freeze and Serve Later: Let loaves cool completely. Place on baking sheet and freeze until firm, about 2 hours. Wrap each loaf in heavy-duty foil; freeze up to 1 month. Heat foil-wrapped, frozen loaves in 400° oven 30 minutes or until heated through.

Banana Nut Batter Muffins

Seasoned with a hint of ground nutmeg, these yeast muffins are moist and tender with a robust banana flavor.

1 pkg. active dry yeast
½ c. sugar
1 tsp. salt
½ tsp. baking soda
½ tsp. ground nutmeg
2½ c. sifted flour
¼ c. water
¼ c. milk
3 tblsp. butter or regular margarine
1 c. mashed, ripe bananas (about 3 medium)
1 tsp. vanilla
1 egg
1 c. chopped walnuts

In large bowl, stir together first 5 ingredients and ½ c. flour; set aside.

In 1-qt. saucepan over low heat, heat water, milk and butter until very warm (120 to 130°).

Using mixer at low speed, gradually beat water mixture into yeast mixture until well blended. Increase speed to medium; beat 2 minutes. Add bananas, vanilla, egg and ½ c. flour; beat 2 minutes more.

Using wooden spoon, gradually stir in walnuts and remaining 1½ c. flour until mixture is well blended and forms a stiff batter. Cover with towel and let rise in warm place until doubled, about 50 minutes.

Using wooden spoon, stir down batter. Spoon batter evenly into 12 well-greased 3″ muffin-pan cups, filling about two-thirds full. Let rise, uncovered, until batter is level with tops of cups, about 25 minutes.

Bake in 350° oven 25 minutes or until golden brown. Immediately remove from pans. Serve warm. Makes 12 muffins.

Apple Crumb Batter Muffins

Fashioned after a German kuchen, these little yeast cakes make excellent breakfast or lunch-box treats.

> 1 tsp. ground cinnamon
> ⅓ c. sugar
> ¼ c. flour
> 2 tblsp. butter or regular margarine
> 1 pkg. active dry yeast
> ½ tsp. salt
> ½ c. sugar
> 2¼ c. sifted flour
> ¼ c. milk
> ¼ c. water
> ⅓ c. butter or regular margarine
> 2 eggs
> 1½ c. chopped, peeled apples
> ½ recipe Confectioners' Glaze (see Index)

In small bowl, stir together cinnamon, ⅓ c. sugar and ¼ c. flour. With pastry blender, cut in 2 tblsp. butter until crumbs form; set aside.

In large bowl, stir together yeast, salt, ½ c. sugar and 1 c. flour; set aside.

In 1-qt. saucepan over low heat, heat milk, water and ⅓ c. butter until very warm (120 to 130°).

Using mixer at low speed, gradually beat milk mixture into yeast mixture until well blended. Increase speed to medium; beat 2 minutes. Add eggs and ½ c. flour. Increase speed to high; beat 2 minutes more.

Using wooden spoon, gradually stir in apples and remaining ¾ c. flour until mixture is well blended and forms a stiff batter.

Spoon batter evenly into 12 well-greased muffin-pan cups, filling one-half full. Sprinkle cinnamon mixture over batter. Cover with towel and let rise in warm place until doubled, about 50 minutes.

Bake in 375° oven 30 minutes or until browned. Immediately remove from pans. Cool on racks 5 minutes.

Meanwhile, prepare Confectioners' Glaze; drizzle over warm muffins. Serve warm or cold. Makes 12 muffins.

Raised Breakfast Rolls

Let the dough rise while you sleep; in the morning, roll it out and bake fresh cinnamon rolls. This heirloom recipe comes from Texas.

1 pkg. active dry yeast
¼ c. sugar
4 c. sifted flour
1¼ c. milk
1 c. butter or regular margarine
2 eggs
2 tblsp. butter or regular margarine, melted
2 tsp. ground cinnamon
½ c. sugar

In large bowl, stir together yeast, ¼ c. sugar and 1½ c. flour; set aside.

In 2-qt. saucepan over low heat, heat milk and 1 c. butter until very warm (120 to 130°).

Using mixer at low speed, gradually beat milk mixture into yeast mixture until well blended. Increase speed to medium; beat 2 minutes. Add eggs and 1 c. flour; beat 2 minutes more.

Using wooden spoon, gradually stir in remaining 1½ c. flour until mixture is well blended and forms a thick batter. Cover tightly with plastic wrap and foil. Refrigerate 6 to 24 hours.

Using wooden spoon, stir down batter. Turn out batter onto lightly floured surface; divide in half. With lightly floured rolling pin, roll out each half into a 12″ square. Brush squares with 2 tblsp. melted butter.

In small bowl, stir together cinnamon and ½ c. sugar. Sprinkle sugar mixture over each dough square; roll up tightly, jelly-roll fashion. Pinch seams to seal.

Place a long piece of thread under 1 roll. Cross ends of thread and pull, cutting through dough. Repeat at ½″ intervals to cut roll into 24 slices. Place slices, cut-side down, 1″ apart, on greased baking sheets. Repeat with remaining roll. Do not let rise.

Bake in 350° oven 12 to 15 minutes or until brown. Immediately remove from baking sheets. Serve warm. Makes 48 rolls.

11
Pancakes, Waffles and Other Griddle Breads

Some of the easiest and fastest breads you can make are "baked" outside the oven on a griddle—Flapjacks, Johnnycakes, Crumpets and French Toast, to name just a few.

Although some griddle breads are made with yeast, such as our Silver Dollar Sourdough Pancakes and English Muffins, most are considered quick breads and are made from batters leavened with baking powder, baking soda or a mix of both. The method is the same one used to make many other quick breads: add liquid ingredients to the dry ingredients, then stir just enough to make a lumpy batter.

Waffles can be prepared from the same batter you'd use to make pancakes. Whichever you're making—pancakes or waffles— the griddle or waffle baker must be well seasoned to prevent the batter from sticking. Griddles and waffle bakers also should be preheated until they're hot enough to set the batter immediately, but not so hot that they burn the batter. Test the temperature of a griddle by sprinkling a few drops of water on it; if the droplets dance on the griddle, it's ready to use. To preheat your waffle baker, follow the manufacturer's directions.

In this country we call our griddle breads pancakes; in Mexico, flat griddle breads are Flour Tortillas; in France, they have paper-thin pancakes called Crêpes. In the Netherlands, the Dutch use a skillet to bake one large puffy pancake that yields four servings. For these recipes and more, turn the page.

Country Pancakes

Just add an egg, milk and a bit of sugar to our All-purpose Baking Mix and you'll have light, tender pancakes ready to serve in minutes.

  2½ c. All-purpose Baking Mix (see Index)
  1½ c. milk
  1 egg
  1 tblsp. sugar

In large bowl using mixer at medium speed, beat all ingredients just until blended. (Batter should be slightly lumpy.)

Using about ¼ c. batter for each pancake, pour batter onto lightly greased hot griddle. Bake until tops of pancakes are covered with bubbles and edges look dry. Turn and bake until bottoms are golden brown. Serve hot. Makes 12 (4½") pancakes.

COUNTRY WAFFLES: Bake batter in preheated waffle baker following manufacturer's directions. Makes 6 (7") round waffles.

Favorite Buttermilk Pancakes

Thick flapjacks that can be topped with fresh berries for brunch, or coupled with sausage and apples for dinner.

  2 c. sifted flour
  2 tblsp. sugar
  1 tsp. baking soda
  1 tsp. salt
  2 c. buttermilk
  2 tblsp. butter or regular margarine, melted
  2 eggs

Into large bowl, sift together flour, sugar, baking soda and salt.

In small bowl, mix buttermilk, melted butter and eggs until well blended. Add buttermilk mixture to dry ingredients; stir just until moistened. (Batter should be slightly lumpy.)

Using about ¼ c. batter for each pancake, pour batter onto lightly greased hot griddle. Bake until tops of pancakes are covered with bubbles and edges look dry. Turn and bake until bottoms are golden brown. Serve hot. Makes 16 (4") pancakes.

FRUITED FAVORITE BUTTERMILK PANCAKES: Add 1 c. of one of the following to batter: diced bananas; diced, peeled apples; fresh or frozen blueberries; or well-drained canned pineapple. Makes 18 (4") pancakes.

Flapjacks

A basic batter that's good for making silver dollar-size pancakes, whole-wheat pancakes, cinnamon pancakes, or waffles.

> 1¼ c. sifted all-purpose flour
> 2 tblsp. sugar
> 2 tsp. baking powder
> ½ tsp. salt
> 1¼ c. milk
> 3 tblsp. vegetable oil
> 1 egg

Into large bowl, sift together flour, sugar, baking powder and salt; set aside.

In medium bowl with wire whisk, beat milk, oil and egg until well blended. Add milk mixture to dry ingredients. With whisk, beat just until moistened. (Batter should be slightly lumpy.)

Using about ¼ c. batter for each flapjack, pour batter onto lightly greased hot griddle. Bake until tops of flapjacks are covered with bubbles and edges look dry. Turn and bake until bottoms are golden brown. Serve hot. Makes 14 (4") flapjacks.

SILVER DOLLAR FLAPJACKS: Use 1 tblsp. batter to make each silver dollar-size flapjack. Makes 40 (2") flapjacks.

CINNAMON FLAPJACKS: Add ½ tsp. ground cinnamon to dry ingredients, and ¼ tsp. vanilla to milk mixture.

WHOLE-WHEAT FLAPJACKS: Substitute ½ c. stirred whole-wheat flour for ½ c. sifted all-purpose flour.

WAFFLES: Increase milk to 1⅓ c. and increase oil to ¼ c. Bake batter in preheated waffle baker following manufacturer's directions. Makes 6 (7") round waffles.

Buckwheat Pancakes

An American favorite that's also popular in Brittany. Buckwheat is rich in iron, calcium and phosphorus.

  1½ c. sifted all-purpose flour
  1 tblsp. sugar
  1 tblsp. baking powder
  1 tsp. salt
  ½ c. stirred buckwheat flour
  2 c. milk
  1 tblsp. butter or regular margarine, melted
  1 egg

Into large bowl, sift together flour, sugar, baking powder and salt. Stir in buckwheat flour until well blended; set aside.

In small bowl, mix milk, melted butter and egg until well blended. Add milk mixture to dry ingredients; stir just until moistened. (Batter should be slightly lumpy.)

Using about ¼ c. batter for each pancake, pour batter onto lightly greased hot griddle. Bake until tops of pancakes are covered with bubbles and edges look dry. Turn and bake until bottoms are golden brown. Serve hot. Makes 15 (4") pancakes.

Yeast Pancakes

Make this batter in the evening and refrigerate overnight. Next morning, just heat the griddle or waffle baker and bake.

  1 pkg. active dry yeast
  2 c. sifted flour
  1 tblsp. sugar
  ¾ tsp. salt
  ½ tsp. baking soda
  1½ c. milk
  ½ c. butter or regular margarine
  3 eggs

In large bowl, stir together first 5 ingredients; set aside.

In 2-qt. saucepan over low heat, heat milk and butter until very warm (120 to 130°).

Using mixer at low speed, gradually beat milk mixture into yeast mixture until well blended. Add eggs. Increase speed to medium; beat 3 minutes. Cover tightly with plastic wrap. Refrigerate 2 to 24 hours.

Stir down batter. Using about ¼ c. batter for each pancake, pour batter onto lightly greased hot griddle. Bake until tops of pancakes are covered with bubbles and edges look dry. Turn and bake until bottoms are golden brown. Serve hot. Makes 16 (4″) pancakes.

YEAST WAFFLES: Bake batter in preheated waffle baker following manufacturer's directions. Makes 8 (7″) round waffles.

Silver Dollar Sourdough Pancakes

These thin, moist pancakes with a tangy flavor are especially popular in the West, where they originated.

> 1½ c. Sourdough Starter (see Index)
> ½ c. sifted flour
> ⅓ c. warm water (105 to 115°)
> ¼ c. nonfat dry milk
> 1 egg, beaten
> 2 tblsp. sugar
> 2 tblsp. vegetable oil
> ½ tsp. salt
> ¼ tsp. baking soda
> 2 tsp. water

In large glass or stoneware bowl, stir Sourdough Starter, flour and ⅓ c. warm water until smooth. Cover loosely with plastic wrap and let stand in warm place (85°) overnight.

Add dry milk, beaten egg, sugar, oil and salt. With wooden spoon, stir just until well blended. (Batter should be slightly lumpy.)

In small cup, stir together baking soda and 2 tsp. water. Gently stir baking soda mixture into batter.

Using about 1 tblsp. batter for each pancake, pour batter onto lightly greased hot griddle. Bake until tops of pancakes are covered with bubbles and edges look dry. Turn and bake until bottoms are golden brown. Serve hot. Makes 46 (2½″) pancakes.

Blue Ridge Pancakes

Southern-style pancakes made with corn meal—light and fluffy, with a buttermilk flavor.

1 c. sifted flour
1 tsp. sugar
1 tsp. baking soda
1 tsp. baking powder
¾ tsp. salt
1 c. white or yellow corn meal
3 eggs, separated
2 c. buttermilk
2 tblsp. butter or regular margarine, melted

Into large bowl, sift together first 5 ingredients. Stir in corn meal until well blended; set aside.

In small bowl using mixer at high speed, beat egg whites until stiff, but not dry peaks form; set aside.

In medium bowl, mix buttermilk, melted butter and egg yolks until well blended. Add buttermilk mixture to dry ingredients; stir just until moistened. Fold beaten egg whites into batter, leaving a few puffs of egg white showing.

Using ⅓ c. batter for each pancake, pour batter onto lightly greased hot griddle. Bake until tops of pancakes are covered with bubbles and edges look dry. Turn and bake until bottoms are golden brown. Serve hot. Makes 20 (4½") pancakes.

Corn Meal Pancakes

With our Corn Bread Mix, you can make these corn meal cakes in a hurry—just add milk and eggs!

> 1 c. milk
> 2 eggs
> 2½ c. Corn Bread Mix (see Index)

In medium bowl, with wire whisk, beat milk and eggs until well blended. Add Corn Bread Mix; beat just until moistened. (Batter should be slightly lumpy.)

Using about ¼ c. batter for each pancake, pour batter onto lightly greased hot griddle. Bake until tops of pancakes are covered with bubbles and edges look dry. Turn and bake until bottoms are golden brown. Serve hot. Makes 12 to 14 (4½") pancakes.

Johnnycakes

Over the centuries, these dense, slightly thick, corn meal cakes, which originated in Rhode Island, have been the subject of serious debate. Sometimes called journeycakes or Shawnee cakes, they were first made with only corn meal, water and salt. We've added a little sugar and an egg to improve their flavor and texture. We like them topped with butter and warm syrup or honey.

> 1 c. yellow corn meal
> 2 tblsp. sugar
> ½ tsp. salt
> 1 c. boiling water
> 1 egg

In medium bowl, stir together corn meal, sugar and salt. Gradually stir in boiling water until smooth. Add egg; beat until well blended.

Using 1 heaping tblsp. batter for each cake, pour batter onto lightly greased hot griddle. Bake until tops of cakes are covered with bubbles and edges look dry. Turn and bake until bottoms are golden brown. Serve hot. Makes 10 (3") cakes.

Crêpes

*Use these paper-thin French pancakes to make a main dish of
Cheese Blintzes or a dessert of Crêpes Suzette with a buttery
orange sauce.*

¾ c. sifted flour
1 tblsp. sugar
¼ tsp. salt
1 c. milk
3 eggs
2 tblsp. butter or regular margarine, melted

Sift together flour, sugar and salt; set aside.

In medium bowl using mixer at medium speed, beat milk and
eggs until well blended. Add dry ingredients; beat until batter is
smooth and well blended. Cover and refrigerate at least 30
minutes or up to 24 hours.

Brush 7 or 8" skillet with melted butter. Over medium-high
heat, heat skillet until hot. Pour a scant ¼ c. batter into skillet;
tip skillet to coat bottom with batter. Bake about 2 minutes, or
until edge of crêpe is browned and top loses its gloss.

With metal spatula, lift edge of crêpe all around. Shake skillet
to loosen crêpe and invert onto sheet of waxed paper. Repeat with
remaining batter, brushing skillet with melted butter as needed.
Stack crêpes between sheets of waxed paper. Makes about 12 (7 or
8") crêpes.

CRÊPES SUZETTE: Prepare crêpes. Fold each crêpe in quarters;
set aside.

In chafing dish or 10" skillet over medium heat, bring ½ c.
orange juice, ⅓ c. butter or regular margarine, 3 tblsp. sugar and
¾ tsp. grated orange rind to a boil, stirring constantly. Boil 1
minute. Reduce heat to low. Dip each folded crêpe in hot orange
mixture, arranging them around edge of skillet; keep warm.

In 1-qt. saucepan over medium heat, heat ⅓ c. orange-flavored
liqueur just until warm. Carefully ignite warm liqueur with match
and pour over crêpes. Serve immediately. Makes 6 servings.

STRAWBERRY CRÊPES: Prepare crêpes; set aside.

In medium bowl using mixer at medium speed, beat ¾ c. heavy cream, ¼ c. confectioners' sugar and ¼ tsp. vanilla until soft peaks form. Fold in 1 c. sliced strawberries.

Spoon 2 tblsp. strawberry mixture in center of one crêpe; fold over sides to make a roll. Repeat with remaining crêpes and whipped cream mixture. Sift confectioners' sugar over rolls. Serve immediately. Makes 6 servings.

CHEESE BLINTZES: Prepare crêpes; set aside.

In blender container, place 1 (8-oz.) container cream-style cottage cheese, 1 (3-oz.) pkg. cream cheese, softened, ½ tsp. vanilla, ⅛ tsp. ground cinnamon and 1 egg; cover. Blend at high speed until smooth.

Place 1 rounded tblsp. cheese mixture in center on browned side of one crêpe. Fold in 2 opposite sides of crêpe. Then fold in remaining 2 sides, overlapping cheese mixture, to form an envelope. Repeat with remaining cheese mixture and crêpes.

In 10″ skillet over medium heat, melt 2 tblsp. butter. Cook blintzes until browned on all sides. Top blintzes with warm cherry pie filling and a dollop of sour cream, if desired. Serve immediately. Makes 12 blintzes or 6 servings.

SWEDISH PANCAKES: Using 1 tblsp. batter for each pancake, pour batter onto lightly greased hot griddle. Bake until golden brown around edges. Turn and bake until bottoms are golden brown. (If you have a Swedish pancake griddle with indentations, by all means use it to make these pancakes.)

For each serving, arrange 6 pancakes in a circle with edges overlapping, on a small plate. Place a spoonful of raspberry or lingonberry jam in center of circle and top with a dollop of whipped cream. Serve immediately. Makes 5 servings.

Dutch Pancake Batter

A simple batter of flour, milk and eggs can be used to make a tempting variety of puffy pancakes for breakfast or dessert.

> ½ c. unsifted flour
> ½ c. milk
> 2 eggs
> ¼ tsp. salt

In small bowl, using mixer at medium speed, beat flour, milk, eggs and salt 2 minutes or until smooth. Use batter as directed to make the following three recipes.

Dutch Pancake

This big skillet pancake bakes in the oven into a golden brown puff.

> 1 recipe Dutch Pancake Batter
> 1 tsp. vanilla
> 1 tblsp. vegetable oil
> Orange Sauce (recipe follows)

Prepare Dutch Pancake Batter as directed; stir vanilla into batter.

In 450° oven on lowest rack, heat 10″ round casserole pan or oven-safe skillet, 5 minutes.

Add oil to hot pan, tilting pan to coat bottom and side. Pour batter into pan. Bake 10 minutes. Reduce temperature to 350° and bake 10 minutes more, or until pancake is puffy and browned. (As pancake bakes, it rises like a popover; as it cools, it will shrink slightly.)

While pancake is baking, prepare Orange Sauce.

Cut pancake into wedges. Serve immediately with warm sauce. Makes 2 to 3 breakfast servings.

ORANGE SAUCE: In 1-qt. saucepan, stir together ½ c. packed brown sugar, ¼ c. orange juice, 3 tblsp. butter or regular margarine and 1 tsp. grated orange rind. Over medium heat, bring mixture to a boil, stirring constantly. Reduce heat to medium-low and simmer 5 minutes, stirring frequently. Makes about ⅔ c. sauce.

Dutch Apple Pancake

Tastes like apple pie, but has fewer calories than its pastry-crusted cousin—plus it's much easier to make!

> 3 tblsp. butter or regular margarine
> 2 medium Golden Delicious or other baking apples,
>   peeled, cored and sliced
> 1 recipe Dutch Pancake Batter
> 1 tsp. vanilla
> ½ tsp. ground cinnamon
> Confectioners' sugar

In 10" oven-safe skillet over medium heat, melt butter. Add apples and cook until tender.

Meanwhile, prepare Dutch Pancake Batter; stir in vanilla.

When apples are tender, stir in cinnamon. Pour batter over apples in skillet.

In 450° oven on lowest rack, bake 10 minutes. Reduce temperature to 350° and bake 5 to 10 minutes more, or until pancake is puffy and browned. Generously sift confectioners' sugar over pancake. Cut pancake into wedges. Serve immediately. Makes 2 to 3 breakfast, or 4 to 6 dessert servings.

Sausage 'n' Pancake Bake

Sausage links are baked right in this pancake which resembles Yorkshire pudding. You may know this as "Toad-in-the-Hole."

> ¼ c. vegetable oil
> 3 recipes Dutch Pancake Batter
> 12 pork sausage links, cooked and drained

Pour oil into 13x9x2" baking pan. Place in 450° oven on lowest rack and heat 5 minutes.

Meanwhile, prepare a triple batch of Dutch Pancake Batter. Pour batter into hot pan and evenly arrange cooked sausage links in batter.

Bake in 450° oven 15 minutes. Reduce temperature to 350° and bake 10 minutes more, or until pancake is puffy and browned. Cut into squares. Serve immediately. Makes 6 servings.

French Toast

In France, country cooks soaked day-old bread in an egg mixture, fried it and called it "lost bread." For a real treat, try using thick slices of Challah, French or Italian bread.

> 3 eggs
> 1 c. milk
> 1 tblsp. sugar
> ¼ tsp. salt
> 8 slices bread
> Confectioners' sugar

In pie plate with fork, beat eggs, milk, sugar and salt until well blended. Quickly dip bread slices into egg mixture, turning to coat both sides.

Place toast on well-greased hot griddle. Bake, turning once, until toast is golden brown on both sides. Sift confectioners' sugar over toast. Serve hot. Makes 8 slices.

CINNAMON FRENCH TOAST: Stir 1 tsp. vanilla and ¼ tsp. ground cinnamon into egg mixture.

LEMON FRENCH TOAST: Substitute 2 tblsp. confectioners' sugar for sugar. Add 1 tsp. grated lemon rind to egg mixture.

THICK FRENCH TOAST: Substitute 6 (1"-thick) slices Challah (see Index), 12 (1"-thick) slices French Bread (see Index) or 8 (1"-thick) slices Italian Bread (see Index) for bread.

Sunday Supper Waffles

These savory waffles can be made with white or whole-wheat flour.
Bake them plain, or fold pecans or bacon bits into the batter.

> 1 c. sifted all-purpose flour
> 2 tsp. baking powder
> ¼ tsp. salt
> 2 eggs, separated
> 1 c. milk
> ¼ c. butter or regular margarine, melted

Into large bowl sift together flour, baking powder and salt; set aside.

In small bowl, using mixer at high speed, beat egg whites until stiff, but not dry peaks form; set aside.

Add milk, melted butter and egg yolks to dry ingredients. Using mixer at medium speed, beat just until well blended. Do not overbeat. Gently fold beaten egg whites into batter, leaving a few puffs of egg white showing.

Bake batter in preheated waffle baker following manufacturer's directions. Serve hot. Makes 14 (7") round waffles.

SUNDAY SUPPER PECAN WAFFLES: Fold ½ c. chopped pecans into batter before baking.

SUNDAY SUPPER BACON WAFFLES: Fold 6 slices bacon, cooked, drained and crumbled into batter before baking.

SUNDAY SUPPER WHOLE-WHEAT WAFFLES: Substitute ½ c. stirred whole-wheat flour for ½ c. sifted all-purpose flour.

Southern Corn Meal Waffles

Capture the flavors of down-home cooking—serve corn waffles with honey-flavored butter and thick slices of country ham.

1 c. sifted flour
2 tsp. sugar
1 tsp. baking powder
½ tsp. baking soda
½ tsp. salt
1 c. white or yellow corn meal
2 c. buttermilk
¼ c. vegetable oil
2 eggs

Into large bowl sift together first 5 ingredients. Stir in corn meal until well blended; set aside.

In small bowl, mix buttermilk, oil and eggs until well blended. Add buttermilk mixture to dry ingredients; stir just until well blended. (Batter should be slightly lumpy.)

Bake batter in preheated waffle baker following manufacturer's directions. Serve hot. Makes 8 (7") round waffles.

Belgian Waffles

These extra-thick waffles are traditionally served topped with sweetened whipped cream and fresh strawberries.

4 eggs, separated
2 tblsp. sugar
½ tsp. vanilla
¼ tsp. salt
3 tblsp. butter or regular margarine, melted
1 c. sifted flour
1 c. milk
Confectioners' sugar

In small bowl using mixer at high speed, beat egg whites until stiff, but not dry peaks form; set aside.

In another small bowl using mixer at high speed, beat egg yolks, sugar, vanilla and salt until thick and lemon colored. Beat in melted butter. Reduce speed to low; beat in flour alternately with milk just until smooth. Fold beaten egg whites into batter, leaving a few puffs of egg white showing.

Bake batter in preheated Belgian waffle baker following manufacturer's directions. Sift confectioners' sugar over waffles. Serve hot. Makes 4 (7") square or 16 (3½") square waffles.

Gingerbread Waffles

For a delectable dessert, serve these spicy waffles à la mode.

        2 c. sifted flour
        1½ tsp. baking powder
        1 tsp. ground cinnamon
        1 tsp. ground ginger
        ½ tsp. salt
        ¼ tsp. ground allspice
        2 eggs, separated
        ¼ c. butter or regular margarine
        ½ c. packed brown sugar
        ½ c. molasses
        1 c. milk

Sift together first 6 ingredients; set aside.

In small bowl using mixer at high speed, beat egg whites until stiff, but not dry peaks form; set aside.

In large bowl using mixer at medium speed, beat butter and brown sugar until light and fluffy. Beat in egg yolks, molasses and milk until well mixed. Reduce speed to low; beat in dry ingredients just until well blended. Fold beaten egg whites into batter, leaving a few puffs of egg white showing.

Bake batter in preheated waffle baker following manufacturer's directions. Serve hot. Makes 8 (7") round waffles.

Flour Tortillas

You don't need a tortilla press to make the basic "bread" staple of Mexican cuisine. Unlike corn tortillas, which use a special blend of corn meal called masa harina, flour tortillas are made from flour, shortening, salt and water. Use flour tortillas for tacos, burritos, enchiladas, or serve plain as chips.

2 c. sifted flour
1 tsp. salt
2 tblsp. shortening or lard
8 to 10 tblsp. warm water

In medium bowl, stir together flour and salt. With pastry blender, cut in shortening until fine crumbs form.

Sprinkle warm water over crumb mixture, 1 tblsp. at a time, tossing with fork until dough forms. Knead briefly in bowl until mixture forms a ball. Cover with towel and let rest 15 minutes.

Divide dough into 12 pieces. Shape each piece into a ball.

On lightly floured surface with floured rolling pin, roll out each ball to a 7" circle. (Keep remaining pieces of dough covered.)

In 10" skillet over medium-high heat, bake tortillas one at a time, turning once, about 3 minutes, or until tortillas are blistered and small brown spots appear on both sides. Remove from skillet. Stack tortillas between sheets of waxed paper. Makes 12 tortillas.

Green Onion Cakes

Also known in China as scallion cakes, these simple, pan-fried cakes go well with stir-fried chicken or beef dishes.

2 c. sifted flour
¾ c. iced water
Vegetable oil
½ c. finely chopped green onions
2 cloves garlic, minced
1 tsp. salt

Place flour in medium bowl. Gradually add iced water in a steady stream, stirring until mixture forms a stiff dough that leaves side of bowl.

Turn out dough onto lightly floured surface. Knead until smooth, 1 to 2 minutes. Cover with towel and let rest 15 minutes.

Knead dough until no longer sticky, adding additional flour if necessary.

On lightly floured surface with floured rolling pin, roll out dough into a 17" circle. Brush with 1 tblsp. oil. Sprinkle green onions, garlic and salt evenly over dough.

Roll up tightly, jelly-roll fashion; pinch seam and ends to seal. With sharp knife, cut roll into 4 pieces. Pinch cut ends of each piece to seal.

Coil each piece into a circle; tuck ends under. Press between hands to make a 1"-thick cake. Cover cakes with plastic wrap.

On heavily floured surface with floured rolling pin, roll out each cake into a 7" circle.

In 10" skillet over medium-high heat, heat 1 tblsp. oil until hot. Add one cake. Bake 30 seconds; cover. Reduce heat to medium-low; continue baking 2 minutes. Turn cake; cover and bake 2 minutes more, or until cake is slightly puffy and small brown spots appear on bottom.

Remove from skillet; drain briefly on paper towels. Keep warm in 300° oven. Repeat with remaining cakes. Cut each cake into 4 wedges. Serve warm. Makes 4 (7") cakes.

Paratha

The breads of India have unique shapes and most are unleavened.
Their answer to the tortilla is this whole-wheat bread.

> 1½ c. stirred whole-wheat flour
> ½ tsp. salt
> 1 tblsp. vegetable oil
> ½ to ⅔ c. water
> ¼ to ⅓ c. butter or regular margarine, melted

In medium bowl, stir together whole-wheat flour and salt. With fork, stir in oil and enough water to make a very stiff dough. Knead in bowl until smooth and pliable, about 10 minutes.

Divide dough into 8 pieces. Shape each piece into a ball. Flatten balls slightly. Cover with plastic wrap to prevent balls from drying out.

On whole-wheat floured surface with whole-wheat floured rolling pin, roll out one ball to a 5" circle. Brush with some melted butter. Fold circle in half and brush with melted butter. Fold in half again, you now have a pie-shaped wedge.

Flatten wedge slightly and roll from center to each point until sides are about 6"-long. Cover with plastic wrap to keep from drying out. Repeat with remaining balls.

Over medium-high heat, heat 12" skillet until hot. Brush skillet with some melted butter. Bake wedges, 2 at a time, in skillet 2 minutes or until lightly browned.

Brush tops with some melted butter. Turn and bake 2 minutes more or until lightly browned. Remove from skillet. Brush again with some melted butter. Wrap in single layer in foil. Keep warm in 300° oven. Repeat with remaining wedges. Serve warm. Makes 8 paratha.

To Reheat: Store foil-wrapped paratha in refrigerator up to 4 days. Heat wrapped paratha in 300° oven 10 minutes or until heated through. Or, unwrap paratha and brush both sides with melted butter. In 12" skillet over medium heat, heat paratha about 2 minutes, turning once.

Lefse

A South Dakota woman's recipe for a pancake-like Norwegian potato bread that's baked on a griddle. On Christmas Eve, it's customary to serve this flat bread with oyster stew.

2 lb. baking potatoes (4 large), peeled and quartered
1 tsp. salt
¼ c. half-and-half
¼ c. butter or regular margarine, melted
2¼ c. sifted flour
⅓ c. butter or regular margarine, softened
Granulated white or brown sugar

Place potatoes and salt in 2-qt. saucepan; add enough water to cover potatoes. Over high heat, bring to a boil. Reduce heat to low. Cover and simmer about 20 minutes, or until potatoes are tender. Drain; rice potatoes using potato ricer. Cover and refrigerate at least 8 hours.

Firmly pack potatoes into measuring cups. You will need 3½ c.

In large bowl, stir potatoes, half-and-half and ¼ c. melted butter until well blended. Gradually stir in flour until soft dough forms. Shape dough into 12"-long rope, making sure to remove air bubbles. Divide rope into 12 pieces.

On well-floured pastry cloth using floured, stockinet-covered rolling pin, roll out one piece of dough into 12" pancake. The pancake should be very thin, about ¹/₁₆" thick. Carefully roll pancake around rolling pin so it can be easily transferred to griddle.

Bake pancake on ungreased hot griddle or in 12" skillet until small brown spots appear on the underside. Using long metal spatula, turn and bake until brown spots appear on other side. Using metal spatula, fold lefse into fourths. Place on towel (do not use a terry towel). Cover with another towel.

Roll out remaining dough pieces and bake. Place folded lefse on top of each other and cover with towel.

Cool lefse to room temperature. Use immediately, or wrap in plastic wrap, placing 6 lefse in a package. Place packages in plastic bag to keep lefse soft. Refrigerate up to 5 days.

Lefse should be served at room temperature. Unfold lefse and cut in half. Spread each half with softened butter; sprinkle with sugar. Fold each half into thirds, forming pie-shaped wedges. Makes 24 lefse.

English Muffins

Plump, golden brown rounds that bake on a griddle. Split them open with a fork, then toast.

        1 pkg. active dry yeast
        1 tblsp. sugar
        1½ c. warm water (105 to 115°)
        2 tblsp. butter or regular margarine, melted
        1 tsp. salt
        4¼ to 4¾ c. sifted flour
        Yellow corn meal

In large bowl, sprinkle yeast and sugar over warm water; stir until dissolved.

Using mixer at low speed, gradually beat butter, salt and 2 c. flour into yeast mixture until well blended. Increase speed to medium; beat 2 minutes. Add ½ c. flour; beat 2 minutes more.

Stir in enough additional flour to make a soft dough. Turn out dough onto lightly floured surface. Knead until smooth and elastic, about 5 to 8 minutes.

Place in greased large bowl, turning over dough so that top is greased. Cover with towel and let rise in warm place until doubled, about 45 minutes.

Punch down dough. Cover and let rest 5 minutes.

On lightly floured surface with floured rolling pin, roll out dough to ½" thickness. Cover and let rest 5 minutes. With floured 3" biscuit cutter, cut dough into 18 circles.

Sprinkle corn meal over greased large baking sheets. Place rounds, 2" apart, on baking sheets.

Cover and let rise until doubled, about 30 minutes.

Over medium heat, heat lightly greased griddle until hot. With wide metal spatula, carefully transfer 6 rounds to griddle. Bake, turning once, 16 to 20 minutes, or until muffins are browned on both sides and sound hollow when tapped. Remove and cool on racks. Repeat with remaining rounds.

Split, toast and serve. Makes 18 (3") muffins.

Crumpets

The honeycomb texture of these thin yeast cakes results from the fast-rising action of the yeast when it hits the hot griddle. If you don't have round metal crumpet rings, use 7-oz. tuna cans and remove both tops and bottoms.

> 1 pkg. active dry yeast
> 1 tsp. sugar
> ⅔ c. warm water (105 to 115°)
> 2 c. sifted flour
> ⅔ c. milk
> 2 tblsp. butter or regular margarine, melted
> 1 tsp. salt
> ¼ tsp. baking soda
> 1 tblsp. hot water

In large bowl, sprinkle yeast and sugar over warm water; stir until dissolved.

Using mixer at low speed, gradually beat in flour, milk, melted butter and salt until well blended. Increase speed to medium; beat 4 minutes.

Cover with towel and let rise in warm place until doubled, about 1 hour.

In small bowl, stir together baking soda and hot water. Using wooden spoon, stir baking soda mixture into batter, beat 30 seconds. Let rise, uncovered, until doubled, about 1 hour.

Over medium-high heat, heat griddle until hot. Place 4 well-greased 3¼" crumpet rings on griddle. (If you don't have the rings, use 7-oz. tuna cans and remove both tops and bottoms.)

Pour ¼ c. batter into each ring. Reduce heat to medium-low. Bake 8 to 10 minutes, or until surface appears dry and crumpets are set. Remove rings. Turn crumpets; bake 8 to 10 minutes more or until golden brown. Remove and cool on racks. Wipe off griddle and regrease rings before using again. Repeat with remaining batter.

Split, toast and serve. Makes 10 to 12 crumpets.

12
Doughnuts,
Fritters and More

Golden brown on the outside, light and tender on the inside—
fresh doughnuts are one of America's favorite breakfast treats.
Whether they be Peach Doughnuts, Cinnamon Swirls, or Vanilla-
glazed Doughnuts, they're not hard to make and take only
minutes to cook.

The trick in making doughnuts, fritters or any fried bread is to
keep the hot oil at an even temperature. A deep-fry thermometer
is the tool that'll help you maintain the right temperature (specific
temperatures are given in our recipes).

Other than this measuring device, you don't need any special
equipment, not even a deep fryer—any deep, heavy pan will do. As
you're frying Cake Doughnuts or rich New Orleans Beignets,
remember to fry only a few pieces of dough at a time. Adding too
much dough quickly lowers the oil temperature, causing greasy,
unevenly fried breads.

Not all fried breads are sweet. Among the savory recipes in this
chapter are vegetable fritters; whole-wheat puffs called Poori;
Langos, rectangular-shaped rolls that are rubbed with garlic
before serving; and corn meal nuggets named Hush Puppies.

Other breads, such as Bagels and Soft Pretzels, are boiled in
water before baking to give them their characteristic chewy
texture. Chinese Steamed Pork Buns—filled with spicy
ground pork—can be kept frozen and are ready to steam when
needed. For a sweet finale, steam a loaf of Boston Brown Bread.

Cake Doughnuts

Lightly spiced with cinnamon and nutmeg, these doughnuts have a dense, cake-like texture that makes them ideal for dunking.

> 3½ c. sifted flour
> 1 tblsp. baking powder
> ¾ tsp. salt
> ½ tsp. ground cinnamon
> ¼ tsp. ground nutmeg
> 4 eggs
> ⅔ c. sugar
> ⅓ c. milk
> ⅓ c. shortening, melted and cooled
> About 1 qt. vegetable oil
> Confectioners' sugar or granulated sugar

Sift together first 5 ingredients; set aside.

In large bowl using mixer at medium speed, beat eggs and ⅔ c. sugar until light. Beat in milk and melted shortening.

Reduce speed to low. Beat in dry ingredients until well blended. Cover dough and refrigerate until well chilled, about 2 hours.

In 4-qt. Dutch oven over medium heat, heat 1" oil to 375° on deep-fat thermometer.

On floured surface with floured rolling pin, roll out dough to ³/₈" thickness. Cut dough with floured 2¾" doughnut cutter.

Using metal spatula, carefully lift and slide 5 doughnuts and 5 centers into hot oil. Fry, turning once, 5 minutes or until golden brown on both sides. Remove and drain on paper towels. Repeat with remaining doughnuts and centers.

Place confectioners' sugar in paper bag. Gently shake warm doughnuts, one at a time, in sugar until coated. Makes about 24 doughnuts and 24 centers.

COCONUT CAKE DOUGHNUTS: Prepare and fry doughnuts as directed, but do not coat with confectioners' sugar.

In small bowl, stir 2¼ c. sifted confectioners' sugar, 3 tblsp. milk and ½ tsp. vanilla until smooth. Dip tops and centers of warm doughnuts in glaze and then in 1¾ c. toasted coconut.

Potato Doughnuts

Mashed potatoes provide these yeast-risen doughnuts with added lightness, and the honey glaze gives them a beautiful sheen.

1 pkg. active dry yeast
½ c. sugar
1 tsp. salt
6¼ to 6¾ c. sifted flour
¼ c. water
¼ c. butter or regular margarine
1½ c. milk
½ c. mashed potatoes
2 eggs
About 1 qt. vegetable oil
3 c. sifted confectioners' sugar
3 tblsp. honey
1½ tsp. vanilla
5 tblsp. milk

In large bowl, stir together yeast, sugar, salt and 1½ c. flour.

In 2-qt. saucepan over low heat, heat water, butter and 1½ c. milk until very warm (120 to 130°).

Using mixer at low speed, gradually beat milk mixture into yeast mixture until well blended. Increase speed to medium; beat 2 minutes. Add potatoes, eggs and ¼ c. flour; beat 2 minutes more.

Stir in enough additional flour to make a soft dough. Turn out dough onto lightly floured surface. Knead until smooth and elastic, about 5 minutes. Dough will be soft.

Place in greased large bowl, turning over dough so that top is greased. Cover with towel and let rise in warm place until doubled, about 1 hour 30 minutes.

Punch down dough. On lightly floured surface, gently knead dough 1 minute. Divide dough in half. Cover and let rest 5 minutes.

With floured rolling pin, roll out dough to ³/₈" thickness. Cut dough with floured 2¾" doughnut cutter. Place doughnuts and centers on lightly floured baking sheets.

Cover and let rise until doubled, about 45 minutes.

During last 10 minutes of rising time: In 4-qt. Dutch oven over medium heat, heat 1" oil to 375° on deep-fat thermometer.

Using metal spatula, carefully lift and slide 5 doughnuts and 5 centers into hot oil. Fry, turning once, 3 minutes or until golden brown on both sides. Remove and drain on paper towels. Repeat with remaining doughnuts and centers.

In small bowl, stir confectioners' sugar, honey, vanilla and 5 tblsp. milk until smooth. Dip tops and centers of warm doughnuts in glaze. Serve warm. Makes about 24 doughnuts and 24 centers.

Peach Doughnuts

You'll want to make a double batch of these tender morsels because they'll disappear as fast as you can fry them.

> About 1 qt. vegetable oil
> ⅓ c. water
> 2 eggs
> 3 tblsp. sugar
> 2 c. All-purpose Baking Mix (see Index)
> ½ c. chopped, drained, canned peaches
> Confectioners' sugar

In 4-qt. Dutch oven over medium heat, heat 1″ oil to 365° on deep-fat thermometer.

Meanwhile, in large bowl, mix water, eggs and sugar until well blended. Stir in All-purpose Baking Mix just until moistened. Gently stir in peaches.

Drop 6 rounded tblsp. of batter, 1 tblsp. at a time, into hot oil. Fry, turning once, 3 minutes or until golden brown on both sides. Remove and drain on paper towels. Repeat with remaining batter. Roll doughnuts in confectioners' sugar. Serve warm. Makes 18 doughnuts.

Cinnamon Swirls

Pinwheel-shaped, yeast-risen doughnuts that are filled with sugar and spice and iced with a cinnamon-scented glaze.

        1 pkg. active dry yeast
        ¾ tsp. salt
        3 to 3½ c. sifted flour
        ⅓ c. sugar
        1 c. milk
        3 tblsp. butter or regular margarine
        1½ tsp. ground cinnamon
        1 tblsp. sugar
        About 1 qt. vegetable oil
        Cinnamon Glaze (recipe follows)

In large bowl, stir together yeast, salt, 1 c. flour and ⅓ c. sugar; set aside.

In 2-qt. saucepan over low heat, heat milk and butter until very warm (120 to 130°).

Using mixer at low speed, gradually beat milk mixture into yeast mixture until well blended. Increase speed to medium; beat 2 minutes. Add 1 c. flour; beat 2 minutes more.

Stir in enough additional flour to make a soft dough. Turn out dough onto lightly floured surface. Knead until smooth and elastic, about 5 minutes.

Place in greased large bowl, turning over dough so that top is greased. Cover with towel and let rise in warm place until doubled, about 50 minutes.

Punch down dough. Cover and let rest 10 minutes. Meanwhile, mix together cinnamon and 1 tblsp. sugar; set aside.

On floured surface with rolling pin, roll out dough to an 18x8" rectangle. Sprinkle cinnamon mixture evenly over rectangle. Starting with one long side, roll up rectangle, jelly-roll fashion. Pinch seam to seal. Cut roll into 18 (1") slices.

Place slices, 2" apart, on lightly floured baking sheets. Flatten each slice slightly.

Let rise, uncovered, in warm place until doubled, about 30 to 45 minutes.

During last 10 minutes of rising time: In 4-qt. Dutch oven over medium heat, heat 1" oil to 365° on deep-fat thermometer. Prepare Cinnamon Glaze; set aside.

Using metal spatula, carefully lift and slide 5 doughnuts into hot oil. Fry, turning once, 3 minutes or until golden brown.

Remove and drain on paper towels. Repeat with remaining doughnuts. Dip tops of warm doughnuts in glaze. Serve warm. Makes 18 doughnuts.

CINNAMON GLAZE: In small bowl, stir 1 c. sifted confectioners' sugar, ½ tsp. ground cinnamon and 5 tsp. milk until smooth.

Vanilla-glazed Doughnuts

Once you bite into a warm homemade jelly doughnut, you'll never want to settle for store-bought again.

> 1 pkg. active dry yeast
> ¼ tsp. sugar
> ¼ c. warm water (105 to 115°)
> 1 tsp. salt
> 1 egg
> 3 to 3½ c. sifted flour
> ¾ c. milk
> ¼ c. vegetable oil
> 3 tblsp. sugar
> ⅓ c. jelly, jam or preserves (raspberry, strawberry, grape or apricot)
> 1 egg white
> About 1 qt. vegetable oil
> 1½ c. sifted confectioners' sugar
> 1 tsp. vanilla
> 2 tblsp. milk

In large bowl, sprinkle yeast and ¼ tsp. sugar over warm water; stir until dissolved. Add salt, egg, 1½ c. flour, ¾ c. milk, ¼ c. oil and 3 tblsp. sugar.

Using mixer at medium speed, beat 2 minutes. Stir in enough additional flour to make a soft dough. Turn out dough onto lightly floured surface. Knead until smooth and elastic, about 5 minutes.

Place in greased large bowl, turning over dough so that top is greased. Cover with towel and let rise in warm place until doubled, about 1 hour.

Punch down dough. Cover and let rest 10 minutes.

On lightly floured surface with floured rolling pin, roll out dough to ¼" thickness. With floured 3" biscuit cutter, cut dough into 28 circles. Place 14 circles on lightly floured baking sheet.

Spoon 1 tsp. jelly in center of each circle. Brush edge of each circle with egg white. Top each circle with another circle. Press edges of circles together to seal.

Cover and let rise until doubled, about 1 hour.

During last 10 minutes of rising time: In 4-qt. Dutch oven over medium heat, heat 1" oil to 365° on deep-fat thermometer.

Using metal spatula, carefully lift and slide 5 doughnuts into hot oil. Fry, turning once, 3 minutes or until golden brown on both sides. Remove and drain on paper towels. Repeat with remaining doughnuts.

In small bowl, stir confectioners' sugar, vanilla and 2 tblsp. milk until smooth. Frost tops of doughnuts with sugar mixture. Serve warm. Makes 14 doughnuts.

Funnel Cakes

A traditional German recipe for fried doughnuts. Each one has its own lacy shape, because the batter is poured into a funnel, then drizzled into hot oil and fried to a golden brown.

About 1 qt. vegetable oil
2½ c. sifted flour
¼ c. sugar
2 tsp. baking soda
1½ tsp. baking powder
½ tsp. salt
1½ c. milk
2 eggs
Confectioners' sugar

In 4-qt. Dutch oven over medium heat, heat 1" oil to 375° on deep-fat thermometer.

Meanwhile, into large bowl, sift together flour, sugar, baking soda, baking powder and salt; set aside.

In small bowl, mix milk and eggs until well blended. Add milk mixture to dry ingredients; stir until batter is smooth.

Holding forefinger over tip of funnel, pour ½ c. batter into funnel. Remove finger and move funnel in a circle to drop batter into hot oil, forming a spiral.

Fry, turning once, 2 minutes or until golden brown. Remove and drain on paper towels. Repeat with remaining batter. Sift confectioners' sugar over cakes. Serve warm. Makes 6 cakes.

Fastnachts

Small German doughnuts, dusted with cinnamon and sugar, are traditionally served on Shrove Tuesday, the day before the beginning of Lent.

> 1 pkg. active dry yeast
> ½ tsp. salt
> 3¾ to 4¼ c. sifted flour
> ⅓ c. sugar
> 1 c. very warm water (120 to 130°)
> ¼ c. butter or regular margarine, softened
> 1 egg
> About 1 qt. vegetable oil
> 1 tsp. ground cinnamon
> 1 c. sugar

In large bowl, stir together yeast, salt, 1¼ c. flour and ⅓ c. sugar.

Using mixer at low speed, gradually beat warm water into yeast mixture until well blended. Increase speed to medium; beat 2 minutes. Add softened butter, egg and ½ c. flour. Beat 2 minutes more.

Stir in enough additional flour to make a soft dough. Turn out dough onto lightly floured surface. Knead until smooth and elastic, about 5 minutes.

Place in greased large bowl, turning over dough so that top is greased. Cover with towel and let rise in warm place until doubled, about 1 hour.

Punch down dough. Cover and let rest 10 minutes.

On lightly floured surface with floured rolling pin, roll out dough into a 16x8" rectangle. Cut into 2" squares; then cut a 1"-long slit completely through each square. Place squares on lightly floured baking sheet.

Cover and let rise until doubled, about 45 minutes.

During last 10 minutes of rising time: In 4-qt. Dutch oven over medium heat, heat 1″ oil to 375° on deep-fat thermometer.

Using metal spatula, carefully lift and slide 4 squares into hot oil. Fry, turning once, 2 minutes or until golden brown on both sides. Remove and drain on paper towels. Repeat with remaining squares.

In small bowl, stir together cinnamon and 1 c. sugar. Roll warm doughnuts in sugar mixture. Serve warm. Makes 32 doughnuts.

Rosettes

Add interest at your next buffet dinner—serve Chicken à la King spooned over crisp, fried rosettes. Simply omit the sugar and vanilla when you make the batter.

> About 1 qt. vegetable oil
> 2 eggs
> 2 tblsp. sugar
> ¾ tsp. vanilla
> ¼ tsp. salt
> 1¼ c. sifted flour
> 1 c. milk
> Confectioners' sugar

In 4-qt. Dutch oven over medium heat, heat 1″ oil to 365° on deep-fat thermometer.

Meanwhile, in small bowl, using mixer at medium speed, beat eggs, sugar, vanilla and salt until blended. Reduce speed to low. Add flour alternately with milk to egg mixture, beating well after each addition.

Immerse rosette iron in hot oil to heat, about 1 minute. Dip hot iron into batter, being careful not to let batter run over the top of the iron. (This will make it difficult to remove the rosette from the iron after frying.)

Immerse batter-dipped iron in hot oil and fry until golden brown, 30 seconds to 1 minute. Remove. Using fork, remove rosette from iron, and drain on paper towels.

Repeat, immersing iron in hot oil each time before dipping into batter. Store in airtight container. Before serving, sift confectioners' sugar over rosettes. Makes 40 (3″) rosettes.

Spice Puffs

After a winter's outing, adults and children alike will welcome a snack of cinnamon-coated doughnuts and hot chocolate.

About 1 qt. vegetable oil
2¼ c. sifted flour
1 tblsp. baking powder
½ tsp. salt
½ tsp. ground mace
⅓ c. sugar
½ tsp. ground cinnamon
¾ c. milk
1 egg
¼ c. vegetable oil
1 c. sugar
1 tsp. ground cinnamon

In 4-qt. Dutch oven over medium heat, heat 1″ oil to 375° on deep-fat thermometer.

Meanwhile, into large bowl, sift together flour, baking powder, salt, mace, ⅓ c. sugar and ½ tsp. cinnamon.

In small bowl, mix milk, egg and ¼ c. oil until well blended. Add milk mixture to dry ingredients; stir just until blended.

Drop 8 tsp. of batter, 1 tsp. at a time, into hot oil. Fry, turning once, 2 to 3 minutes or until golden brown on both sides. Remove and drain on paper towels. Repeat with remaining batter.

In small bowl, stir together 1 c. sugar and 1 tsp. cinnamon. Roll warm doughnuts in sugar mixture. Serve warm or cold. Makes 7 doz. doughnuts.

Blueberry Fritters

Folding beaten egg whites into the batter makes these bite-size morsels tender and light.

About 1 qt. vegetable oil
2 c. sifted flour
¼ c. sugar
2 tsp. baking powder
1 tsp. salt
½ tsp. ground cinnamon
4 eggs, separated
¾ c. milk
2 tsp. lemon juice
1 tsp. grated lemon rind
1 pt. fresh or frozen blueberries
Confectioners' sugar or maple syrup

In 4-qt. Dutch oven over medium heat, heat 1″ oil to 365° on deep-fat thermometer.

Meanwhile, into large bowl, sift together flour, sugar, baking powder, salt and cinnamon; set aside.

In small bowl using mixer at high speed, beat egg whites until stiff, but not dry peaks form; set aside.

In another small bowl using mixer at medium speed, beat egg yolks, milk, lemon juice and lemon rind until well blended.

Gently stir egg yolk mixture into dry ingredients, just until blended. Then, gently fold in egg whites and blueberries.

Drop 3 tblsp. batter, 1 tblsp. at a time, into hot oil. Fry, turning once, 3 minutes or until golden brown on both sides. Remove and drain on paper towels. Repeat with remaining batter. Sift confectioners' sugar over fritters or serve with syrup. Serve warm. Makes 24 fritters.

CORN FRITTERS: Omit sugar, cinnamon, lemon juice and lemon rind. Substitute 1½ c. fresh or frozen corn, cooked and drained, for blueberries.

Beignets

These are a French version of fritters, made from a simple dough that's deep-fried to a golden brown. Sprinkled with sugar, they make a great dessert.

About 1 qt. vegetable oil
1 c. water
⅓ c. butter or regular margarine
1 tsp. granulated sugar
¼ tsp. salt
1 c. sifted flour
4 eggs
1 tsp. vanilla
Confectioners' sugar

In 4-qt. Dutch oven over medium heat, heat 1" oil to 375° on deep-fat thermometer.

Meanwhile, in 2-qt. saucepan over medium heat, bring water, butter, granulated sugar and salt to a boil. Remove from heat. With wooden spoon, stir in flour all at once.

Return to heat; stir until mixture forms a ball that leaves side of pan, about 2 minutes. Remove from heat; cool 5 minutes. Add eggs, one at a time, beating well after each addition until smooth. Beat in vanilla.

Drop 10 tsp. of dough, 1 tsp. at a time, into hot oil. Fry, turning once, 2 minutes or until golden brown on both sides. Remove and drain on paper towels. Repeat with remaining dough. Sift confectioners' sugar over beignets. Serve warm. Makes about 6 doz. beignets.

New Orleans Beignets

In the French Quarter of New Orleans, you'll find little square doughnuts called beignets. The sweet, rich yeast dough is chilled for easier handling before it's rolled.

1 pkg. active dry yeast
3 tblsp. sugar
½ c. warm water (105 to 115°)
¾ tsp. salt
1 c. heavy cream
1 egg
3 c. sifted flour
About 1 qt. vegetable oil
Confectioners' sugar

In large bowl, sprinkle yeast and sugar over warm water; stir until dissolved. Stir in salt, cream and egg until well blended.

Gradually stir in flour until mixture forms a soft dough that leaves side of bowl. Cover tightly with plastic wrap. Refrigerate 2 to 24 hours.

Turn out dough onto heavily floured surface. With floured rolling pin, roll out dough to a 15x12½" rectangle. Cut dough into 2½" squares. Cover and let rest 10 minutes.

Meanwhile, in 4-qt. Dutch oven over medium heat, heat 1" oil to 375° on deep-fat thermometer.

Using metal spatula, carefully lift and slide 5 squares into hot oil. Fry, turning once, 2 minutes or until golden brown on both sides. Remove and drain on paper towels. Repeat with remaining squares. Sift confectioners' sugar over beignets. Serve warm. Makes 30 beignets.

Hush Puppies

Did you ever wonder how these got their name? It's said that fishermen would fry these corn meal nuggets along with their catch and toss them to the hounds to keep them quiet.

About 1 qt. vegetable oil
1¼ c. yellow corn meal
¾ c. sifted flour
½ tsp. salt
½ tsp. baking soda
¼ tsp. dried thyme leaves
⅛ tsp. ground red pepper
¼ c. finely chopped green onions
2 cloves garlic, minced
1 c. buttermilk
1 egg

In 4-qt. Dutch oven over medium heat, heat 1″ oil to 375° on deep-fat thermometer.

Meanwhile, into medium bowl, sift together corn meal, flour, salt, baking soda, thyme and red pepper. Stir in green onions and garlic until well blended; set aside.

In small bowl, mix buttermilk and egg until well blended. Add buttermilk mixture to dry ingredients; stir just until moistened.

Drop 6 tsp. of batter, 1 tsp. at a time, into hot oil. Fry, turning once, 2 to 3 minutes or until browned on all sides. Remove and drain on paper towels. Repeat with remaining batter. Serve hot. Makes 18 to 20 hush puppies.

Sopaipillas

Dip these puffy pillow-shaped breads into guacamole as an appetizer to start off your next Mexican meal, or top them with honey or sugar as a dessert.

> 1¾ c. sifted flour
> 2 tsp. baking powder
> 1 tsp. salt
> 2 tblsp. shortening
> ⅔ c. iced water
> About 1 qt. vegetable oil
> Honey or confectioners' sugar

Into medium bowl, sift together flour, baking powder and salt. With pastry blender, cut in shortening until fine crumbs form.

Sprinkle iced water over crumb mixture, 1 tblsp. at a time, tossing with fork until dough forms. Press dough into a ball.

Turn out dough onto lightly floured surface. Knead just until smooth, about 1 to 2 minutes. Cover with towel and let rest 10 minutes.

Meanwhile, in 4-qt. Dutch oven over medium heat, heat 1" oil to 400° on deep-fat thermometer.

On lightly floured surface with floured rolling pin, roll out dough to a 15x12" rectangle. With pastry wheel or knife, cut dough into 20 (3") squares.

Using metal spatula, carefully lift and slide 3 squares top-side down, into hot oil. Fry, turning once, 1 to 2 minutes or until golden brown on both sides. Remove and drain on paper towels. Repeat with remaining squares. Drizzle with honey or sift confectioners' sugar over sopaipillas. Serve warm. Makes 20 sopaipillas.

Poori

Watching these rounds of dough puff into crisp balloons as they fry is as much fun as eating them. The recipe originated in India.

> 1 c. sifted all-purpose flour
> 1 c. stirred whole-wheat flour
> ½ tsp. salt
> 2 tblsp. vegetable oil
> ½ to ⅔ c. water
> 3 c. vegetable oil

In medium bowl, stir together all-purpose flour, whole-wheat flour and salt. With fork, stir in 2 tblsp. oil and enough water to make a very stiff dough. Knead in bowl until smooth and pliable, about 7 minutes.

Divide dough into 20 pieces. Shape each piece into a ball. Flatten balls slightly. Cover with plastic wrap to prevent balls from drying out.

In 3-qt. saucepan over medium-high heat, heat 3 c. oil to 400° on deep-fat thermometer.

Meanwhile, on whole-wheat floured surface with whole-wheat floured rolling pin, roll out each flattened ball into a 4″ circle, dusting frequently with more whole-wheat flour to prevent sticking. Cover with plastic wrap to keep circles from drying out.

Fry poori, 1 at a time, in hot oil about 10 seconds, using back of slotted spoon to gently hold poori down in the oil until it puffs up. Turn and fry 10 to 20 seconds more or until lightly browned. Remove and drain on paper towels. Serve immediately. Makes 20 poori.

To Reheat: Wrap poori in single layer in foil. Store at room temperature up to 3 days. Heat wrapped poori in 325° oven 5 minutes or until heated through. Poori may flatten during reheating.

Langos

These little fried breads (pronounced langosh) are native to Hungary. Any leftover dough from daily bread-making was rolled and fried, then served hot with cloves of garlic. Before eating the langos, each person rubs them with garlic.

1 pkg. active dry yeast
2 tsp. sugar
1¼ c. warm water (105 to 115°)
½ c. mashed potatoes
⅓ c. nonfat dry milk
¼ c. vegetable oil
1 tsp. salt
1 egg
2 cloves garlic, crushed
4¾ to 5¼ c. sifted flour
About 1 qt. vegetable oil
Peeled garlic cloves

In large bowl, sprinkle yeast and sugar over warm water; stir until dissolved. Add potatoes, dry milk, oil, salt, egg, 2 cloves crushed garlic and 2 c. flour.

Using mixer at low speed, beat until well blended. Increase speed to medium; beat 2 minutes.

Stir in enough additional flour to make a soft dough. Turn out dough onto lightly floured surface. Knead until smooth and elastic, about 5 to 8 minutes.

Place in greased large bowl, turning over dough so that top is greased. Cover with towel and let rise in warm place until doubled, about 1 hour.

Punch down dough. On lightly floured surface, knead until dough is no longer sticky, about 30 seconds, adding additional flour if necessary. Cover and let rest 10 minutes.

With floured rolling pin, roll out dough to ½" thickness. With floured 3" biscuit cutter, cut dough into 20 circles. Cut 3 slits, 2"-long, through each circle. Cover; let rest 20 minutes.

During last 10 minutes of resting time: In 4-qt. Dutch oven over medium heat, heat 1" oil to 375° on deep-fat thermometer.

Using metal spatula, carefully lift and slide 2 circles, top-side down, into hot oil. Fry, turning once, 3 minutes or until browned on both sides. Remove and drain on paper towels. Repeat with remaining circles. Serve warm. Rub with peeled garlic cloves before eating. Makes 20 langos.

BREAKFAST LANGOS: Increase granulated sugar to ¼ c. Substitute ¾ tsp. ground ginger for crushed garlic. Sift confectioners' sugar over langos. Serve warm.

Soft Pretzels

Germans and Austrians deserve the credit for the original soft, chewy pretzel, introduced to America in the mid-1800s.

> 1 pkg. active dry yeast
> 1 tblsp. sugar
> ½ c. warm water (105 to 115°)
> 1 c. warm milk (105 to 115°)
> 1 tsp. salt
> 3½ to 4 c. sifted flour
> 1 tblsp. baking soda
> 1 egg
> 1 tblsp. water
> Coarse salt

In large bowl, sprinkle yeast and sugar over ½ c. warm water; stir until dissolved. Add milk, salt and 1½ c. flour.

Using mixer at medium speed, beat 2 minutes. Stir in enough additional flour to make a soft dough. Turn out dough onto lightly floured surface. Knead until smooth and elastic, about 10 minutes.

Place in greased large bowl, turning over dough so that top is greased. Cover with towel and let rise in warm place until doubled, about 1 hour 30 minutes.

Punch down dough. Cover and let rest 10 minutes.

On lightly floured surface, roll out dough into a 10x8" rectangle. Cut rectangle into 10 (8"-long) strips. Roll each strip into 20"-long rope.

To form pretzels: Hold both ends of one rope. Form a large loop. Twist rope once, 3" from ends. Bring down ends of rope and pinch to opposite side of loop to make a pretzel shape. Place on floured baking sheet.

Repeat with remaining ropes, placing pretzels, 3" apart, on floured baking sheets.

Let rise, uncovered, until doubled, about 30 minutes.

During last 10 minutes of rising time: In 4-qt. Dutch oven over high heat, bring 2 qt. water to a boil.

Add baking soda to boiling water. Add 2 pretzels to boiling water; boil 1 minute. With slotted spoon, remove pretzels and drain well. Place pretzels, 3" apart, on well-greased foil-lined baking sheets. Repeat with remaining pretzels.

In small bowl, mix together egg and 1 tblsp. water. Brush pretzels with egg mixture. Sprinkle with coarse salt.

Bake in 400° oven 18 minutes or until golden brown. Serve warm. Makes 10 pretzels.

To Reheat: Wrap pretzels in single layer in foil. Store at room temperature up to 3 days. Heat wrapped pretzels in 400° oven 10 minutes or until heated through.

Bagels

You can make these German rolls with all-purpose or whole-wheat flour. Bake them plain, or top with sesame, poppy or caraway seed.

> 1 pkg. active dry yeast
> 2 tsp. salt
> 5¼ to 5¾ c. sifted all-purpose flour
> 3 tblsp. sugar
> 1½ c. very warm water (120 to 130°)
> 1 tblsp. sugar
> 1 egg white
> 1 tblsp. water
> Sesame, poppy or caraway seed

In large bowl, stir together yeast, salt, 1½ c. flour and 3 tblsp. sugar. Using mixer at low speed, beat in 1½ c. very warm water until well blended. Increase speed to medium; beat 2 minutes. Add 1 c. flour; beat 2 minutes more.

Stir in enough additional flour to make a stiff dough. Turn out dough onto lightly floured surface. Knead until smooth and elastic, about 8 to 10 minutes.

Place in greased large bowl, turning over dough so that top is greased. Cover with towel and let rest in warm place 20 minutes.

Punch dough down. Turn out dough onto lightly floured surface and divide into 12 pieces. Cover and let rest 10 minutes.

Shape each piece into ball and flatten into 1½" circle. With floured index finger, make a hole in the center of each circle. Twirl circle around finger to widen hole. Make hole bigger by pulling edges of dough into a ring, about 2½" wide. Cover and let rest 20 minutes.

Meanwhile, in 6-qt. Dutch oven over medium heat, bring 4 qt. water and 1 tblsp. sugar to a boil. Using metal spatula, carefully lift and slide 3 rings into simmering water. Simmer, turning once, 6 minutes. Remove rings and drain on paper towels 5 minutes. Place, 2" apart, on greased baking sheets. Repeat with remaining rings.

In small bowl, mix egg white and 1 tblsp. water until well blended. Brush each bagel with egg white mixture. Sprinkle with sesame, poppy or caraway seed.

Bake in 375° oven 35 minutes or until golden brown. Immediately remove from baking sheets. Serve warm. Or, cool completely on racks; split and toast before serving. Makes 12 bagels.

WHOLE-WHEAT BAGELS: Substitute 1½ c. stirred whole-wheat flour for 1½ c. sifted all-purpose flour.

CINNAMON-RAISIN BAGELS: Omit poppy, sesame or caraway seed. Add 1½ tsp. ground cinnamon to yeast mixture and knead ½ c. raisins into dough.

ONION BAGELS: Omit poppy, sesame or caraway seed. In small bowl, pour 3 tblsp. water over 3 tblsp. instant minced onion. Let stand 5 minutes; drain.

Brush bagels with egg white mixture and sprinkle with onion before baking.

Steamed Boston Brown Bread

In colonial times, frugal housewives used molasses to sweeten and flavor their steamed breads and baked beans.

1 c. stirred whole-wheat flour
½ c. sifted all-purpose flour
½ c. raisins
½ c. chopped walnuts
1 tblsp. sugar
½ tsp. baking soda
½ tsp. salt
⅔ c. buttermilk
⅓ c. molasses

In large bowl, stir together first 7 ingredients.

In small bowl, mix buttermilk and molasses until well blended. Add buttermilk mixture to dry ingredients; stir just until moistened.

Pour batter into greased 1-lb. coffee can. Grease a piece of foil larger than the top of can. Place foil, greased-side down, over can and secure with string.

Place can on rack in 6-qt. Dutch oven. Add water to a level of 1". Over high heat, bring to a boil. Reduce heat so water maintains a steady simmer. Cover and steam 2 hours 30 minutes or until toothpick inserted in center comes out clean.

Cool bread in can on rack 5 minutes. Remove; cool on rack. Wrap loaf in foil. Let stand, overnight, in cool dry place before serving. Makes 1 loaf.

SLOW COOKER METHOD: Prepare batter, pour into 1-lb. coffee can and cover as directed. Place can on trivet in 3½-qt. slow cooker. Pour 2 c. hot water into cooker. Cover and cook at high setting 2 hours to 2 hours 30 minutes or until toothpick inserted in center comes out clean.

PRESSURE COOKER METHOD: Prepare batter as directed. Pour batter into 2 greased 16-oz. fruit or vegetable cans, filling each two-thirds full. (Do not use 1-lb. coffee can; it's too big to fit in the pressure cooker.) Cover cans as directed. Place cans on trivet in 6-qt. pressure cooker. Pour 3 c. water into cooker.

Close cover securely and place cooker over high heat. Bring cooker to 15 lb. pressure according to manufacturer's directions. When pressure is reached (control will begin to rock), reduce heat immediately to maintain a slow, steady rocking motion and cook 35 minutes. Remove from heat. Let pressure drop of its own accord. Makes 2 loaves.

Chinese Steamed Pork Buns

Traditionally served as a midday snack, these soft rolls are filled with a mixture c f vegetables and pork.

¼ c. chili sauce or ketchup
¼ c. dry sherry or water
2 tblsp. cornstarch
2 tblsp. soy sauce
1 tsp. sugar
1 tsp. minced fresh ginger root or
    ½ tsp. ground ginger
¾ lb. ground pork
½ c. finely chopped cabbage
½ c. finely chopped celery
¼ c. finely chopped water chestnuts
¼ c. finely chopped green onions
1 pkg. active dry yeast
1 tblsp. sugar
1¼ c. warm water (105 to 115°)
3½ c. sifted flour
1 tsp. salt

In small bowl, stir together first 6 ingredients.

In 10″ skillet over medium heat, cook ground pork, cabbage, celery, water chestnuts and green onions until pork is browned and vegetables are tender.

Add chili sauce mixture; cook, stirring constantly, until mixture boils and thickens. Transfer mixture to medium bowl. Cover and refrigerate until ready to use.

In medium bowl, sprinkle yeast and 1 tblsp. sugar over warm water; stir until dissolved.

Using wooden spoon, gradually stir flour and salt into yeast mixture until mixture is well blended and forms a ball that leaves side of bowl. Turn out dough onto lightly floured surface. Knead until smooth and elastic, about 5 minutes.

Place in greased large bowl, turning over dough so that top is greased. Cover with towel and let rise in warm place until doubled, about 1 hour 30 minutes.

Punch down dough. Divide dough into 16 pieces. Cover and let rest 15 minutes.

On lightly floured surface with lightly floured hands, pat and flatten each piece into a 3" circle. (Keep remaining pieces of dough covered.)

Place 1 tblsp. pork mixture in center of a circle. Bring edges up over filling and gather together. Pinch gathers well to seal. Place, gathered-side down, on small piece of waxed paper. Repeat with remaining dough and filling.

Place buns, ½" apart, in two tiers of bamboo or metal Chinese steamer. Cover and let rise until doubled, about 30 minutes.

During last 10 minutes of rising time: In wok over high heat, bring 1" of water to a boil. Reduce heat so that water maintains a steady simmer.

Place stacked and covered steamer tiers over boiling water. Steam 12 minutes, or until toothpick inserted in center of bun comes out clean.

Remove steamer tiers from wok. Remove buns and carefully peel off waxed paper. Serve warm or cold. Makes 16 buns.

Note: If you don't have a Chinese steamer, you can improvise, and use a 6-qt. Dutch oven or 12" skillet with dome lid and 2 round wire racks.

Wrap racks with foil; randomly prick foil to vent steam. Place 8 buns on each rack and let rise as directed.

During last 10 minutes of rising time: Invert several custard cups in bottom of Dutch oven. Add water and heat as directed.

Balance 1 rack on custard cups. Cover and steam as directed. Repeat with remaining rack.

To Freeze and Serve Later: Prepare buns as directed; but do not let rise. Immediately after shaping, place on baking sheet and freeze until firm. Wrap each bun in foil. Freeze up to 1 month. Unwrap and steam frozen buns 24 minutes.

Index

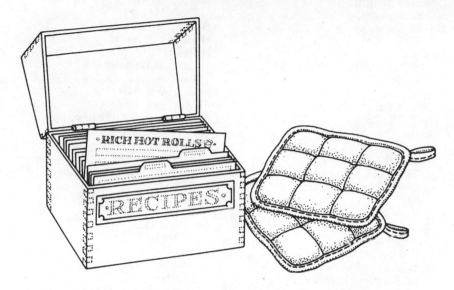

References to illustrations are in **bold type.**

Coffee Breads, 47. *See also*
   tea loaves
   recipes for, 199, 201, 209
Coffeecakes, recipes for,
   50-51, 53, 196, 204,
   210-212, 227, 254, 275. *See
   also* cake(s); Danish
Coffee Rings, Danish, 253
Colonial Gingerbread, 52
compressed yeast, 12
Confectioners'
   Glaze, 256
   Sugar Icing, 229
      Creamy, 206
Convection Oven, Baking
   in a, 26
Conventional Method of
   mixing yeast dough, 114
Conventional Oven, Baking
   in a, 25, 26
cooling racks, 30
Coolrise
   Best-ever White Bread, 135
   Brioche Dough, 246
   Pizza Dough, 171
   Sweet Dough, 191
Corn Bread, 54. *See also* Corn
      Fritters; corn meal; Corn
      Muffins; Corn Sticks
   Golden, 55
   Skillet Mexican, 56
   Mix, 53
      in Corn Bread, 54
      in Corn Meal Pancakes,
         293
      in Spoon Bread, 54
Cornell Formula Bread, 138
corn flour, 9
Corn Fritters, 319
corn meal, 9
   Biscuits, 95
   -Bran Muffins, 88
   Crackers, 108
   Pancakes, 293
   Rolls, 181
   Waffles, Southern, 300
Corn Muffins, 55
cornstarch, 9
Corn Sticks, 55
Cottage Cheese Rolls, 180
Country Pancakes, 288
Country Waffles, 288
cracked wheat
   Bread, 154
      Casserole, 264
   flour, 6

crackers, 83. *See also* Flat
   Breads
   recipes for, 104-108, 109
   to store, 83
Crackling Biscuits, 98
Cranberry
   -Banana Loaf, 76
   Bread, 77
   Muffins, 85
Cream Cheese Filling, 254
Cream Cheese Spread,
   Spiced, 75
Creamy Confectioners' Sugar
   Icing, 206
Crêpes, 294, 295
Crescent(s)
   Butter, 215
   Cloud Biscuits, 97
   Peanut Butter, 215
   Rolls, 176
Crisp Bread Sticks, 179
Croissants, 257, 259
Crumb
   Batter Muffins, Apple, 284
   Cake, French, 48
   Coffeecake, Citrus, 275
   Ring, Sour Cream, 49
   Topping, 49
      Cinnamon, 89
      Citrus, 275
Crumpets, 307
Crusty Rolls, 175
Currant Scones, 102

D

Dairy Bread, Melissa's, 168
Daisy Coffee Breads, 201
Danish. *See also* Coffeecakes
   Coffee Rings, 253
   Pastry Dough, 252
   Twists, 255
   Wreaths, 256
Dark Pumpernickel, 162
Dark Raisin Bread, 152
Date
   Bread, Honey-, 75
   Muffins, 85
   Nut Coffeecake, 196
   Nut Filling, 196
Deep-dish Pizza, 172
deep-fried breads. *See* fried
   breads
Dilly Casserole Bread, 265

French Bread (continued)
  Sourdough, 147
    Rolls, 148
  Whole-Wheat Processor, 145
French Crumb Cake, 48
French Toast, 298
Fresh Orange Sauce, 278
fried breads, 309. *See also*
    doughnuts; Fritters
  recipes for, 315, 317-318,
    320-325, 326
Fritters, 319
Frosting. *See also* glazes; Icing
  Lemon-Orange Butter, 199
  Viennese Striezel, 232
Fruit Bread, Gluten-free, 61
Fruited Favorite Buttermilk
    Pancakes, 289
fruit juices, as ingredients, 15
Funnel Cakes, 315

G

Garden Biscuits, 96
German Pumpernickel, 161
Giant Brioche, 247
Giant Cinnamon Swirl, 227
Gingerbread, 52
  Waffles, 301
glaze(s). *See also* Finishing
    Touches; Frosting
  Butter-Almond, 79
  Cinnamon, 314
  Confectioners', 256
  egg, 118
  Orange, 213
  Orange-Nut, 214
  Quick Orange, 218
  Quick Vanilla, 202
  Thin Confectioners', 205
Glazed
  Doughnuts, Vanilla-, 314
  Lemon Bread, 78
  Raisin Bread, Orange-
    Nut, 213
gluten, 5, 6, 8, 114, 115, 116,
    117, 121
  -free Bread, 60
  -free Cheese Bread, 60
  -free Fruit Bread, 61
Golden
  Apricot Filling, 202
  Corn Bread, 55
  Pecan Cinnamon Buns, 222
  Pumpkin-Raisin Bread, 167

Gouda Loaves, 236
Gougère, 67
Graham Crackers, 104
graham flour, 8
grease pans, how to, 23
Grecian Feast Loaf, 200
Green Onion Cakes, 303
griddle breads, 287. *See also*
    Flapjacks; pancakes;
    waffles
  recipes for, 298, 302, 303,
    305-307
griddles, 287
grits, 9
Gugelhupf, 273

H

Hamburger Rolls, Whole-
    Wheat, 150
Health Crackers, 106
Hearts
  Cherry, 205
  Cinnamon-Sugar, 220
Herb Loaves, Individual
    Onion-, 282
Herb Ring, Pull-apart, 68
high altitude(s)
  baking breads at, 33
  deep-frying breads at, 33
  making yeast doughs at, 33
  storing flour at, 32
Holiday Bread, 226. *See also*
    Christmas recipes; Easter
    recipes; Valentine's Day
    recipes
Honey
  -Date Bread, 75
  -Wheat Buns, 184
  -Zucchini Bread, 62
Hot Cross Buns, 216
Hot Rolls, Rich, 174
Houska, 195
Hush Puppies, 322

I-J

Icing. *See also* Frosting; glazes
  Brown Butter, 223
  Confectioners' Sugar, 229
  Creamy Confectioners'
    Sugar, 206
  Vanilla, 275

N

Naan, 103
New Orleans Beignets, 321
No-knead Dinner Rolls, 177
nonfat dry milk, 15
nonstick pans, 23
nut(s), 16
  Bread
    Apricot, 73
    Banana, 80
    Pumpkin, 65
    Sweet Potato, 64
    Zucchini, 62
  Coffeecake, Date, 196

O

oat(s), 9
Oatmeal
  Bread, Old-fashioned, 163
  -Raisin Muffins, 89
  Scones, 103
Old-fashioned
  Oatmeal Bread, 163
  oats, 9
One-Hour Rolls, 179
  Spoon, 278
Onion
  Bagels, 328
  Bow Ties, Sesame-, 187
  Cakes, Green, 303
  -Herb Loaves, Individual, 282
orange
  Glaze, 213
  juice, as ingredient, 15
  -Nut Glaze, 214
  -Nut Glazed Raisin
    Bread, 213
  Sauce, 296
  Sauce, Fresh, 278
  Twist Coffee Breads, 209
  Twists, 209
oven(s)
  -baked Boston Brown
    Bread, 70
  convection, 26
  conventional, 25, 26
  microwave, 27, 28, 29
  spring, 119
  thermometer, 26, 31
Oyster Crackers, 106

P

pancakes, 287. *See also*
  Flapjacks; griddle breads
  recipes for, 288, 290-297
Panettone, 230
Pan Rolls, 175
  Quick, 280
pans
  choosing, 22, 23, 24
  substituting (chart), 24
Paratha, 304
Parker House Rolls, 176
pastry
  blender, 31
  brush, 31
  Dough, Danish, 252
Peach Doughnuts, 312
Peanut
  Batter Bread, 270
  Butter Bread, 70
  Butter Crescents, 215
Pear Bread, 74
Pecan Cinnamon Buns,
  Golden, 222
Pecan Waffles, Sunday
  Supper, 299
Pilgrim's Bread, 165
Pineapple
  -Bran Muffins, 87
  Bread, Carrot-, 66
  -Cheese Ring, 251
  Spice Loaf, 76
Pinwheels
  Apricot-Prune, 208
  Buttermilk Biscuit, 101
  Cinnamon Biscuit, 92
  Texas Biscuit, 92
Pita, Whole-Wheat, 240
Pizza, 170-172
  Batter Bread, 269
plastic wrap, 31
Polenta Bread, 140
Poori, 324
Popovers, 111
Poppy Seed
  Crescents, 241
  Filling, 242
  Tea Bread, 72